T0367623

# ONLY A BAD DREAM?

*Childhood Memories of the Holocaust*

Sahbra Anna Markus

iUniverse LLC
Bloomington

ONLY A BAD DREAM?
CHILDHOOD MEMORIES OF THE HOLOCAUST

iUniverse books may be ordered through booksellers or by contacting:

iUniverse
1663 Liberty Drive
Bloomington, IN 47403
www.iuniverse.com
1-800-Authors (1-800-288-4677)

Because of the dynamic nature of the Internet, any web addresses or links contained in
this book may have changed since publication and may no longer be valid. The views
expressed in this work are solely those of the author and do not necessarily reflect the
views of the publisher, and the publisher hereby disclaims any responsibility for them.

Any people depicted in stock imagery provided by Thinkstock are models,
and such images are being used for illustrative purposes only.
Certain stock imagery © Thinkstock.

ISBN: 978-1-4917-2194-0 (sc)
ISBN: 978-1-4917-2196-4 (hc)
ISBN: 978-1-4917-2195-7 (e)

Library of Congress Control Number: 2014901175

Printed in the United States of America.

iUniverse rev. date: 02/27/2014

*In loving memory of my parents,*
*Devorah Efroimowitz Markus and Ze'ev 'William' Volfe Markus*

# Contents

# Acknowledgments

Without the capable assistance of Shirley Knapp, this book would have taken much longer to publish. When our paths crossed a few years ago, we became friends. When she offered to have a look at my story, I doubted she would succeed at editing where others had failed because they decided my story was too graphic and painful. Not my Shirley! She persevered as I relived myriad details. She cried, laughed, and prayed with me, persistently encouraging me to keep going. I am grateful for her literary, editing, and computer skills, as well as her careful attention to detail as the story of my young life took shape on paper. This is one Christian Zionist *Goya* (Gentile) of whom Jesus must be very proud. She knows and loves the Jewish heart. I also extend my sincerest gratitude to Shirley's husband, Reg, for his friendship and for allowing me to borrow his wife for many long hours of hard work over the past years. I will always be grateful for their loving friendship.

Thank you, Natalie May, for your constant supportive encouragement to tell my life story and for being my very dear friend for many years.

Thank you, Alexandra Andreassen, for your many years of friendship, loyalty, and valuable assistance.

Thanks to Dr. Alan Quinn for your support and encouragement.

I appreciate the time, effort, and constructive input of Pamela Berry and Sandra McDonald in early proofreading of the manuscript. With gratitude, thanks, ladies.

The editorial team at iUniverse has provided much constructive and encouraging assistance to this project, for which I am grateful.

Sahbra

# Introduction

To the Reader:

The events recorded in this book are personal recollections of the early years of my life in World War II Europe and later in Israel. I learned some of the anecdotal information in the 1960s from several of Mama's cousins and then again in the 1980s from her cousin Mindy Klein from Toronto, Canada.

I have been assembling this record over the past several decades. My now-deceased parents related some details over time. Other family members and friends have contributed bits of information. Mainly these are the personal memories of the life I have lived.

Obviously, in the chaos and trauma of those Holocaust years, I was very young and did not record events as they transpired.

The passage of time and the effects of a stroke accidentally caused during extensive heart surgery have dulled some recall. This may account for some incongruity within the stories themselves, in that some events and details may not conform to a strict timeline.

For example, I have no conscious memory of the Warsaw ghetto where I was born and lived for the first few months of my life. Traipsing as a young child across Europe with my family amidst the upheaval of war makes some confusion inevitable.

Many events I recall in detail, though their exact sequence may be uncertain. Some locations and my precise age at the time may be questionable. However, it was my life, and for any inconsistencies, I ask your indulgence.

Sahbra Anna Markus

# Chapter 1

# The First Martyr of Brzezine

*Aaron Efroimowitz*

*Poland—1939*

B rzezine, a vibrant city in Poland, was home to a large Jewish population. Many men and women worked in the tailor shops, factories, and stores of the large textile fashion center. Others were successful shopkeepers or tended their farms in the surrounding countryside. My grandparents owned a large hardware store, a factory, and several small tailor shops.

To serve the Jewish community, several *shuls* (synagogues) and many *shtibls* (one-room studies) were available.

There was one very large, beautiful house of worship in the center of the city known as the Big Synagogue. However, the one I will tell you about was small and very much loved by my family.

Rabbi Chaim Meir and Rivkah Efroimowitz attended services there. Reb Chaim's family had lived in Brzezine for many generations or, as he would declare, "since the beginning of the Diaspora." The Efroimowitz family had five daughters and a son, the youngest child being Aaron.

Now a young man almost nineteen years old, Aaron spent his days studying the Torah in the synagogue. Handsome, tall, and slender, he was very pale from rarely spending time in the sun. His long, shiny dark-brown *payos* (sidelocks) curled in front of his ears. His beautiful, big brown eyes always had a hint of a smile in them.

The bright-eyed, serious student of the Torah lived with his secret hope of one day becoming a respected rabbi and having his very own congregation.

One fateful Friday afternoon, he was delayed in his study. It was becoming late, and he needed to go home and prepare himself for *Shabbat* (the Sabbath). As he was completing the last few lines in a chapter of the Torah, a noise from outside caught his attention. Stopping his study to investigate, he opened the front door just a bit to look out. He saw trucks and Jeeps arriving in front of the synagogue.

Aaron was confused. He had never seen vehicles quite like those before. It was certainly the first time anyone had seen red flags with the black swastika in the middle waving in the Brzezine breeze.

Aaron closed the door and quickly and quietly made his way through the *shul* toward the back door. He was too late. The Nazis had seen him through the windows.

One of the German officers yelled out, "Go after him; catch him! Bring him out! Let's make an example of him."

Soldiers burst through the large front doors as others came in through the back. Aaron stopped running. He was trapped. There was no way out. He could not comprehend what was happening and didn't know what to do.

Two of the soldiers grabbed him by the arms and started to drag him out. A Nazi officer came in and told other soldiers to take all the Torah scrolls from the big ark where they were stored and take them to the back yard.

Aaron, frightened and bewildered, glared at the men as they gathered up his precious sacred scrolls and carried them outdoors. *Why would they do this?*

Standing captive outside the synagogue, Aaron watched in horror as all the Holy Torah scrolls were thrown to the ground in front of him, and the soldiers laughed mockingly in his face.

Aaron understood some of the German words they were speaking to one another. His horror was magnified when an officer came to him with a box of matches and announced, "If you do as I say, you will have your life and go home. You must light the fire. You must burn the books!"

To make them burn faster, the officer poured a large full can of benzene (gasoline) on the scrolls.

Aaron stood shaking his head as he mumbled, "No, I cannot and will not do that!"

The first blow to his face from the officer's fist was a painful surprise. Blood poured from his nose to his mouth. Wiping his face on his sleeve, Aaron asked, "Why are you doing this? My books and I have done nothing to any of you. We are innocent."

"You will burn the books, or you will die!" the Nazi barked.

Aaron repeated the question. "Why are you doing this?"

They answered with more blows to his body, and he stumbled to the ground. Again they told him to light the matches and burn the books; once more, he refused.

They picked Aaron up roughly and dragged him to the far end of the yard. There they put ropes around his waist and bound him to a tree. They tore off his blood-soaked shirt and *tzitzit*—the undergarment that signified his devotion to G-d. (Many devout Jews use this English spelling to indicate their reverence and respect for the name of G-d, which in Hebrew is never spoken aloud.) Then two soldiers took turns beating him with a wide leather belt as Aaron continued to declare, "No, I will not burn my sacred scrolls."

Blood now covered Aaron's chest, the skin broken in many places where the belt buckle cut deeply. With each blow, the soldiers laughed at him. One yelled, "Stupid little Jew, save yourself. Burn the dammed books!"

Aaron, realizing he may not come out of this alive, mumbled the words of the *Shema*, the last words every devout Jew speaks when he knows his death is near. Then he raised his voice loud and clear, declaring, "*Shema Yisrael Adonai Eloheinu Adonai Echad*. Hear, O Israel, the L-rd our G-d, the L-rd is One."

Yet another fist hit his nose and mouth, and the man ordered him to shut up. Even that did not stop him from invoking the prayer repeatedly.

The Nazi officer became frustrated with his lack of progress with this stubborn young Jewish man. He wanted results. Ordering his soldiers to remove the rest of Aaron's clothing, they pulled off his pants and underclothes, which by now were blood-soaked. Pointing to his genitals, the soldiers doubled over with laughter.

"Have you ever seen anything this ugly? He is mutilated!" one of them yelled in amusement.

Another mocked, "I have never seen a mutilated organ before. Look how ugly it is. Somebody, take a picture!"

The officer thrust the matches out to him. Again, he shook his head no and continued reciting the *Shema*. The blows to his head and body came faster and faster. At one point, they stopped for a moment, thinking he was finally dead. However, Aaron's young body did not give up his life to them; his spirit was fighting.

The Nazi officer approached again menacingly. "You will burn the books, or I will start shooting you. I will use you for target practice!"

Aaron summoned a loud *"No! I will not."* The officer took his revolver out of its holster, aimed it at Aaron's right leg, and fired. As the bullet hit Aaron, a look of disbelief came over his face. Then the pain came, and he screamed.

Now the officer leaned close and implored quietly, "Just burn the books. I don't want to kill a child like you."

This time Aaron did not say a word. He only shook his head.

Silence fell on the back yard. They all gaped at the brave, stubborn, young Jewish boy-man as his last moments were near.

The officer tried one more time, gun in hand, this time yelling at Aaron, "Will you do what I say?"

Aaron didn't move. He appeared to be dead. The Nazi took aim and shot him again, this time in the left leg. Aaron screamed with the new pain.

The Nazi torturer, furious at his failure to make Aaron comply, raged, "How much longer will I have to torture you? What will it take to make you burn the books?" Then he methodically took aim and put a bullet into each arm of his helpless victim.

A short time later, as Aaron and the tree stood together in a growing pool of blood, another officer approached and lit the fire himself. "We need to move on. We have lost too much time over this one miserable Jew. Get back to your vehicles," he barked as the flames consumed the scrolls. Taking out his gun, he shot young Aaron Efroimowitz point-blank in his heart.

*HaShem yakum damo*—for murdered martyrs. G-d will avenge his blood.

✡ ✡ ✡

The caretaker/groundskeeper of the synagogue, who was hiding nearby, witnessed this grizzly event from beginning to end. As soon as the Nazis left, he ran to Aaron. Taking off his own coat, he spread it on the ground. Then he cut the ropes and gently laid Aaron's body on the coat.

This kind man then ran to a neighbor, told him what had happened, and asked to borrow a horse and cart so he could take Aaron back to his family. The groundskeeper put Aaron into the cart and walked slowly through the streets of Brzezine.

People stopped to look. Some asked, "What has happened? Who is this boy? Who did this?"

"This is Aaron Efroimowitz. The Nazis have come!" he answered sadly, as he kept walking.

Arriving at the lovely, big home of the Efroimowitz family, the groundskeeper knocked on the door and, without waiting for an answer, returned to the cart. He gathered Aaron and the blood-soaked coat in his arms and carried him gently to the house.

A servant, as was usual, did not answer the knock. Aaron's mother Rivkah (nee Schotland) opened the door. She first registered surprise to see the synagogue's caretaker, whom she recognized. Then her eyes took in the whole unbelievable scene of her only son—his lifeless body covered in blood.

Her screams pierced the neighborhood. In that one moment, her heart was broken, and she was never the same again. With the death of her beloved son, she totally lost her mind.

My uncle Aaron was prepared in his final moments to sacrifice his own life rather than transgress G-d's law—an ultimate act of *Kiddush HaShem* (for the glory of our G-d—for the sanctification of G-d's name). He was the first Holocaust victim murdered in the city of Brzezine.

Each evening after that horrific day, my grandmother Rivkah and her youngest daughter, twenty-one-year-old Bluma (*Bliema'le*), went from house to house all around the Jewish neighborhood with aprons full of candles. They stopped people in the streets and at every house, handing each of them a candle as Rivkah implored, "Please light this candle for my son, Aaron. He died *Kiddush HaShem*."

When this happened, my mother, Devorah (Rivkah's daughter), was married and living in Warsaw. Mama and Papa learned of Aaron's murder from a former neighbor who fled Brzezine right after it happened. Mama was devastated and blamed herself for not being there to protect her baby brother.

Mama and Papa were proud parents of twin boys, but the four of them were soon evacuated to the Warsaw ghetto. One terrible day, often repeated, Nazi trucks came, loaded many children and others onto trucks, and took them to Treblinka and other death camps. My brothers were among the children taken.

Some weeks later, Rivkah Schotland Efroimowitz and her beautiful daughter Bluma were sent to Auschwitz along with most of the city's Jewish population. In 1947, while in a displaced persons' camp in Germany, my mama—Devorah (nee Efroimowitz) Markus—met two witnesses who told her of the death of her mother and sister. Mama never accepted that they were also murdered. She kept searching for them until her death in 1962.

I was born in the ghetto not too long after Aaron's death. They named me Anna, a derivative of Aaron, in memory of Mama's beloved brother. Knowing this heritage, I have worked hard all my life to be worthy of this honor.

So why the name Sahbra?

Miriam and Ze'ev Turi, a young Jewish couple, left home and family in Poland and walked to faraway Palestine. They were among the Zionists drawn to return to the land of their ancestors, the Promised Land, in the 1930s. Once there, they continued the work of early *halutzim* (pioneers), rebuilding the once desolate land described in the writings of Mark Twain. Miriam Turi was my father's older sister.

Papa received a letter from his sister, enthusiastically describing their life in the Holy Land—a land of great challenges but with much potential. Though there were ongoing problems with the British and the Arabs, they foresaw a great future there for themselves and their family and for many Jews who were making *aliyah* (immigrating to Israel, then known as Palestine).

Miriam described the beautiful city of Haifa on the shores of the Mediterranean Sea and the flowery slopes of the Carmel Mountains. She also told of massive cactus hedges that served as fences between properties. These native cacti, called *sabras,* produced a delicious fruit— the prickly pear. The name *sabra* has come to signify a native-born Israeli, a Jew born in Palestine. The comparison is quite appropriate— Israelis may seem to be tough and prickly outwardly, but when you get to know them, they are often soft and sweet on the inside.

Aunt Miriam thought Papa should consider giving this name to one of his children should he someday have them. Of course, she hoped her brother Ze'ev and other family members would one day follow them to live in this very special place. When I was born, Papa wanted to name me Sabra, but Mama insisted my name be Anna in memory of her brother, Aaron. Anna I was! Only years later did Papa mention to me his sister's letter and her name suggestion.

In the mid-1960s, I began to perform professionally, having trained in various genres of dance in Haifa, Tel Aviv, and later New York City. On the eve of the reopening of the beautiful Taft hotel in mid-Manhattan, the show's producer asked for my stage name. I didn't know I would need a special name for my belly dancing performance. My new friend, Morocco, another dancer on the bill, asked, "Are you not from Israel? What is that name for all Israeli natives? Is it not Sabra?"

I laughed, recalling Aunt Miriam's suggestion. "Of course! That is the name I will use!" *Thank you, Aunt Miriam.*

In the 1960s, people often had problems with the pronunciation of my name, so I changed the spelling and had my name legally changed to Sahbra Anna Markus.

**Aaron Efroimowitz**

**Rivkah Efroimowitz, nee Schotland**

# Chapter 2

# Escaping from Poland into Russia

ecause I was very young when we escaped the Warsaw ghetto,
it is impossible to recount those earliest days with any degree of
certainty. I have no memory or explanation of how we got out. Papa
never talked about it. It's most likely that my parents sought shelter and
protection from tenant farm families who had worked for our Jewish
ancestors for many generations. We probably moved from place to place,
hiding out with Polish Catholic Gentiles who sympathized with our
situation. Eventually, a plan was formulated to help us escape to the
relative safety of Russia.

In the story I am about to tell you, I have combined my mother's,
father's, and some of my own memories of that journey. Through the
years, Mama recounted these events and asked me many times to repeat
the story so I would never forget my first encounter with a bad Jew, an
anti-Semite Communist.

Mama's voice calling "It's time to go" awakened me from a deep
sleep. She said, "Everyone has arrived—wake up, my little *Anna'le*."

I looked around; it was no longer daytime. The sun had gone away.
I did not like it when the sun left; it made me feel sad and cold.

It was now the beginning of the evening. It would soon be very dark
in the woods where we were all hiding. The trees around us moved only

a little from side to side. I could hear them whispering to each other. The breeze was still warm, but Mama said we must put on most of the clothing we owned so nobody could steal it from us.

I looked at the faces of the people who came into the woods with us. They all looked just like Mama and Papa—very thin, tired, and hungry. No one was talking; nobody spoke a word. The first thing they did was go off to the side and, in a whisper, talk to the two big men in charge of us. After talking a little while, they took out paper money and gold things. Mama said it was to pay for our trip.

They would all go with us to a place called Russia and Freedom. *Then why is no one happy? Why do all the faces look so afraid?* They looked at the ground—not at each other—and no one was talking.

I looked up at the tall trees, and I thought they too looked very sad. Many of them had their heads bowed to the ground. I did not know why. *Were they sad to see us go away? Did they know something we did not? Should I be frightened?*

A tall man came to tell us. "There will be no turning back once the hike has started. You have a child? Nobody told me about this! Keep her silent, or she will get us all killed!" He hissed his words through his teeth, just like a little snake.

Papa, Mama, and I were the only small family in this group. The man was very angry with my papa. I did not understand why he hated us. I told myself I was not going to like him very much either.

The march started. We walked slowly and silently through the woods with our small bundles of extra food, water, and belongings on our backs. Everyone had one or two bundles. Very few people had suitcases. I thought we waddled like ducks because of all the extra clothing we were wearing.

I was in my papa's arms at first, but soon he could no longer carry me. I was not a baby; I was much too big for that. When Papa put me down, I walked holding onto Mama's hand.

I looked around me for something fun to see. The moon started climbing up and floating slowly to the middle of the sky—up and up, getting bigger and brighter by the minute. Mama said she was very worried. "So much light could get us into trouble; someone might see us! They will catch us before we cross the river to safety!"

I liked what the moon was doing. I could see many things no one else noticed. The brighter the moon shined, the louder the sound of the singing wolves surrounding us became. Every few moments, I could hear more of them join in the songs. They were everywhere—all around us! My friends, the wolves, were singing again; they sounded happy tonight. It was a love song to the moon, Papa told me. I don't think anyone else cared about my happy friends.

*Bug? Is that the name of the river? I think so.* I kept hearing that word, but I was only able to remember it many years later. Then I found it on a map, so I know it is real.

We walked many long nights, only stopping for sleep in the daytime so no one would see us. We ate whatever we had while we kept walking. If someone wanted to sit down and rest, the men told us there was no time for that. We still had some distance to go. "If we get to the river late, they will not take you across, and we will leave you there!" So we walked on in silence.

Because I was the only child in this group, Mama was very worried about me. "The wolves are getting closer," Mama said to Papa. "I am very concerned."

"They will not hurt us, Mama," I said. "They are my friends." I smiled back at my new friend, the moon. It became my moon, just as all the wolf packs in the forest belonged to me. The moon had joined our friendship circle, and now I was happy. I had a new and very bright friend. *He will light our way to Russia and Freedom.*

I fell asleep in my papa's arms. Sometime later, I awoke to hear voices speaking another language. We had finally arrived at the agreed meeting place on the riverbank.

I could see the moon reflected in the water. I know it smiled only for me. Somehow, I knew tonight was special. We had arrived at the river.

The people waiting for us by the river were pacing back and forth, talking to each other in whispers, and smoking something that smelled very bad. Some of the people were dressed in soldiers' uniforms and looked very angry. I was frightened.

A large rowboat was waiting for us at the riverbank. "We will cross the wide river into Russia in that boat," Mama said.

Mama walked away from us to talk to the men on the riverbank and to the soldiers who were smoking. I watched as Mama paid a soldier with gold and some small pretty stones that sparkled in the moonlight. I saw people give lots of paper money, gold jewelry, and some other things to the soldiers again, just as they had a few nights earlier at the beginning of this hike.

After each person or family paid for the crossing, we were permitted to climb into the boat. Mama was afraid that the boat was too small for all of us, that if we all got in, we might sink, but there was no other choice.

I didn't think my friend the moon would let me be harmed; he was still smiling.

Not one person helped another, and no one helped us get into the boat. Mama got in first, and then Papa gave her our two bundles. She put one under herself to sit on, and the next one she put between her legs so no one could take it away from her.

Papa picked me up, waded into the river, and put me into my mama's arms where I sat on the bundle. Papa was in the water all the way up to his waist. He made sure Mama and I were settled, and then he climbed into the boat with another big bundle on his back.

We began to move in the water, very slowly at first. The rhythm of the oars splashing in the water added to the night's music all around us.

I looked at the oars as they kept dipping and splashing in and out, distorting the face of my new friend the moon. They dipped in and out, on and on. I leaned back against my mama. *Is my new friend the moon a boy or a girl?* I had important questions to ask, but Mama said I was not to speak at all on this night.

"The sound will travel down the river valley, and we will be in big trouble," she whispered.

The wolves, the moon, and I could only speak to each other in my head.

It was very late at night. Mama whispered in my ear, "Close your eyes and go to sleep."

I wanted to look at the river and the moon and listen to the singing of my friends the wolves. The men told everyone on the boat to be very quiet. No talking! Not a whisper! Mama didn't listen to them very well. Only I did.

Four big men were at the oars. Papa said there were too many of us in this little boat. Mama whispered, "It will be a miracle if we don't drown." We were now in the middle of the river. *I think we will get to the other side.*

We kept moving across the river, faster and faster. The oarsmen rowed faster, and the current carried the boat and us downstream a few kilometers to the other side. This was the first time I remember having fun. I was not afraid. I liked this ride very much, and I didn't want it to end.

It was still night when our boat touched the bank on the Russian side of the river. The moon was very big and bright and had moved a little lower in the sky. My friends the wolves didn't sing as much anymore, and as we reached the other side of the river, even the wolves knew to be quiet.

We made it across the big Bug River with our belongings. So did all the other people with us. No one was hurt. We had arrived.

Mama had been teaching me some Russian words; now she told me to pretend I couldn't speak. That way, no one would discover Mother was lying. On that very long walk, Mama had told everyone we were Russians going to visit her aunt who lived in a small farming village not far from the river.

There were men in uniforms waiting for us. Mama warned me again not to say a word. I must be silent, just like my wolves. "Maybe we will get out of this with our lives," Mama said.

They called out to us to get out of the boat quickly. Quickly! Mama whispered that they were speaking Russian.

Two of the oarsmen left our boat and went to the Russian soldiers. One gave sparkling stones and gold jewelry to one of them, and the soldier hugged him. They stood together talking for some time. Soon they started shaking hands and slapping each other on the shoulders. They looked very happy. They gave each other cigarettes and lit them with matches. I could see their faces very clearly. They looked just like everyone in Poland. *So what is the difference between all of us? Why will we be safe in this Russia and not back home in Poland?* I didn't understand any of this.

Mama interrupted my conversation with myself and told me lots of money was paid to these people to allow us to cross the river and go into Russia. Everybody paid—no exceptions!

Once we were out of the rowboat, the soldiers pushed us to walk faster in the direction of a small house near the riverbank. They told us to sit on the ground. We would all have to see someone they called Comrade Commissar. "Wait your turn till someone comes for you."

Our turn came. Mama and I went in holding hands, gripping our treasured bundles. They shoved Papa in, and he stood behind us. Next to the walls, soldiers stood listening to voices coming from a black box. We were in a small room with papers all over the walls. The papers had lines on them in many colors; they looked pretty. The soldiers made marks on those papers on the wall. In front of us was a large desk. From where I stood, I could only see the head and shoulders of the man talking to Mama.

For years, Mama mentioned that man's name to me—many, many times after that night. For many years, I did remember his name. Unfortunately, I am no longer sure whether it was Weintroub or Weinshtock. I think it was Weintroub.

He had bright red hair, a big round head, and a red face; he also had very small blue eyes with white eyelashes and eyebrows. He was ugly! Mama said later that he looked like a pink pig. The man stopped talking to us and turned away to speak with someone else.

I could tell Mama didn't like him. She whispered that he was not a good man. She called him an anti-Semite, and Mama was never wrong.

"Why did you say that, Mama? What is that word?" I asked quietly.

She whispered back, "This is a bad Jew; he is going to send all of us back into Poland." She had warned me not to talk, so I just kept shaking my head *No!* I wanted to tell her he would not do that, because if he did, the Germans or the Poles would kill us all.

Mama said this man didn't care what would happen to us. "Remember this for as long as you live—the worst anti-Semite on earth is the Jew who is ashamed of his own religion and his people."

I promised Mama I would remember always. "The worst anti-Semite in the world is a Jewish anti-Semite," I repeated. "I will never forget."

She was right; he didn't care. I did not forget my promise. My mother was right then, and she would still be right today.

As the pig-man looked back at us, he looked very angry and asked many questions. Mama answered him, but the man was not happy with her answers.

Certain she was lying, he yelled, "Where are you going?" He yelled a third time, looking at Papa.

Papa, with a strange expression on his face, just looked straight ahead and didn't say a word. My mother squeezed my hand tight, letting me know not to say anything.

As Papa didn't speak or look at him, the ugly man with the red face asked my mother if she had married an idiot. He roared with laughter, and the soldiers in the room laughed with him.

"And another thing! Why is your little girl not talking? Does she speak Russian? Or is she an idiot like her father?" Everyone was having fun laughing at Papa and me. I wanted to let go of Mama's hand and run to help my papa. Mama held my hand so tightly it hurt—she just would not let go.

"My child can't speak at all," Mama told him. "She is mute. We are Russians, and we are going to stay with my aunt. She lives in a small village not far from here."

"Where does your aunt live?" Mama told him the name of a farming community not far from the river. My mother spoke Russian very well, but because my father didn't speak it well enough to pass for a Russian, they had decided he would also pretend to be mute.

The next time the red-faced man spoke to my mother, he roared, "Well, take your *pekalach* and go." He spoke Yiddish for package or bundle. "Get out before I change my mind! Get out! Go! Leave!"

He was allowing us to go! We hurried out of the little room, afraid he would change his mind. Several steps away from the little house, we slowed down. He stood in the doorway with some of his soldiers watching us to see if Mama had told him the truth. Had she really been here before, and did she know the way to her aunt's home?

Mama whispered, "Don't run; walk slowly. I need time to think."

"Mama," I asked, "why did he let us go? We are the only people he didn't turn back to the river!"

Mama kept walking very slowly as she looked at me. After a short pause, she finally said, "Is it possible he has taken pity on us? He thinks you, little one, are not able to speak. He also thinks Papa is sick in the head. Could it be some small part of his heart might not be completely dead? I don't know, but for tonight, we may be safe. I just hope he will not have a bad surprise waiting for us up the road."

Did Mama know where to go? We walked a short distance, very slowly. She took a deep breath, and as I looked at her, I could see fear in her eyes. Although her body was shaking, she kept walking.

We were not very far from the little house or the river, and we were coming to a fork in the road. "Do we go to the right, or do we go left? One of those roads is the wrong road," Mama said. Papa picked me up, and we kept walking very slowly.

"If we take the wrong road, he will shoot us in the back or send us back across the river, back to Poland and death." Mama kept saying it to herself—again and again.

My father asked, "*Devorah'le*, do you know where you are going?"

"No, I don't know!" Mama said to him finally. "When in doubt, go to the right!" She had traveled on business for my grandma's farm equipment factory and the hardware store she and my grandpapa owned. It was her mother's advice many years ago, and she heeded it now.

"Well, you only have two choices," Papa said.

We went to the right, as Mama said we must.

I could not hear Mama or Papa breathing; they had stopped breathing. I was afraid. *Should I also stop breathing? Will that help us?* After a few steps on the right fork of the road, the bad Jewish man shouted from far behind us, "Keep going; it's a lucky guess! It's your lucky day!"

"That bastard," Papa whispered, "is an anti-Semite!"

I looked at my papa. "Is he Jewish?"

"Yes, my little one, he's a very bad Jewish man. He is a big man in Russia—a Comrade Commissar with the Communist Party."

I didn't know what it meant then. I didn't understand everything he said, so I asked Mama what it meant. All she would say was, "*Shpeter, shpeter.* Later. I will tell you later."

I never relented until she told me everything. For many years, I have remembered those words: "Lucky guess." That horrible man! He could have sent us all back to die in Poland if Mama hadn't guessed right. He wanted to; he did send most of the others back that night. Papa told me they were all Jews.

As we continued walking slowly away from the house, we could hear the oars once again slapping the water as those denied sanctuary in Russia were returned to Poland. Now farther away from the river, we could still hear the crying voices coming from the boat, wailing, "Why? How could a Jew do this to his own people?" I could also hear the men in charge of the boat telling them all to be quiet. Their voices did travel on the water, just as Mama had said.

"Morning will soon be here," Papa said. "We have to get off the road very soon, and we need to find a place to get some sleep and some food and then hide for the day."

We started to walk faster as fear chased after us for hours.

Mama didn't have family near the river. Our family in Russia lived in Moscow. Mama's Uncle Chaim Schotland was Grandmama Rivka's brother. His family—his wife, four sons, and daughter Galina lived in Russia. Mama still hoped one day to get to the capital to be with her uncle and his family. They were to be our new family, home, and future.

On that night, I heard for the first time the words: "The worst anti-Semite in the world is a Jew." Much to my sadness, I know my mother was right. In my travels all over the world as an artist, I have more than once come across people like that pink-faced pig-man. I have met some of them. They live everywhere, even today.

# Chapter 3

# Angels in Russia

*The City of Mary, Turkmenistan—1944*

My parents didn't know much about the city of Mary (pronounced Marie) before we arrived there. They couldn't know the summer heat would be scorching or that it would be burning hot both day and night.

One evening, Papa told us we would soon feel much better. At first, we didn't understand what it was he planned to do. He had a small ladder in his arms, which he said we would need that night.

We lived on the second floor, right beneath the flat roof of the small two-story building. The heat was stifling; Mama felt sick. When nighttime came, Papa put the ladder against the wall near a square in the ceiling. He asked Mama to climb more than halfway up, and then Mama pushed on the square and opened a strange door in the ceiling. As she pushed it up, it fell outward with a big bang. I could see the moon. Papa picked up my baby brother, Chaim, and handed him to her.

Mama lifted him up and out through the hole and put him outside of the hole. *Did she throw him away?* I didn't know, but when she came back halfway down the ladder again, Chaim wasn't in her arms anymore. I didn't know what was or wasn't up there. I had never seen or been on a rooftop before. She leaned over, and Papa picked me up and handed me up to my mother.

"Hold on till we get to the top," Mama said as Papa helped me climb onto her back. Then I scrambled over her back and out onto the roof right next to Chaim. He was safe!

My father repeated the trip several times, bringing up two buckets of water and several sheets. I had no idea what this was about, and I didn't care. Sitting on the roof, I was able to look all around and down at the city below. Papa was whistling nice songs, as he often did when he was happy. The air seemed to shimmer in the moonlight, although the heat made it difficult to breathe. It was a quiet night, and Papa kept whistling.

On every roof were figures with big white wings. They looked as if they were dancing to the sound of Papa's happy tunes, moving slowly at first and then faster. This sight was all around me—everywhere! *Are they ghosts? Angels?* Mama had told me stories about angels and ghosts, but I had never seen anything like this before! Huge white squares spread out in the dark that started to move, first slowly unfolding arms, and then rolling up into a human form. Then they would disappear into the dark background again. I had no idea what I was watching or what was happening. It frightened me a little, but it was also very exciting and interesting. I didn't know what ghosts or angels looked like, but Mama said this was it.

From large white squares, the figures slowly changed into huge white birds. First, they opened their wings wide and waved them several times—up, down, and to the sides before folding them around themselves and vanishing. Then I noticed they went down off the rooftops and perched on the ground for a short time before rising to repeat the same dance. I liked that dance, and I wanted to dance prettily just as they did. It all looked very fascinating. I watched for some time until Papa joined us on the roof.

Papa took a big bed sheet, dunked it into a bucket of water, and then opened it up wide. He shook it a few times and wrapped my mother in it. Papa then wrapped Chaim and handed him to Mama. Papa dunked a smaller sheet and began to wrap me in it. As he did, he told me to spread my arms wide, hold onto each end of the small sheet with my fingers and flap my arms like a bird to straighten it out. Then Papa helped me wrap the sheet around myself.

When he had us all wrapped in the wet sheets, he did the same for himself, still whistling a happy tune. As he moved to his own music, Papa looked as if he too was a great big dancing angel or bird, just like everyone else on the rooftops. It was all so beautiful and lots of fun. *Are we ghosts? Angels?* It didn't matter, really. We were no longer alone but part of a group of many who looked the same in the moonlight.

We were birds for only a short time before the sheets began to dry. Then Papa put them all back into the water bucket, and when they were soaked once more, we'd wrap ourselves again in those cool, wet sheets and dance like angels. That is how everyone kept from dehydrating in the heat. That was how we could be cool enough to sleep during the hot Turkmenistan summer. Papa, my papa, was so smart to learn this secret to keep us cool and happy.

We had three buckets—one for dunking, one for drinking, and another on the far side of the roof for our toilet. Papa made us drink continuously. He would often come to us with a cup of water and tell us to drink. If we were not drinking or dunking sheets and playing as birds or angels, we had a few moments to sleep.

It was like this every night for many nights. That must be why everyone was always so very cranky and angry in the morning. Though we all needed a long nap by noon, baby Chaim was the only one who slept.

# Chapter 4

# The Candy Factory

*Mary, Turkmenistan—1944*

It was a very restless night, as were most summer nights in Mary. One hot morning as we came down from the rooftop where we had spent the night, Papa said to Mama, "We should be able to save up a few rubles from my job."

Papa was working for the army as a baker. He also did something else he would not tell us about—something "on the side." He wanted to open a small business so he would not have to work for the military branch of the Soviet government. He planned to earn some extra money so we could continue on our journey to Moscow.

Mama said Papa knew only a little about business. My opinion was that my papa knew how to do everything! At this point, all I wanted was for them to be quiet so my little brother Chaim and I could get some more sleep.

Papa rented the small room on the ground floor of the house where we lived. The following week a three-wheeled truck arrived with three big crates on the back. A few days later, a little truck brought some more wooden boxes, which Mama and Papa piled one on top of the other in the room.

Papa and Mama opened the crates. "These are the molds I will use to make candies," Papa announced. The metal forms had many strange and pretty designs.

Mama and Papa assembled the machine parts, while I took care of and played with Chaim. We were going into the business of what was to become the Candy Factory.

Within three days, all was ready. Then a horse and buggy arrived and delivered two sacks of sugar, some bottles with pretty, colored liquid in them, and several other boxes.

Papa and Mama dragged the sacks of sugar into the room. Mama said the sugar was worth almost as much as gold. "Do you know what gold is?" she asked. "It's what my ring is made with." (Mama still had her wedding ring at that time.) "And it's the yellow metal we use to pay for things."

"Yes, Mama, I know gold. I saw you use it to pay the man at the river."

Where did Papa get the money? Mama would not tell me. All she would say was, "I don't know." Many years later, Mama told me they sold some of her jewelry every week for our survival. In addition, Papa was doing something secret to "help out." Something that later got us all into big trouble.

Soon Papa started making hard candy with this new machine. "My waltz machine," he called it. He cooked the sugar in big pots and added lemon juice to some of them. He put other things in the other pots for a good taste, with many different colors to make them all very pretty. "This will pave our road to freedom, my little one."

"Papa, why do you call this machine a waltz machine? Is that its name?"

"Yes it is, but also because I think it has the rhythm of the dance. As the wheels turn, it sounds like it wants to make you dance. Listen to the knocking. Can you hear the rhythms?"

Papa picked me up off the ground and whirled the two of us around a few steps as he started to count in time with the beat of the machine: "*One*, two, three, *one*, two, three." I was in my papa's arms, and we were dancing. We were just like the trees in the wind, moving from side to side. I had seen the trees dancing in the forest; the branches moved, and the leaves twirled. Papa said I could be a great dancer someday, because I was so very light on my feet. Papa was very funny. Papa helped the machine's rhythm by whistling a Viennese waltz. We kept dancing until Mama came into our new little factory room.

"Have the two of you lost your minds? The world is in flames, and like the mad Caesar Nero who played music and thought he was singing while the fires of Rome consumed the city, the two of you are dancing to the sounds of a machine? Volfe!" Mama used Papa's Russian name when she was not happy. "Why do you fill her head with such fantasies? We will be lucky to be alive next week, next month, and next year!"

Papa and I stopped dancing, and Papa's big smile disappeared. I did not see him smile again for a very long time. Papa was sad. Papa loved music and dance, and I loved to be with him when he wanted to dance. We didn't dance together again for many years—not until the *bat mitzvah* of his granddaughter Sherry in Brooklyn, New York.

One week after the small factory was set up and Papa started to make the candy, my parents brought home a strange, large box. It looked like a small table with four legs. On top of it was a large, glass lid. Mama told me we would be able to see into it, but flies would not be able to get in and eat from the candy. I wondered to myself, *How much candy could flies eat?* I didn't dare ask. Mama didn't like most of my questions.

Mama told me she would organize the candy according to color in nice little rows and colored designs, so all the different candies Papa made would look very pretty. She said by next morning she and I would be in the marketplace with our new candy store. I would help with the candy and watch over Chaim as he slept on a small carpet at her feet.

Our new store consisted of this one small table with a glass lid. I was so happy when people came over, paid for our candy, and smacked their lips with delight. They loved it! My papa was so smart. He knew how to make things everyone liked. Mama said candy was a luxury beyond words, but some people would even buy candy and sweets instead of bread.

All was well with Mama and Papa, and they looked happy—until the morning when we had the first disaster.

Papa was very tired. He was not getting much sleep on the roof at night. He didn't like the heat, and he worked in that small room in the heat all day long, from sunrise till long after dark.

The room was always very hot. One day, Papa fell asleep on one of the empty sugar sacks in a corner of the room. All the while, those big cauldrons were cooking the sugar to make the candy for the next week's inventory.

Papa had just a little bit of time before he would need to add the fruit and the zests of oranges and lemons—fruit he had bought at a considerably high price. However, he fell soundly asleep.

Papa awoke with a start to the smell of the burning sugar. Was it a complete disaster? Would we have to throw it all away? My mother was not happy. She was very angry. My poor papa was exhausted. He looked so sick, and he had worked so hard.

"Weeks of money and sugar and survival and bread are all going down the drain, or is it up in smoke?" she accused.

Papa looked at Mama, and then a big smile appeared on his face. "Now," he declared, "since this mistake has happened, we will make ten times the money!"

"How? With what?" she demanded. "You've burned the merchandise! That is all the sugar we had!"

Papa answered, "No, it is not burned. It is now coffee candy! Caramelized sugar smells and tastes like coffee! We will double the price for the new coffee candies. Do you know we are the only candy store in the entire city or country that has coffee-flavored candies?"

Mama finally agreed. "We will try this for one week. We have no other choice."

So the next day, off we went, Mama and I, to the market to set up our small table-store. Mama started calling out loudly, telling everyone about our special new candies. A few stalls down the road from Mama, I imitated her yell: "Coffee candy!"

"Coffee candy!" the two of us yelled. "We are the only booth in the city with coffee candy!"

The line-up was very long. Everyone could smell the coffee from our factory room. Now everyone wanted coffee candy.

In no time, Mama shouted, "*Anushka*, come quick! Help me here! I am out of candy!"

I began running back and forth—from my father in the factory to get the small paper bags full of coffee candy and quickly back to Mama, doing my best not to step on Chaim on his carpet at my mother's feet.

I could hardly keep up! As soon as I got the candy to Mama, she sold it all, again and again. The coffee candy was a great success. We more than doubled our profits in one day, all because of a big mistake. This was also my first job. Mama told me I was a very good, hard worker.

I was three years old, and I was able to help my parents. I felt proud and so very grown up.

Mama asked Papa to remember from now on to do one batch with the fruit, colors, and proper cooking time, and he would burn the sugar just a little bit in the other big pot so we could have coffee candy again. Now we had three products to sell—coffee candy and the lemon- and orange-flavored candies.

From now on things would be very good. We would save lots of money so we could get out of Turkmenistan, Papa told us. We would go back home to Poland to look for our families, Mama said. "But first, we go to Uncle Chaim in Moscow."

# Chapter 5

# Princesses of the Night

*Mary, Turkmenistan—1944*

With Papa's hard work in the candy factory and Mama's and my work at our market table-store, we were now earning a good income. There was enough money to purchase food for our family but not enough for many other necessities. Still, Papa had hope.

Then one day, two men wearing uniforms came to see Papa. I think they were policemen. They told Papa he must stop his work and close his little factory that very day, or he would get a big fine and they would confiscate the candy machines. They said he was operating without a special permit, and if he didn't get one immediately, he would be going to prison. They also said Papa didn't have a permit to sell his goods in the marketplace, so Mama and I would not be able to work at our one-table store any longer.

All work came to a stop immediately. Since we were in the country illegally, Papa did not dare go to city hall for the necessary permits, even if he could have afforded the high cost. A bribe to get the permits would cost even more.

Papa's and Mama's hearts were broken, and I was sad for them.

When the men left, Papa told Mama those Russian swine were just looking for a big handout to leave us alone. I thought a handout was like a bribe. He said graft and corruption in Russia was outrageous. It would cost at least two weeks of hard labor—half of our month's livelihood—to get them to leave us alone so we could work and survive.

Because we did not have any extra money to pay them off, we had to close our big business.

The next day, Mama and Papa saw a policeman stationed not far from our home, watching to see that we did not open the doors to our little candy factory. It was clear we could not stay.

Papa soon found another place for us to live, so we left everything but our personal belongings and moved across the city.

Papa already had his part-time job in the military bakery while he worked in our candy factory. The bakery job alone would not be enough to provide for the family's needs, so Papa took a full-time position with the military to earn more money. It would still take a few months of working to be able to save enough to leave Mary and go on to Moscow.

He started his new work baking bread and pastries for the officers' dining hall. Papa, grateful for the job, was proud and happy to be able to bring home in his big pockets some leftover food from the mess hall almost every night. However, he was very sad inside because he missed the candy factory and had to be away from us for such long hours.

Now Papa would leave for work very late in the evening after putting us up on the roof for the night. It was cooler to sleep there in the heat of summer. He came home in the afternoon to eat and go to sleep for a short while. We did not see much of him during that time.

He also missed making all the wonderful cakes and tortes like he once did in Warsaw. Mama said Papa had been a great pastry chef. They had three small stores, and people respected and admired Papa for the beautiful works of art he created with cakes. This new job was menial, low-class labor, and he didn't like doing it. He felt ashamed to be only baking bread and simple pastry.

As I have told you before, Papa was doing something else "on the side." Well, I think that was the reason for what happened next.

A man who worked with Papa in the bakery came running to our new residence. He yelled Mama's name through the open window.

"Dora! Dora! Your husband said to hide it all now! They are coming! They are on the way! Hide it all now!"

I looked at Mama standing in the middle of the room. For just a moment, she looked frightened. Her black eyes flashed a worried look, and her cheeks started to get red. When Mama became frightened or angry, her cheeks would get very red. That is how I knew my mother was in some sort of trouble.

Taking Chaim in her arms, she said, "Quick! Go outside the room and keep watch."

Of course I knew how to do that. I would just stand outside our door and look all around, watching back and forth in the street. Then if I saw someone, I was to yell, "Mama." That would mean people were coming up the steps to our building.

After a few minutes of watching, I saw three big men walking toward our little house, so I yelled, "Mama! Mama!" as I ran inside our little room and back to my mama for safety.

The men pushed the door open and came into our room. They began searching the room, wrecking things and turning everything upside down.

Then I saw Mama do something to Chaim. Whenever the men were not looking, Mama pinched Chaim on his thigh, and he started crying and then screaming. Chaim was a happy baby and almost never cried, but now he was shrieking. The more he shrieked, the angrier the policemen became. And the harder Mama pinched my poor brother, the louder he cried.

The bad men looked everywhere, but could not seem to find what they were looking for. They yelled and threatened Mama, waving fists in her face. They made her cry. One yelled, "Unless we find the saccharin package immediately, we are going to send your husband away to hard labor camp, and you will never see him again!"

Finally, after what seemed like a very long time, everything was left broken and on the floor. We didn't have much to destroy, but now it was a big, broken mess. On their way out the door, one of the men said, "We will catch him stealing one day, and you will all go to prison!" With that final threat, they left. Mama asked me to look outside the door to be sure they were gone.

Chaim had stopped screaming, because Mama wasn't pinching him anymore. "Mama, Chaim stinks! Please change his rags!"

Mama laughed—for the first time in a long time. "He does stink very badly, doesn't he? I'll change him now."

Still laughing, she said, "Anna'le, what is the only place in this room those men did not look? What is the only thing they did not open or tear apart in their search?"

As I thought about it, Mama was taking off several sets of rags from Chaim's bottom. First, the outer clean ones and next to his bum some dirty, stinky cloths. Hidden between those layers was a well-wrapped bundle I had never seen before.

There, concealed in my brother's stinky diapers was about a half kilo of the precious contraband Papa had collected.

"Mama, what is that?"

"This, Little One, will be our ticket to freedom. This is what the men did not find in their search. No man in his right mind would think to look here for the saccharin."

Mama explained that Papa *had* to take saccharin, an artificial sweetener, because with the small wages they paid him for his work, our family could not survive. Saccharin on the black market was worth lots of money. It was worth its weight in gold, she said.

Each day just before Papa left work, he would take two or three big pinches of saccharin from a very secure closet where only the bakers could enter. He would quickly put it into his pocket and come home. Then Mama would collect it, and when she had a quarter of a kilo or more saved up, she would go to the black market to sell it.

There she would buy some things we needed—bread, eggs and butter, a little milk, and even some medicine and second-hand clothing. What we really needed was money to pay our travel costs to get out of Russia, so she would hide most of the money in a secret pocket in her underwear for when we could go back home to Poland.

My father, Mama told me, was one of the most honorable men she had ever met. However, since the war was on, he temporarily had to do things he did not like. He was not a thief, but he had no choice, because he wanted to feed his wife and children. He had taken the saccharin even though he risked prison or death for stealing from the armed forces. It was a serious crime at any time, but especially during wartime.

I couldn't stop thinking about what Mama did. "Mama, you hurt my Chaim. You hurt my brother! You made him cry. Don't do that again. I will take him and run away!"

Mama just nodded.

A few days later, three big policemen came to our house, and they grabbed my mother's arm. She fought against their touch and snatched up Chaim, but they started to pull her out of our home. I grabbed her dress pocket and hung on tight.

They dragged us all out, and though I do not remember how we got to that new, big house, we were in a room Mama said was a police station and prison. The room had iron bars, and Mama and I could only find space to sit on the filthy floor. Chaim and I sat in her lap, because there was no room anywhere else.

There were some other people in the big room, sitting on two long benches against the wall. They were pretty ladies, and their faces were very painted. Their lips were bright red, and they had lots of black around their eyes. Such strange, pretty, and colorful clothing they wore; it only half-covered their very big breasts.

I asked Mama, "Do they have babies? Do they have lots of milk? They have big breasts! Will they give Chaim and me a drink?"

"Anna, be quiet!"

"Mama, look! Their lice are even bigger than mine are! Oh, look! There's a mouse!"

"No, Anna, it's a rat."

Sitting there on the dirty floor, Mama tried to answer my questions. She said the women probably didn't have babies but only big breasts without any milk. No, you can't have a drink from a total stranger.

Mama said the lice were on everyone and everything all over the world. She saw the lice running down my arm. She brushed them off and looked so sad. Poor Mama!

Sitting there on the floor, Chaim was on one breast, and I was holding onto the other breast. I remember Mama saying to me, "You're over three years old, so you have to stop suckling."

"I am hungry, Mama." I was always hungry.

"Chaim needs my breasts now. I don't have much to give either one of you. He is still so little, and he needs me more than you do."

I will never forget those words. I asked her in my new language, Russian, "*Potom ychoe mne dash?* If I let go now, later will you give me more?"

Mama's face was in pain as she promised that if she felt well, I would get more much later.

Soon the police sent a doctor to see Mama. She had been coughing for weeks now, and I often saw blood come out of her mouth when she coughed. She also had pain in her chest. The doctor examined Mama and then us, and he told her sternly, "You don't have any milk!"

"If I stop feeding them, they will starve."

The doctor yelled at my mother, "You are killing your children! You have no milk, and from the blood you are coughing up, it is most likely you also have tuberculosis! If you keep trying to feed them your bloody milk, then the three of you will all die of TB together! However, if you stop breast-feeding your kids, there is a chance you might survive if we can get some medication for you."

Mama looked him in the eye and said, "We will have to live or die together, because if I stop feeding them, they will starve. I have nothing else to give them, and without them, I don't wish to live!"

Mama started feeding Chaim while the ladies watched, and the doctor stomped out of the room. Then those painted creatures—that's what Mama called them—spoke to her. "Those children are not worth your life! Quit suckling them. Save yourself."

They thought she had long empty sacks she was trying to pass off as breasts. They were right—Mama's breasts were empty; just long empty sacks. I don't know what we swallowed when we suckled, because there was no milk.

That first day in prison was the last time Mama gave me her breast.

Some of the painted women had food hidden in pockets under their skirts. One of them, the prettiest and most painted one, came to us and helped Mama up onto her spot on the bench. Then she pushed another woman off and sat down with me in her lap.

She was very pretty, and she smelled nice. She took a big chunk of bread and some cheese from her big underskirt pocket. She gave a chunk of black bread to Mama for us to eat. Mama did not look in her face, but her tears said, "Thank you for your help."

Mama broke off a piece of bread and put it into my mouth. I told Mama to eat too, but she said we didn't have enough for more than one good meal. "You can't have a breast anymore to suckle, so you have to eat the bread. You have teeth, so I want you to eat more bread and live. I cannot give you a breast now. I need to give Chaim what little milk I have."

I ate the bread, and she kept stuffing more bread and some cheese into my mouth, piece after piece. The pretty woman saw Mama give it all to me, so she gave Mama another chunk of bread just for herself.

The ladies who shared the room with us were different from all the other women I had ever seen. "Mama, why do they look like this?"

"They are princesses of the night. They make people happy."

I only knew of princesses from the stories Papa told me. I had never met a princess before, and none had ever helped me before that day. I decided I must be nice to any princess I might meet in the future. As it was, many more princesses came to visit and stay awhile in that big prison room. Many of them gave us a bit of food to help keep Mama, Chaim, and me from being hungry.

I was learning to say words in Russian. By that time, I knew many words, but I did not understand everything people said. I did understand the policeman who warned that if "it" ever happened again, they would keep us in jail until we died. I think he was talking about Papa and Mama taking the saccharin.

We were able to leave the prison after what seemed like a very long time. I'm not sure how long we were there, although it was probably only a few days. I don't know, and years later Mama would say very little about it.

I remember being back in our shabby little room. Not long afterward, Papa was sent away to serve time in the coal mines in the Ural Mountains.

I remember Mama writing letters, trying to locate her cousin Gala Schotland who lived in Moscow and was a very important person in the military. Mama was sure if she could find her cousin we would be able to get our papa back and could have a better life for the whole family.

# Chapter 6

# The Coal Mines

*Ural Mountains—1944*

We watched as the truck pulled away. Mama held baby Chaim in her arms, and I stood sadly beside her. Papa yelled, "Don't worry, Devorah. Take care of yourself and the children; I will be back very soon!"

Mama didn't cry, but her face was worried, and her eyes looked troubled. I noticed Mama had not been eating much lately. What little food we had, she had been giving to Papa and me.

"Mama, what will we do now?"

"First," Mama said, "we will go to the bakery and get some bread. Then we will go home to eat, have hot tea, and think."

Fresh bread and hot tea seemed like a big meal to me. We stood in line for the bread for a very long time. Suddenly, Mama fell to the ground in a dead faint. I was very frightened. Chaim and I started to cry and scream, but no one cared or moved to help us for fear they would lose their place in the line.

One finely dressed couple, a man and a woman, walked by Mama with hate in their eyes and yelled at her. "You should be ashamed of yourself. You, a mother, and you're drunk in the middle of the day? Are you now sleeping off your drunken stupor in the streets? You are disgusting!" They spat on her as they walked away.

I wiped the spit from Mama's face with my shirt. Chaim was still in her arms. Opening her eyes, Mama immediately asked, "Did we lose our place in the line?"

"No, Mama, the line did not move at all while you were not well."

After many hours, we got to the front of the line. Mama was only able to get one large, round black bread, which she quickly put inside her coat. She tightened the belt around the waist of her coat and put Chaim inside to sit on top of the bread, with only his head visible under her chin. Then she told me to grab hold of her coat and hang on tight for the long walk back to our little one-room home.

"We will have to survive the best way we can till your Papa comes back."

Papa was not there with us. He was still doing hard labor in the coal mines in the Ural Mountains. After Papa left, Mama contacted her cousin Gala—or Galina as we called her affectionately. She was the daughter of Uncle Chaim from Moscow and was in charge of army convoys—the big transports that took soldiers, ammunition, and provisions to the front.

Cousin Gala promised to help. She was trying to get Papa released and returned to his family. She also brought us food.

In the apartment next door to us lived a very beautiful young woman. Her hair was very blond and her eyes more blue than Galina's eyes. She was a tall, big-breasted woman. Everyone thought she was beautiful, because men came to visit in her room all the time, day and night.

I learned about their uniforms. I asked who these important people were, and she told me they were infantrymen or sailors. I thought it was wonderful that she had so many friends. I wanted to grow up to be just like her.

I asked Mama if I could be friends with that lady. "No, you may not be friends with that kind of lady." I didn't know what she meant. Perhaps she was too pretty, and Mama didn't want me to play with her.

One day I opened our door, and there she was, talking to one of the sailors in the hallway. She looked a bit strange. She was wearing garments that didn't cover very much of her body. Her breasts were pushed up very high. One leg was all naked, and she was leaning against the doorframe.

The sailor asked her, "When I come back next time, what would you like me to bring you?" Aunt Galina had once asked me the same question.

The young woman replied with a deep sigh and whispered, "I do *so* love *chocolate!*"

The way she said *chocolate* sounded so wonderful that I also wanted some! I did not know what it was, but if she loved it so much, I knew I would love it too!

When Galina came the following day and asked what I would like her to bring for me the next time she came, I strutted like the lady next door, leaned against the doorframe, pushed up my nonexistent breasts, and in the deep, sensuous voice of a child, I said, *"Chocolate!* I also love *chocolate!"*

Mama and Galina looked at each other. My mother was bewildered. "I don't know why she said this. She has never had chocolate."

I stamped my foot. I knew what I was saying, and I wanted some! I had no idea what it was I demanded to have. I only knew I must have it.

Galina smiled and said, "Don't get all upset. I will bring you some, even if I have to steal it from Stalin himself." She said she was in and out of the Kremlin to give reports and knew she could find me some chocolate, even in Mary. That must be why Mama called Gala the big *macher*—a person who can accomplish important things. She was one who got things done regardless.

When Cousin Galina returned, she handed me a small package. I took it and looked at the picture of a little girl on the paper wrapper. I said, "Pretty baby."

Galina and Mama glanced at each other as Galina said, "You don't know what this is?" I shook my head no. Impatient, she ordered, *"Kushay, kushay!* Eat! Eat!"

*What? I should I eat the pretty paper?*

Galina took it from my hands and tore the pretty girl in half. I gasped at the sight of the torn picture but watched in amazement as a large brown bar appeared from inside the paper. Then speaking more softly, Galina handed the bar to me, saying, "Eat, my little girl; you will like this. It is chocolate."

I held the chocolate bar in my small hands. Now I could smell it, and it was wonderful. I was so proud of myself that I had known to ask for something that smelled so good and was even edible.

Then I licked it a few times. I could not believe my great luck. It was sweet and tasted wonderful.

By now, Galina was losing her patience. "Bite it!" she ordered.

A small chunk fell into my mouth. *This must be the "heaven" Mama talked about,* I thought.

I promised myself that when I grew up, I would always have lots of dark chocolate to eat. I love good dark chocolate to this day.

*(Papa told me the rest of this story when I was seven.)*

It was a short trial. No one came to defend Papa or any of the other accused and now convicted men. They were simply dragged out of the building and put on a tarp-covered truck. Without any evidence, Papa was found guilty of theft from the army supply of saccharin and ordered to serve a one-year sentence of hard labor in the Ural Mountains coal mines.

That transport truck took Papa and a group of other convicts to the train station. Guards watched the prisoners with rifles pointed at them at all times during the long trip so they would not try to run away. Many trains arrived amid screeching brakes and belching smoke. Finally, with rifles in their backs, Papa and those in his group were herded forward on the platform and shoved onto a train for the long trip.

The trip took several days, as the train had to stop on sidetracks to give way to military transport trains rushing through on their way to the front lines of the war.

The prisoners received no food on the train, though they did receive water in buckets. Some of the men had not eaten in days. Papa said the men themselves didn't care if they lived or died, as most of them had been given a life sentence in the coal mines.

Before they took Papa to prison, Mama made him a special belt with a pouch, which he could wear under his shirt so no one would see it. Mama packed some bread, cheese, and dried fruit into it, and on the train, Papa covered his head with the front part of his coat when he broke off a small bite of food. He ate slowly, without a sound, pretending to be asleep.

The men did hard, physical work in the coal mines without much food or water and hardly any rest. The guards were brutal, and the slightest infraction would precipitate a beating frenzy. The word *murder* did not apply to the daily killing of prisoners.

Papa did the work as he was told and kept to himself as much possible. He did not wish to make friends. Papa feared they would find out he was a Jew and would kill him. He was certain no one would come to his defense.

Shortly after arriving at the coal mines, Papa got sick. The coal dust, cold air, and dampness of the mines were affecting his lungs. He was coughing up black phlegm with blood in it, but he kept working. Had he stopped, they would have shot him.

Late one morning, he heard rumors about a planned prison break. Three of the men were talking about killing some of the guards. Papa did not wish to have anything to do with that, so he kept working. About noon, he heard shooting, and he stood against the wall behind a coal wagon. Men went running past.

Two of them saw Papa and yelled, "Come, Markus! Run! They are near. They will kill you if you stay!"

Papa started running with them. Some distance from the base camp, Papa fell to the ground in pain. He could not run anymore; he could barely breathe. He was coughing very hard and spitting up black phlegm again. The other two men kept running, leaving my papa behind.

Sitting on the ground and struggling for each breath, Papa wondered what to do next. Was it wise to run with all the others? Or should he have remained to serve out the rest of his sentence? He wasn't sure he could survive much longer in the prison with his lung condition.

Just then, a man dressed in a guard's uniform approached and yelled at Papa. "What are you doing out here, so far from the camp? Are you with the criminals who are escaping?"

Papa caught his breath. "They threatened me and made me leave with them!"

"Well you better get back to base camp and make sure no one sees you. No one must know you ran away!"

Papa asked why he must go back when all the others are running away in all directions. "And why are you treating me differently now?"

"Your imprisonment was a big mistake. You should not have been sent here. You, Markus, must know someone very big in Moscow. You have received a pardon! The orders came from Moscow this morning to let you go back home to Moscow. I will help you with the paperwork."

Papa did his best to hide his confusion. *A pardon? Go back home to Moscow?* He had never been to Moscow. *Do they have the wrong Markus?* Could he get away with claiming to be that person? First, he must get back into that terrible prison camp without anyone seeing him. But how?

It took him the rest of the day to make his way back inside the camp, hiding from prisoners and guards alike. The place was in chaos. No one paid much attention to him. People were running in the opposite direction, some yelling for him to get out of the way. Guards and now even some prisoners had guns and were shooting at most anything that moved.

Papa managed to get back to his cell late into the night, out of breath and feeling very ill.

One of his cellmates was on the floor, badly wounded by what appeared to be gunshots. There was blood everywhere. He looked at Papa and gasped, "Markus, why are you here? They will kill you! Get going! Run away. You know no one likes a Jew." Papa wondered about that comment, as he had told no one there of his heritage. However, there was no time then to think about it.

"No, I will not run away now," Papa said. "I've just learned I have received a pardon. A letter came from Moscow, and I will be going back home!"

"You're a ... fool, Markus. They must have told ... everyone ... the same story ... just to get them back ... to the mine."

Papa stood frozen, looking at him. "I never thought of that," he said. "What can I do for you right now?" Papa asked the wounded man.

He was gasping for each breath. "A letter. In my pocket. Send it ... to ... my mother. I won't ... see her ... I won't ... make it."

Papa took the letter, put it inside his shirt next to his body, and promised to send it as soon as he could. He left the cell to get some water, and when he returned, the man was dead. Papa stood for a moment in front of the lifeless form, silently promising that his mother would get his letter. Later in our town of Mary, Papa read the letter, added a few hundred rubles of his own money, and mailed it to the dead prisoner's mother.

Papa was exhausted and too sick to think of anything but getting some rest. He sat down on some rags by the wall and soon fell into a deep sleep. He had not slept very long when kicks from a guard's boot jolted him awake.

"Get up, Markus! Where have you been? What took you so long to get back in?"

Papa told him he was hiding throughout the prison and in the mine. He said at one point he was frightened of other prisoners who wanted him to run away with them again.

"It is lucky you did not run. You would have been shot or have to stay as a prisoner for life in this mine. Instead, we will take you to the train station with your documents of freedom, and you can go on home. Mother Russia takes good care of her innocent children!"

Papa did not dare to say a word. He just nodded his head in agreement.

"Come with me," the guard said. "Let's get out of this hell hole. I have been ordered to personally escort you to the train station. It is two or three days away from here. Tell me, did your cellmate say or give you anything before he committed suicide?"

Papa shook his head no. "He was dead when I came back from the latrine."

*What suicide?* Papa asked himself. *The poor man was dead, with two bullets in his body, and he did not have a gun.*

Papa did not say another word. He could do nothing now for his dead cellmate. To show any interest in the man would only have brought more trouble down on his head.

Papa had a few moments to wash his face and hands and clean himself up a bit, and they were off, on their way to the train station. Papa's hatred for this guard was great. He had seen him brutalize men, some of them beaten to death while he laughed sadistically.

Papa was watchful, certain that at the first opportunity, the man would try to kill and rob him. So he always walked beside or behind him and did not speak unless he was asked a direct question.

Three days later, they arrived at the busy train station. The guard took a thick envelope from his breast pocket. Papa's letter of freedom—his pardon—was in it, along with a big roll of money.

As Papa watched, this evil man helped himself to most of the money. He said, "If you say anything, I will destroy the documents and keep all the money. Then I will start screaming for help. I will say you are an escaped convict. The hooligans at this station will be happy to tear you apart. So what will it be? What is your choice? The money, or your life? I am sure your cousin Gala in Moscow will have more money to give you when you arrive."

Now for the first time, Papa realized who his benefactor was! Mama's cousin Gala was a high-ranking officer with the Russian military. In Transport and Supply, she had many connections in the right places. Mama had somehow contacted her and asked for her help.

Papa pleaded with the guard to give him as much money as it would take for several trains to Moscow and to get some food for the three- or four-day trip. That was more than what the guard had left in the envelope. Not wanting a confrontation, the guard took some bills from his pocket and returned them to Papa, telling him to get lost in the crowd.

Papa walked away, a free man. First, he looked to get some food. Then he needed to decide which direction to go, which train to take, so he would be far from this place. *Where was his family? Were they in the same town where he had left them? Or did Mama get help to take the family to Moscow?*

After much thought, Papa finally decided he would go back to the city he came from and look for his little family. It was a long journey of several days and many trains. For some, he paid for a ticket. Most he did not. He was able to avoid the few conductors among the masses of people on the trains.

Papa went back to the city of Mary. Mama, Chaim, and I were still in the same small room, having survived by selling the small handful of the saccharin Papa had left behind.

# Chapter 7

# The Train from Russia

*1944*

*(As told to me by Papa and Mama, with some clear memories of my own.)*

Mama's cousin Galina, with her high army rank and connections, had indeed saved our papa from the hell of the coal mines.

When he returned to us, he was very ill and coughing most of the time. However, that didn't keep him from working to support his family. He said, "Being sick is one thing, but if you want to work, you will always find a job, no matter your physical condition."

Papa went to work almost immediately in a bakery—a job he knew well. Bakers were always in demand.

Once more, he started helping himself to the precious saccharin powder in order to pay for our provisions and for our escape out of Russia. This time, however, Papa was far more careful. He did not wish to experience the coal mines ever again.

Papa's cough did not get better. He looked weak, and he was working very hard.

One day not long after Papa came back, Mama asked me to look after Chaim while she went to find a doctor. I was to make sure my little brother did not fall off the small bed. I must also look after Papa, making sure he had water to drink. He had been very sick and in bed for the past two days.

After a while, Mama came back with a doctor. He asked many questions and listened to Papa's chest. He looked very worried.

"Your papa," he said to me, "is very sick, and he will have to stay in bed for a very long time."

"What is wrong?" I asked, just as Mama asked the same question.

"Your papa has a lung infection and a bad sickness called malaria. I will give him some medicine now, and he will start getting better soon." He showed me a yellow powder. "Just make sure he is covered all the time, even when he is very hot and perspiring. He must drink lots of water, even when he is not thirsty!"

Mama gave me the job of keeping Papa covered. So I stayed close by and made sure all the edges of the big, feather-filled comforter were snug around his feet. Papa's face was wet, so I got on top of the bed with a towel and wiped his face and neck. He was shivering so hard.

Papa's eyes were closed, but as I walked away from the corner where the bed was, he whispered, "Wait. Don't go. I am thirsty; water please." Papa was not asleep. His eyes were red and his face was wet again, but he was not shaking as much as before.

I ran to Mama for water. She poured some into an aluminum cup, one that would not break if I dropped it. Mama came with me and put some more powder in the water for Papa to drink. Then she put some more blankets on top of Papa and said, "He will sleep soon for a long time, and when he wakes up, he will feel much better."

I sat on the edge of the bed watching Papa sleep, making sure I could hear his breathing.

I guarded him like this for several days. Papa was getting stronger now and was very hungry. He ate all the food in the house. Mama gave him as much as he wanted, even if it meant she had nothing at all.

Papa wasn't ready to go back to work yet, but because he was feeling somewhat better, he started to tell me stories again. My favorite one was about a land where the Jews once lived in freedom and joy, a land that was home for all Jews. It was where the great kings, David and his son Solomon, once ruled and built a great temple. Papa told me King Solomon made peace with all the nations of the world.

"How did he do that, Papa?"

"He took wives, one from every land, and became the friend of all the kings, and only during his time did the world know a very long peace!"

Once Papa started to tell me stories, I knew it meant he was feeling much better.

"Papa, when can we go to that Jewish land?"

"Soon, my little girl, very soon!"

Papa asked Mama to come to his bed. He had something very important to talk about with her. Papa said, "You do know we will never become Communists. And it is getting more and more difficult for me to keep my job without Communist Party documents. We have to get out of this country as soon as possible!"

"The war is still on all over Europe! Where shall we go, and how will we get there?" she asked.

"Back to Poland!" Papa said. "Some members of our families must have survived this madness! We will search for them there."

"We have small children. How are we going to get out of Russia with them?" Mama asked.

"We will go by train. There are trains going to the border with Poland every day. We can be on one of them!"

"No, we cannot!" Mama declared. "They are all military trains. They will not allow civilians to board, especially a family with small children!"

They both looked angry and very sad.

"Finding a way to get out of Russia must be a priority," Papa said. "It must be the first thing on our minds day and night till we come up with something that will work!"

Now Mama could not get the idea of the train out of her mind. She left Chaim with the old woman next door, and she and I set off on a long walk to the train station.

When we saw the station was full of people all talking at the same time, we knew we were not the only people who wanted to leave this area. "When is the next train to the border?" was the question we heard many people asking.

As we walked around, Mama listened to every voice, hoping to learn something that would be of use to us. However, we went home with bad news for Papa: no trains for the civilian population from this station! Only military transports come and go every few hours moving soldiers and army supplies to the front lines.

Papa knew, or at least suspected, much of what Mama told him. "I will think of something," he said.

Mama again put some of the powder in a glass of water. Papa asked for all the medicine the doctor had given her, so Mama gave him the small bag.

When Mama went to the other side of the room that served as our kitchen, Papa asked me to bring him a large glass of water. When I returned with the water, Papa poured all of the powder into the glass.

"Papa! What are you doing?"

"If a little bit of this is good, all of it at once should be much better! I do not have time to stay sick in bed. I know we have to get out of this land now!"

Papa fell into a deep sleep, and he slept almost continually for two days. When I told Mama what he had done, she looked at me and said, "Well, this may cure him, or it will kill him. We will know soon!"

It was getting to be night outside for the second time since Papa took all the medicine. Chaim and I had to be very quiet for two days and nights. Mama was getting worried. Papa had not eaten for two days. Mama lifted his head and made him drink very often.

It was late in the morning on day three when Chaim and I awakened. Mama was cooking breakfast, and Papa was sitting at the small table drinking tea. Papa was up and well!

I jumped out of the bed Chaim and I shared. "Papa! Papa! Are you all well again?"

I stood before him, but Papa could not pick me up. He said it would be another few days before he would be strong enough to lift me. "Today you will help Mama. We will be packing now to get out of Russia. We will go by train! You will see; it will be fun!"

To Mama he said, "We will do everything we can to get out of this land and go back to Poland."

Mama nodded her head and said, "Yes, we will go back and look for our families. The war should be over very soon!"

✡ ✡ ✡

It was not yet light when Mama got Chaim up and dressed him with all the clothing we had for him. Mama herself was wearing three dresses, two pairs of long socks that came over her knees, two pair of men's pants, two shirts, a sweater, a winter jacket and a thick black winter coat on top of that, as well as big, high boots.

Then it was my turn to get dressed. When Mama completed this task, I could hardly move. Mama told me I would have to help her by keeping an eye on Chaim all day. I agreed. I loved my little Chaim very much.

We left our small room without a word to anyone. We were all very quiet. My parents were afraid to tell anyone of our plans to get out of the country. They knew people would report it to the police. We walked very fast to reach the train station before the streets became full of inquisitive police and other people.

Hundreds of people camped out on the platforms. How long had they been there? Days? Weeks? Months? Very little floor space was available for newcomers. That did not bother Mama. She approached an old woman leaning up against a big post and asked her to move a bit so she could put down a blanket for the children.

The woman asked, "Do you have some bread you could give me?"

"Yes, I will give you some bread, but first, move!"

Mama helped the old woman move her things, and then Mama put down a blanket on the floor. On it, she put two of the three big bundles. She placed Chaim next to one of the bundles and told me to sit on the other one.

A moment later, the old woman reached out her hand to one of our bundles. Quick as a flash, Mama slapped her hard on her hand. "If you touch my bundles or my children, I will kill you!" Mama hissed, eyes blazing. The old woman recoiled, looking angrily at Mama as she moved away, holding her stinging hand.

As Mama promised, she took a big piece of bread from the bundle on her arm and gave it to the old woman. That bundle never did leave Mama's hands. It was the most valuable bundle we had, as it contained all we would need to survive for the next few weeks.

Papa walked around slowly, talking with men, asking questions. Just then, we heard a rumbling sound, distant at first, and then coming closer and closer. As the train neared the station, we could feel its reverberations. Suddenly, most of the people were clamoring, pushing and shoving one another to the edge of the platform.

"The train is coming. A train is coming." They screamed the words repeatedly. People fell off the platform and onto the tracks as those behind them pressed closer. Nobody helped them as they scrambled to get out of the way of the train.

I had never seen a train before. It was very big, black, and angry. It was huffing and puffing, and steam billowed from all sides. It had pretty red flags everywhere.

At the station, the passenger doors never even opened. The train stopped only long enough to take on water and was on its way again. Men left standing on the platform yelled angry words about their bad luck and the war.

Papa came back to where we were on our blanket. "I need to do some serious thinking about how to get us out of this place! I will be back soon with a solution!"

I remember noticing there were no other children on the platform. "Where are all the children?" I asked Mama.

Mama said all the Russian children were at home or in school, and she was not sure if we had many Jewish children still among the living. I did not understand this, but Mama looked very determined about something.

Two days later another train approached the station. Papa announced that this train would be going to the border. With urgency in his voice, he said, "Get ready!"

Papa and Mama hurried to the edge of the platform, carrying one of our large bundles, leaving Chaim and me sitting on the blanket with the other two bundles. The moment the train stopped, Papa hoisted Mama up to a small open window. She scrambled in with the small bundle on her arm and then pulled the big bundle in as Papa pushed it from below.

Papa hurried back for the last two bundles, Chaim, and me. Mama reached out to retrieve a bundle from Papa, struggling to pull it in. Papa lifted Chaim and then me into Mama's arms. She pulled me in and set me on top of the big bundle next to Chaim in the tiniest room I had ever seen. She told me to hold onto Chaim, as she quickly turned back to the window.

As she took the last bundle from Papa, people started to notice what we were doing. Now Papa grabbed onto Mama's arms. Pulling with all her strength, she helped Papa climb through the small window. Then he and Mama stood on the piled-up bundles and forced the little window shut. It was so filthy dirty I couldn't see through it.

Both Papa and Mama were out of breath, and they motioned to me to be quiet. Chaim also stayed silent. I was more interested in listening to what was happening on the platform outside.

People were screaming. One man's voice, the loudest, was yelling repeatedly, "I saw a man. I think he was a Jew. He put his family on this train!"

Others told him to shut up, that it could not be true. Still he kept yelling. "I am sure they were Jews. They are running away from our great Mother Russia. Let's get them out of the train and kill them!"

"You are a fool," another yelled. "There are no Jews in this part of Russia!"

As others joined in the yelling and we cowered in this stinky, tiniest of rooms, I felt the train start to move. Mama's whisper reached me, "*Shema Yisrael Adonai Eloheinu Adonai Echad.* Hear, O Israel, the L-rd our G-d, the L-rd is one."

Mama leaned closer to Papa and whispered, "Well, my dear Volfe, what do we do next?"

Papa smiled a tired, weak smile. "We have our wits and our G-d. We will survive!"

For a very long time, all was quiet. We children were lulled into a good sleep by the motion of the train. Someone banging against the door awakened us. "You in there, hurry up. Others need to use this bathroom!"

Another voice said, "I did not see anyone enter."

"So why is the door locked?" asked the first voice.

Mama whispered, "So *that* is the horrible smell in this little room! We are squeezed into the train's toilet. How many hundreds of soldiers are on this train, and how many toilets are there to service them all?" Mama asked Papa.

The voices outside the door got louder. "Get out and let us in; some of us need to use it!"

Another voice joined in. "At the station, someone was yelling that some people had snuck onto the train! Maybe *that* is who's in there."

"It's not possible," another one said. "The window is much too small and too high off the ground. I don't think anyone could get on board that way."

One yelled, "Go get an officer."

Papa stood up on top of the bundle and straightened his pants and jacket. "Papa, where are you going?" I whispered.

"I must to go out of this room to speak to the officer when he gets here," he explained.

The next voice was of the officer in charge of the train. "Come out right now, or I will shoot through the door!"

Papa answered. "Please, do not shoot; you will kill a Russian child!" Chaim had a Russian birth certificate, but I was born in Poland and had no papers at all.

The silence only lasted a few moments. "Open this door, and we will talk."

Papa opened the door slowly. I looked out and took a deep breath of cleaner air. The officer was talking to Papa. "No civilians are allowed on military trains. I can do one of two things: I can stop the train and have you removed right now, or I can just shoot you where you are and then throw you off!"

Papa was now talking very quickly, as the officer still looked angry. Still, he listened to Papa. "Please do not make us leave. We will get out when we get to the border."

The officer shouted, "You are crazy! It will be five, six, or more days from now, if we are lucky! This train is breaking down every few days!"

Papa interrupted him. "In exchange for the ride, I will work for you. I am a great baker, a *conditore* (pastry chef). And I cook like a great chef. I promise you will eat like kings! Give us a chance to survive this war."

The officer looked into the cubicle where we sat. He ordered that we, with our belongings, exit the room so his soldiers could use the toilet. I looked at the officer's face and could see he was thinking about Papa's proposition.

"What is your name?" he asked Papa.

"Markus," Papa answered.

"Well, Markus, this is your lucky day. We lost our cook a few days ago and have not eaten well since. I will give you the opportunity to show me what you can do."

Papa bravely said, "I have only one condition."

"What?" the officer roared. "You have a condition?"

"Yes," Papa said quietly. "My wife and children must get as much food as they can eat."

Mama and Papa were holding their breath. *Had Papa gone too far?*

The officer started to laugh. "Surely they can't eat so much as to cause us a problem. Hey, you guys, help this man get his family and their belongings out of the bathroom."

As one of the soldiers took me out, a voice in the middle of the train car called out, "Send her down this way; she looks just like my beautiful little Ella back home! Give her to me for a while!"

The soldier holding me looked at Papa. He looked back to see what Mama would say. When she nodded yes, he passed me very carefully over the heads of the soldiers to the man who had asked for me.

"What is your name?" he asked.

"Anna."

He hugged and cradled me in his arms while whispering to me, "My dear little Anushka, go to sleep if you wish. You are safe now. I will protect you!"

I looked around and saw Chaim was also with a soldier, smiling and playing. One of the soldiers gave Mama his seat, and he sat on the floor at her feet, talking to her. I asked my soldier his name, and he said it was Volodia. I was startled. "That is another form of my papa's Russian name!" His beautiful blue eyes and white teeth smiled at me as I fell into a deep, quiet sleep.

Then someone nudged me a few times until I awakened. The train slowed down and came to a complete stop. I looked for my brother; he was still asleep. Papa was talking to the officer. My new friend Volodia asked me if I was hungry. He burst into loud laughter when I said, "Yes, I am always hungry!"

"Well then, we will eat what I have in my bag until your papa cooks for us!" He took out a very nice green cucumber from his bag, broke it in two, and gave me half. He asked me if I could eat all of it. I promised to do my very best.

The young officer, Papa, and a group of soldiers got off the train and started to set up a kitchen for Papa. First, they looked for large, flat rocks to make a stove. Then they brought big vats and large water containers from the supply car, as well as big slabs of pork, sacks of rice, a large container of salt, and nothing more.

Papa asked if they had potatoes or onions. The officer shook his head no. Papa asked for permission to go with some soldiers to one of the farmhouses nearby and see if they could barter for the items he wanted.

The officer agreed it was a good idea and then added, "Why barter? Just take what you want or need. It is war, and all must do the best they can to help Mother Russia."

Papa said he would not do that. All he wanted was two sacks of rice to use for bartering. Rice was a luxury item.

The officer reminded Papa to make sure he did well for the soldiers.

And so he did. Papa came back with a wagon full of goods—two sacks of onions, three sacks of potatoes, two sacks of apples, and five live chickens.

A large group of men helped with peeling the vegetables and killing the chickens. They did everything Papa told them. It was the best meal any of them had had in months. The officer was very happy and wanted to know what it would take to have Papa make bread or even something sweet. Papa asked to see all that was in the supply car. When he came back, he told the officer that in three or four hours, he would be able to make them all happy.

The days went by happily for me. Papa did not have much time for any of us. He was feeding a train full of soldiers. We had dozens of new friends who wanted to play with us. Mama started to look rested and much better after almost a week of good food and some rest on the train.

Then late one afternoon, it was time to say good-bye. The officer in charge of the train sadly informed us we could not go on with them any longer, not even one more kilometer. We could hear artillery fire in the distance. It was the last stop for us. Volodia and I cried. I wanted him to come with us.

The officer thanked Papa for his great work and wished us good luck. He told my parents they were crazy to be this close to the front lines and the war. He gave us lots of food to take with us for the rest of our journey.

We thanked him for the ride and the food. Mama blessed them to go home in peace.

We took the food, and with sad tears and waves good-bye from my friend Volodia and many of the soldiers, we started walking to the nearest village. We hoped there we might get information to help us with decisions for our future.

# Chapter 8

# The Road to the Church
### *1944*

We returned to Poland so my parents could look for survivors of their families, even though they heard that most Jews there were no longer alive. We made our way to the area where our ancestors had lived for generations. Of Poland's prewar Jewish population of three and a half million, some three million were killed in the Holocaust.

It was incomprehensible to Papa; he kept shaking his head, saying no one could or would annihilate so many people. Yes, it was a war, and yes, it was a terrible thing—still, he did not believe anyone would try to murder all the Jews. I remember him using the number eighteen. Papa kept saying there were eighteen million Jews in the world. I am not sure if he meant eighteen million Jews in the entire world or just in Europe; I didn't ask. His pain was too great.

We eventually arrived at the land where generations of my maternal ancestors had lived. A Polish couple were tenant farmers there. They were Gentiles, Polish Catholics. Mama was so happy to see them. To me, they looked very old. Mama said I should call them Grandma and Grandpa. I did not know them, but they were so happy to see me. The old woman could not stop kissing me. She was very blond and had pretty, twinkling blue eyes. They had loved my mother from the time of her birth, as if she were their own.

While they were happy to see us, they were well aware of the danger of sheltering Jews. I could easily pass for the couple's Polish grandchild with my pale blond hair and complexion. I looked just like them. However, my father was always hiding, because if he were ever to be discovered, he would be killed immediately. They would kill us all, as well as the old man and woman for helping us. The only way they could save us was for my papa to become invisible.

My parents decided to join the partisans (resistance fighters). The old woman had a daughter. She agreed to keep my baby brother Chaim to wait for our parents' return at the end of the war. The couple told Mama of a church not far from Brzezine. It had taken in orphaned children from the start of the war. They said they should take me there to save my life. They had heard this church was saving many children. The priests were kind, good people, and they would help every little one. They would hide me while my parents went to join the partisans in the forest, fighting the Nazis.

The old couple had an ox, and they harnessed him to a wagon. They loaded the wagon with an assortment of farm machinery and household furniture, leaving a small space in the back corner for Papa to hide. He would sit on and be covered by pillows and blankets. Then they piled sheaves of hay and straw on top. If someone should stab at the straw with a pitchfork, the hard items would shield him.

We left at night, so no one could see what we were doing. There were packages of food—bread and water—on the wagon. In the daytime, Papa hid under the straw and other household furnishings. At night, he would come out from under all the goods piled high on top of him.

Mama sat in the back of the wagon, and I was usually riding in the front with the two old people when I wasn't asleep in my mother's lap. Mama told me again and again, "Remember you are a Jew, but you must never tell anyone or you will die. Do not forget you are a Jew, and only *after* the war may you be a Jew again. Promise me you will never forget!"

I remember it was always nighttime when the old couple would lie down in the back to get some sleep, and sometimes Papa would drive the wagon. Then I would sit in the front between Mama and Papa, so I could be with my papa and see everything from high up.

One night, I told Papa somebody was following us—I could hear them. "Papa, somebody *is* following us!" I insisted.

"Who's following us?"

"Those little lights." I pointed with my finger. There were lights in the distance, very bright, and they kept following us. I pointed again. "Papa, look over there! There *are* lights; they *are* following us." When Papa looked, he actually saw the lights. "Are they bad people, Papa?"

"No," he said. "They are not people; they are wolves. Wolves are bigger than dogs are, and all those lights—every two lights close together—are the eyes of one wolf. The lights you see are reflections from the bright light of the moon shining in their eyes."

"Why do they want to come with us? Are they going to the church?"

"No, they are hungry. They are looking for dinner." Papa was so clever; he always knew the answers to all my questions.

I looked at him. "Well, we have bread."

Papa whispered back that no, they didn't want bread—they wanted the ox. "They are very hungry, but as soon as it gets to be daylight, we will be safe."

However, it wasn't going to be daylight for a long time, and they followed us all night. I was looking forward to seeing them, but the wolves didn't come to us. Every now and again, we could hear one or more of them howl very loudly. Then another one would join in and then another, while my father would shudder and my mother kept saying, "Oh my G-d, they will get us."

I said, "They sing so pretty! Those wolves *do* sing so pretty. I am going to have a few wolves at home!"

The wolves never came close enough to see. I never heard them snarl; I never saw any viciousness. I have loved wolves ever since then, and even more now that I've learned much more about them.

In the daytime, Mama and I rode on the back of the wagon. Very early every morning, the couple would camouflage Papa so it looked like just they, my mother, and I were on this trip. All manner of junk was piled on top of my poor father; everything that could go on the wagon was heaped on top of him. It looked like a garbage wagon with personal belongings of little value—an unlikely hiding place for anyone.

We were running out of food and water. We were thirsty; we could only have so many sips every day. My mother would cheat. She would take an extra-big swallow and then put her mouth close to my mouth and give it to me. I would get to swallow three or four times and then start coughing as I struggled to swallow the extra water much too quickly. Mama gave me at least half of her water rations each day.

The old woman told Mama she had heard stories of some things many Jewish mothers were doing to their children's faces to help to find them after the war. My mother looked at her with alarm. *What kind of things?* The old woman told her a mother would sometimes take a knife or sharp glass, and carve a design on her child's face, forehead, or cheek so that if they got separated, she would be able to recognize the scar and know her child even years after the war—if they both survived. This grandmama recommended my mother do the same with me now before they left me at the church, just in case we both survived the war.

That same day, my mother found a piece of glass during one of our rest stops. She spat on it and wiped it on her dress to clean it, and then she brought it to my face. She was going to cut lines on my cheek! She held my head tightly with one arm. The more tightly she held me, the more frightened I became and started to struggle and scream. The old woman and Papa tried to hold me down. I must have been a powerful little girl for the skeleton I was. I fought them with all my might, kicking, screaming, and biting.

As Mama came closer to my face with the sharp glass, I was frightened and fought very hard, tossing my head from side to side. Instead of cutting my cheek, she cut me right on my upper eyelid and temple. It's a miracle I was not blinded in my right eye. It was a very bad cut, and I did not allow it to heal for weeks. Every time my mother came near me, I would touch the wound, reminding myself not to trust her again. She hurt me deliberately, but I didn't understand she did this to me for a reason. All I knew was someone I really trusted had hurt me. She had made me bleed, scream, and cry. Years later, I learned Papa blamed me for the pain in his ribs inflicted by my desperate kicking.

Mama was also crying, but I didn't know why. She and the old woman were scared to death I would lose my eyesight, so they used some of the precious little water we had left to clean the cut. It was deep and had grazed the bone at the end of my eyebrow. Mama would press rags against it so it would stop bleeding, but it kept oozing. I didn't want it to heal. It could not heal because I kept scratching and picking at it.

My mother was hysterical, beside herself with pain for having done this. I felt no sympathy for her. All I felt was anger and hate. I did not know what those feelings were, but I had them. For the first time, I did not love my mother or my father. For the first time, I felt something that did not make any sense. Of course, years later, I realized it was anger, fear, and distrust.

It was a very long week of struggling with diminishing food and water. Every now and again, we would pass by an area where the old man or woman would get off the wagon and go to a farmhouse to see if they could barter some of the farm equipment—or anything from the wagon—in exchange for some bread or water. They would say their home had been destroyed in the war, and they had nothing to eat. Could they help a nice Catholic family who was starving? Sometimes the couple came back empty-handed. Sometimes strangers offered food—a few potatoes or an onion. Usually we stunk of onions.

One day, the woman told my mama we only had two days left until we would get to her sister's home—the relative who would take us in and care for us until we gained the strength to continue on the rest of the trip to the church. The plan was still to reach the church and for the old woman to take me to the church as a foundling.

The ground was very hard and dry, and the wagon bounced over rocks and into ruts. Once, we had to stop for an entire day, because one of the spokes in the wheel was broken, and they needed to fix it. After that, we had to travel more slowly.

The old couple usually kept to the dirt country roads. They tried to stay away from big cities and towns, but we were on the road so long that the worst finally happened. We heard vehicles coming down the road behind us.

My father heard them too, and he spoke from underneath all the rubbish on top of him. "Come quickly, Anna'le. Come down here with me." He warned me not to speak to him, not even in a whisper. To be sure I didn't, he put his hand over my mouth. Now I was very afraid. *Were the bad people coming?*

My mother looked around. "Bad people are coming!" she exclaimed with fear in her voice.

Four vehicles arrived—two trucks and two Jeeps. People in the Jeeps wore what I now know to be medals and military insignias. Swastika flags were flying on the Jeeps, and that crooked cross was painted on the vehicles. The soldiers yelled for the wagon to stop. "Halt! Halt!"

The soldiers kept asking questions. I knew some of what they were saying, because I understood Yiddish. Mama spoke German very well, and they kept asking her where my papa was. "Where is your man? Where is your husband?" Mama said he was dead.

*That's not true, Mama! Papa's hiding in the wagon!*

I didn't understanding why Mama said he was dead; he was here with me, hiding in the wagon. Then some motorcycles arrived. They surrounded our wagon. Some of the men said things they thought were funny; they were laughing. They asked the old woman who we were, and she told them Mama was her daughter. The men said, "Dammed dirty Polacks!" and started laughing again.

One of the men said my mother did not look like her "mother," because she had such beautiful, curly black hair, not at all like the old woman. My mama also had black eyes and black eyebrows. I did not look at all like my mother either. I looked like this blond grandmama.

Then one of those men with all the shiny things and ribbons on his chest told the others to take my mother off the wagon.

Hiding under the pile of stuff on the wagon, I clung to Papa, and he held me close. The men were saying things to her. She kept saying no, and then it sounded like they were beating her and doing bad things to her.

They were laughing and saying bad things to my mama. The old woman was screaming and begging them to stop. Mama kept screaming, "No, no, please don't. *No!*"

The old man was crying—Grandpa was crying. Grandma was crying and screaming, "No, no, don't do this to my girl. Don't do this to my girl!" She said it over and over again.

I was so scared and hid my face in Papa's chest as he held me tightly. I heard the men laughing, and then Mama was quiet. I heard the motorcycles and other vehicles drive away.

I scrambled out of my hiding place. Mama's face was bleeding, and her clothes were torn. "Mama, what did those bad men do to you? Why did they beat you? Why, Mama?"

"What are you talking about, my little one? Nothing happened! It was just a bad dream. It will go away."

"No, Mama, it is not a dream. Look! I am awake!"

"It was only a bad dream, dear child. It will all go away very soon."

Shaken and full of fear, we all got back onto the wagon and made our way to the farm. My questions wouldn't go away.

"Mama, those men hurt you! I heard them beating you, Mama! I see you; you have a bad cut across your face."

"No, it was just a bad dream. You will wake up one day and not remember any of this!"

If it was a bad dream, why did Mama's face have such a big wound, and why could she not walk properly? She was torn severely. Those Nazis had raped her repeatedly.

I do not know how long we stayed at the farm. We stayed until Mama's face and body were somewhat healed. Do dreams do that? Do they make you bleed? Will this bad dream ever go away? Will I remember any of this when I grow up?

The family was afraid to have us stay too long, just in case they could not answer all the questions people would ask. Questions like, "Why do you have strangers with you at home?" and "Why are those people here?" They could sell us out for a loaf of bread, which happened when a farmer betrayed Papa's cousin Chaia Rachel, her husband, and their two children—a boy and a girl—in just such a manner. They did not survive the Holocaust. The children were sent to the Janusz Korczak orphanage. Dr. Korczak and all of the orphans perished in the Treblinka extermination camp.

Sometime later, neighbors in the area did start asking too many questions. It was time to leave.

My poor papa had been hiding all this time, in the wagon or in a root cellar. Papa went into his hiding place late at night, and no one knew he was in it. For anyone to stay hidden for a long time had to be a miracle in itself. How he had survived that horrific day on the road is a big puzzle to me—for my papa to be able to stay in the wagon, watching and hearing his wife being raped repeatedly and not jumping out to try to save her. Such horror for him! Of course, if Papa had come out, we would all be dead now. Had he shown himself, all of us, including those two wonderful, caring Gentiles and their families, would surely have been killed. The death of my new grandmama and grandpapa for giving help to a Jewish family would have been worse than our own deaths. However, Papa never forgave himself for not helping Mama.

Both my mother and father tried for years to convince me that what happened on the road that day was all a bad dream. However, I knew what felt and saw and heard. It was not a dream!

We continued our long journey to the church. Every opportunity my parents had—more so Mama than Papa—they demanded I remember this: "Before you remember your name, before you remember your parents, before you acknowledge anything or anyone, remember you are a Jew!" I had no idea what that meant. All I knew was I must never forget I am Jew.

I must also never tell anyone. "Don't tell anyone you're a Jew! Don't forget you're a Jew. This is more important than life itself; remember you're a Jew."

*I must not remember what those terrible men did.* Never, ever tell anyone about this. For as long as my parents are alive, I must never remember anything of what the bad men with all the shiny things on their chests did that day. "It was only a bad dream," they kept telling me.

I was very confused! *Remember you're a Jew! Don't remember the bad men! The most important thing in the world is to remember you're a Jew, and remember G-d. The bad men were not real; nothing happened. It's a bad dream. Don't tell anyone you're a Jew. Don't tell anyone about the bad men. Remember you're a Jew, and you must love G-d.* Every day, all day, Mama kept telling me the same thing as we continued on the road to the church.

We passed some woods. My mother said this was the last time we would see each other for a short while. She promised that before too much time passed, she would come and pick me up again. I should be a good girl and not cause any trouble, so no one would pay too much attention to me. "Do as you are told; be a good girl. You must stay alive! Remember you're a Jew; remember you're a Jew and that G-d loves you. Don't tell anybody, even if they beat you."

*I'll remember, Mama. I will not tell anyone, even if they beat me.*

The wagon went into the woods so Mama and Papa could get off it without anyone seeing them. They took only what they needed and disappeared into the woods.

I stayed on the wagon with Grandma and Grandpa until we got to the church. Grandpa stayed out of sight with the wagon, while Grandma walked me to the big doors and knocked. It was a very big building. She repeated, "Don't tell them I am your grandma. You don't have a grandma. Do not tell them anything; don't tell them who I am. Don't tell them you're a Jew; don't tell them you have a grandpa or a mama and a papa. Don't tell anybody anything." I promised I wouldn't.

She banged on the door a few times, and no one came. I was happy no one came. I thought I was going to go back with Grandma now and find Mama, but then someone came to the door. It was a man in a long black dress. He looked clean and had a very nice smile.

"What do you want, old woman?"

"We found her walking around. You better take her before the wolves get her."

I would rather have gone to the wolves; they were my friends. They had pretty lights in their eyes, and I could see them in the dark.

The priest stood there for a moment and then stepped back into the building, muttering something about me having lice. Everybody had lice; everybody was dirty. I was even cleaner than usual. I was cleaner than most of the kids I had seen.

The old woman bent down to kiss me good-bye. Again, she whispered in my ear, "Remember you're a Jew—don't tell anyone. Remember G-d loves you and all little children."

I answered back, "No! G-d is dead."

"Why do you say that?" she asked.

I thought of the boys and girls I had seen lying still beside the road before we got to the farmhouse. "Because I saw the dead children," I answered. "G-d didn't help them! When I asked Papa why they didn't go home, he said they were dead."

Most of them were lying down on the ground, and they did not move. They had flies all over them. I thought I was doing well, because if the flies came to stand on me, I could chase them away. I was so quick I had even killed a few flies. However, those children didn't come back; they just lay there on the ground. They were dead.

Then the priest returned. He took my hand, pulled me inside, and slammed the door shut in Grandmother's face. She was gone from me forever. He turned to me and said, "Now you will be safe."

Now I wondered, *Where is my G-d, and why must I, a little Jewish girl, live in secret? What awaits me in this strange, new place?*

# Chapter 9

# The Church, Galena, and Me

## 1944–1945

The priest took me inside and closed the heavy wooden door. This was my very first time to be inside a church. It looked so very pretty. I could see light coming through the colored-glass windows high above; the last rays of the day's sun filled the ceiling with many bright, happy colors.

The priest walked me into the main part of the church room where many small beds were lined up in rows against the walls. There were also two rows of beds in the center of the big hall, from the front of the church to the very back. Each bed had a small boy or girl next to it. Most were older than I was—between six and ten years old.

All the children were clean, and so were the long, white sleeping shirts they wore. The priest said I would have a bath and get my very own shirt. Everything was so fresh and clean, and the room smelled like flowers.

He took me to a different room where another man took off all my clothes. I became afraid again, but Mama told me only good people would be in this place. I had to stand in a very big basin. He had something in his hand, and he rubbed it on a rag. He poured water on me from my head down to my toes, and then somebody else came into the room. I thought it was a woman. It wore robes with a lot of cloth down to the floor. It must have been one of the priests, because I never saw any women there.

Whoever it was began to scrub me, and he was saying bad words about the lice. "I will get them all—dead or alive!" he mumbled as he poured benzene over my hair and combed it through. Then more scrubbing. When I was clean, he dressed me in a clean, white nightshirt. It went all the way down to the floor. It was so large I had to hold onto it so I would not trip as I walked barefoot on the cold floor.

The man put me on a chair, handed me a glass, and told me to drink. It was white and cold, and it tasted very nice. I was so very thirsty, but he only let me drink half of the liquid. He told me to put the glass down on the table, and then he gave me something that smelled nice and told me to eat. It was sweet. It was a white bun with honey. I had never seen a white bun. I had never tasted honey before. Then he let me finish my milk. I had not eaten much in a few days, and it all tasted so good.

When I finished eating, the priest took me back to the big room of the church. He took me to a little bed that would be mine to sleep in, so I sat down on it to rest and look around as the priest left me.

There was an older blond girl with long, thick braids on the little bed right next to mine. She must have been eight or nine years old. She was more than double my size. She was sobbing, and her body shook. I asked her why she was crying. She would not talk or even look at me. I thought she did not speak Polish, so I reached out to caress her head. With one hand, she pushed me away, screaming at me, "Don't ever touch me again!" She was speaking Polish.

I went back to her bed again and again, asking for her name. Finally, between sobs she told me, "My name is Gala." She repeated her name several times, as though she was not sure of it anymore. I learned she was eight years old, and she had been in the church since last winter. At first she would not tell me why she was crying; when she could no longer tolerate my persistence, she pushed me hard with both hands. With her teeth clenched, she growled at me, "Wait till this evening when they take you as well. Then you will know what this place is and why I am crying."

Then another priest came and told me to sit on my bed. He pointed to the framed picture at the head of the bed, the picture of a man with long hair. He had things on his head like a crown, but drops of blood were coming down on his face. He also had something in the middle of his chest that made more blood come out. He looked so sad. He looked to be in so much pain. The priest said before I go to sleep every night and when I wake up in the morning, I have to kiss the picture of G-d—his name is *Jezus*—because if I don't kiss the picture and tell him I love him, I will never find my mother and father ever again. They are probably dead anyway and if not, then the man in the picture would let them die if I do not kiss him every day.

I asked the priest if this man could bring my mama and papa back to me. "Why does he have blood all over himself? Why is he sick? If he is a G-d, then why didn't he stop those who were hurting him? My mama had blood all over herself, and nobody helped us!"

The priest didn't say a word; he responded with a slap to my head.

Mama had said, "G-d will save you." But seeing the picture of this G-d Jezus, I knew he was in pain, and he was covered in blood as Mama was on the road to the church! *I was right! He cannot help himself or me. He must be dead! I would not kiss his face! Ever!*

Sitting on my little bed, I couldn't make sense of any of this. I had so much to think about. The priest couldn't answer my questions. Gala had pushed me away. I decided I would call her Galena so she could be my friend. Now it was getting dark outside. No more light shone through the pretty, colored-glass windows.

Children who had been playing and chasing each other around the beds got quieter and quieter. Everyone now sat silently on his or her own bed. Waiting. *For what?* A strange tension filled the church. Galena's muffled sobs became louder as she cried into her pillow.

I was sleepy. It had been a long day. I put my head down on my little pillow and pulled the thin blanket up to my chin. I thought of my mama who had left me in this big, cold place. *Where is she now? Will she and Papa come back for me? Will I see ever them again?*

I was startled out of my thoughts by children's voices. "No … no … no! I don't want to go! Please don't take me!"

Then I heard Galena scream, "I don't want to go! Let me stay in my bed tonight, just one night. Please! Take her. She's new." She was pointing at me.

The nice priest who gave me milk and honey buns tried to calm Galena. He answered, "She'll be going soon enough." He pulled the struggling child from her bed.

A short while later, he returned to me and said, "You have to come with me now." I didn't know where I was going, but this man had been kind to me when I first arrived, so I wasn't too worried.

The floor was cold on my bare feet as we walked toward the back of the church. Then I heard children's voices. Crying. Some were screaming. I didn't understand what was happening to them.

The priest led me into a room. It was white, so clean and white it hurt my eyes. The light was so very bright. There was a bed in the middle of the room. I saw the bed and thought how very lucky I was to have such a big, clean bed all to myself.

I heard laughter to my right, and I turned. Two men stood there, dressed so beautifully. On their chests and shoulders, they had shiny metal things and colorful ribbons. They looked very happy.

One of them spoke to me and said, "*Kommen, meine kind.* Come, my child." I understood what he said; it sounded like Yiddish. I remembered I was not to tell anyone I was a Jew, so I said nothing.

The priest let go of my hand and closed the door behind him as he left.

I walked toward the two men. One touched my hair. He told me I was pretty. He asked his friend if he wanted to put me on the bed, or should he?

I didn't know why I should need anyone to put me on the bed. *I am a big girl,* I thought, *and I can climb up by myself.* I climbed up onto the nice, clean bed, hoping they wouldn't know I understood their language and think I was a Jew.

One of them moved me to the middle of the big bed as I pulled my long nightshirt down over my legs.

I watched as both men took big drinks from two glasses on a small table in the corner and blew smoke from the fat cigarettes they were smoking. The cigarettes were not like the little ones Papa sometimes smoked.

*Are they going to leave now so I can go to sleep?* I wondered.

Sleep was not to be that night or on many other occasions. My screams filled the church, but there was no G-d there, because He didn't come to help me. I was brutally raped by officers and priests in that place where I should have been safe and protected. Some of us children survived those rapes. Many ended up discarded in a heap behind the church.

My stay in this Polish church was dragging on, and still Mama did not come back to take me away from that dark and terrible place! *Mama, why don't you come?* Every day held more pain and torment. *Could it be the priest is right? Is my mama dead just like the rest of the mamas of the kids in the church?* Each day I hoped it would be my last day in that horrible, death-filled place.

The only people who entered the building were more children and Nazi officers. No one ever worshipped G-d there. In fact, I never saw anyone pray.

I often wished to die, to not wake up the next morning. I didn't know how to pray or if it would even help. I did know there was no G-d in that church, neither the priests' nor my mama's G-d. Nobody heard my prayers.

I still carry the physical and emotional scars of that horrendous time—burns on my belly, internal damage, and marks on my soul that no one sees. I was not yet four years old.

One morning in the dead of winter in this cold church, I heard bells ringing. Not the church bells, but little bells. They sounded so very pretty.

*Boże Narodzenie*—the day of G-d's birth. It was Christmastime.

All the children looked as the main doors of the church burst open. There in the doorway stood a large man with a bushy white beard made of cotton strips. He wore tall black boots and was dressed in a long red coat. On his back, he carried a big sack.

Sitting on my small bed with my friend Galena, I said, "*Dzied Maróz.*" I remembered Mama had said those words to me when we lived in Russia.

Galena whispered the words after me. "*Dzied Maróz* is 'Grandfather of Snow' in Russian," she said. My Galena was smart—she knew Polish and Russian, and she was learning German like we all did during our long stay in that church.

"He comes every year at this time of winter," she said. "In Polish we call him *Swiety Mikolaj* (Saint Nicholas). He doesn't have the beautiful Snow Princess with him today. *Snegurochka* is his granddaughter. I wish she was here instead of him; she's pretty!"

The tall, fat man had a big smile on his face, and he called out cheerily, "Come to me, all good little boys and girls who love *Jezus!* I have presents for you!"

I recognized his voice and his face behind the beard as that of the good priest, Father Yevgeny.

Galena and I didn't go to him. She had fear in her eyes; Galena feared everything. She went to sit on her own bed. I didn't love his G-d, and I didn't want a present from him either. He came to Galena and me anyway and gave us each a gift.

I wondered what I might have to do to be able to keep this gift. No one but my papa had ever given me something for nothing before.

The Grandpa of Snow gave me a doll. She was very pretty, just like my beautiful friend Galena. She had beautiful, long blond hair that curled all the way down her back. And big blue eyes with long black lashes.

When the doll was standing up, her eyes were open, and she said "Ma-ma." When you laid her down in your arms, she closed her eyes and went to sleep. This was my new baby! *Now I will have someone to talk to and play with and hold tight,* I told myself.

Sitting across from me on her own little bed, Galena held her gift. It was a bird, an ugly grey-and-yellow stuffed bird. It had an ugly face and a black beak, and the wings were pushed out from its body. Maybe it wanted to be a duck, but it was a bird and was not pretty.

Galena looked at my doll, and then she looked at her bird. I could see by her face that she was very angry. She stood up, came to me, and snatched the doll out of my arms. At the same time, she thrust her ugly bird into my chest.

"Here, you take this. I don't like it. I want the doll!"

"No, Galena! The pretty doll is mine—he gave her to me! This bird is ugly, and I don't want it!"

"Well, you're not so pretty yourself. Pretty dolls go to pretty girls, and she looks like me! You keep the ugly bird."

Galena wouldn't give my baby doll back to me. Now I had no one to hug. Even Galena didn't always let me hug her. She was in a lot of pain most of the time. I was a burden to her, and she tried to get rid of me as often as possible. "Go away! Leave me alone! Everywhere I go, I find you next to me. Go away. I am not your mother!"

"I don't have a mother," I said to her.

"Nobody has a mother! Nobody will ever have a mother—ever! Get used to it! They are all dead." Galena had tears in her eyes, and she was very angry with me.

Soon it was evening, and the priest came to us with the white nightshirts. That meant it was time to go to bed. Everybody, boys and girls, wore the same long white shirts every night.

Those shirts were a signal that nighttime was here. We knew the little lights would go out, and soon the fear, pain, and screaming would start all over again for the rest of the night. Some of us would not see the new morning.

I had no doll to hug. *Wesołych Świąt!* Merry Christmas!

Galena had become my friend. Nearly every night, one of the priests took Galena from her bed so the men in uniforms could do bad and painful things to her in the back rooms, as they were doing to all of us. Galena said their names were Nazis, and they had pretty, shiny things on their chests. They caused her much pain, and when she was brought back to her bed, she cried, but she was still alive and with me. Many children didn't come back after they went away in the night.

One night, things would be different. The big, fat bad priest was on top of my Galena in her little bed. He was making horrible sounds. She screamed and cried and struggled, but he was so big and so strong. Then he put the pillow on her face. He used the pillow to make her be quiet!

I wanted to stop him. I wanted to make him dead. I was afraid to get out of my little bed. I was afraid he would put a pillow on my face as well. I didn't help my Galena; I was too little. No, I didn't help her—I was too scared. I hid under my blanket, peeking out with one eye. I was frightened he would turn around and see me watching him. What would I do if he came to me when she did not move anymore?

Galena stopped screaming. It was quiet all over the church. Complete silence. No one dared to move.

I waited a long time after he left. Then I got out of bed and whispered Galena's name. I started to shake her and kept on shaking her. "Please, Galena, wake up," I urged. "Galena, wake up! I love you, wake up! Please, wake up." I kept kissing her face and telling her I loved her, but she wouldn't wake up.

The nice priest came to me. He was a good man who would wake us in the mornings with milk and little white breads with honey on them. He gave me extra bread when he had it—bread intended for the children who had not survived the previous night. However, the nice priest's visit came much too late that morning to save my little friend. He bent over Galena's bed and tried to waken her.

He looked at me and asked, "*Co sie stalo?* What has happened?" He spoke Polish, like the other priests. Not like the men in uniforms with all the shiny things on their chests; they spoke German. It was a little like the Yiddish my mama and I used. *If they are like us, why are they doing this to all of us?* I couldn't understand.

I told the nice priest about the big, fat bad priest. I pointed my finger at him from far away. "He jumped on top of the bed and then on her. He was making noises like a hungry animal. He put the pillow on my Galena's face, and when he left, she would not move. I tried to kiss her and tell her I loved her to wake her up—but she wouldn't wake up for me. She always wakes up when I kiss her and tell her I love her. Wake up, my Galena. I need you. I love you. I need you."

The good, nice priest said, "It was all a bad dream!"

I remembered every second of what happened!

He looked at me and saw my eyes were swollen. "Did you cry all night?" Then he touched my Galena and told me, "She is cold," and he put another blanket over her face. "My poor little one," he said, "your Galena is now with G-d."

"No!" I screamed. "I need her more!" As he carried Galena away from my sight, I screamed after him, "Are you going to wake her up?"

He answered gently, "I will try, my little one. I will try." He stopped, came back to me, patted my head, and said, "I'll try."

"Bring me back my Galena. I love her, and I have no one else to love."

Eight-year-old Galena had become my mother, as well as my sister. She had become part of my heart. She did not need me as her burden. This poor, beautiful child was trying to survive somehow herself. I was afraid to go to the pee pot by myself. It was too far away, and the one next to me was too full. Still, she had helped me.

All at once, I knew she was gone from me forever.

My parents had joined a group of partisans in the woods. They were fighting the Nazis by attacking small convoys operating in the area.

In early spring, it was warm outside, and there was not much snow on the ground. Sometimes we children could go outdoors for a little while. A high wooden fence surrounded the back yard of the church. That was when I saw the bodies of dead children in a pile beside the church. It frightened me so much; I knew I must run away. How?

Every time I was able to be outside, I dug at the dirt under the fence with my fingers and then with a little stick I found. Always watching that no one saw me, I dug a few more inches of the hard, cold dirt. After many days, I was able to crawl under the narrow space and go into the woods. I hid in the bushes for several hours. Then I heard voices speaking Polish. I crept out of my hiding place. It was the partisans. Suddenly I heard the voices of my parents, and I called to them, yelling, "Mama! Papa!"

Mama grabbed me in her arms as she exclaimed, "My brave little girl! You're alive!" She didn't yet know how I had suffered.

When she observed my difficulty walking and urinating, she asked me what was wrong. Sobbing, I told her everything. After a few moments of silence, she said the words I grew to hate: "It was all a bad dream. All will be well. You will soon forget all about it."

Father was outraged to hear of the horrible abuse I had endured. To Mama he declared, "We will go now and get Chaim from Grandmama's daughter. We'll go back to Russia where we will be safer. We must get as far away from Poland as possible! We cannot stay in a country whose people treat its Jewish citizens like this. We have lived together with them for centuries!" Papa was proud to have served in the Polish army. Now he felt betrayed.

Partisans escorted us and gave us some provisions for our journey eastward. As before, we walked at night and hid during the day, stealing food when necessary. Eventually we reached Russian soil and continued our eastward trek. Sometimes Papa would work for a few days in exchange for food, keeping the family hidden in the woods.

We constantly pushed onward, taking whatever means of conveyance was available to us—oxcart, wagon, truck, and even train.

I don't recall much of this journey, as I was recovering from the physical and mental trauma of the church. Sleep was only a partial reprieve, as nightmares haunted me. Gradually my body healed as we pressed onward with hope for a better tomorrow.

## *Zog Nit Keyn Mol (Never Say)*
### *Hirsh Glik (1922–1944)*

*Zog nit keyn mol az du geyst dem letstn veg,*
*Khotsh himlen blayene farshteln bloye teg.*
*Kumen vet nokh undzer oysgebenkte sho -*
*S'vet a poyk ton undzer trot— mir zainen doh!*

*Fun grinem palmenland biz vaysn land fun shney*
*Mir kumen on mit undzer payn, mit undzer vey,*
*Un vu gefaln s'iz a shprits fun undzer blut,*
*Shprotsn vet dort undzer gvure, undzer mut.*

*S'vet di morgnzun bagildn undz dem haynt,*
*Un der nekhtn vet farshvindn mit faynt,*
*Nor oyb farzamen vet di zun in dem kayor -*
*Vi a parol zol geyn dos lid fun dor tsu dor.*

*Dos lid geshribn iz mit blut un nit mit blay,*
*S'iz not kayn leidl fun a foygl af der fray,*
*Dos hot a folk tsvishn falndike vent*
*Does lid gezungen mit naganes in di hent!*

*To zog nit keyn mol az du geyst dem letstn veg,*
*Khotsh kimlen blayene farshteln bloye teg,*
*Kumen vet nokh undzer oysgebenkte sho—*
*S'vet a poyk ton undzer trot—mir zainen doh!*

# Song of the Partisans

*Translation from Yiddish*
*by Reene Zufi of Melbourne, Australia.*

Never say you are going on your final road,
Although leadened skies block out blue days.
Our longed-for hour will yet come
Our step will beat out—we are here!

From a land of green palm trees to the white land of snow
We arrive with our pain, with our woe.
Wherever a spurt of our blood fell,
On that spot shall spurt forth our courage and our spirit.

The morning sun will brighten our day
And yesterday will disappear with our foe.
But if the sun delays to rise at dawn,
Then let this song be a password for generations to come.

This song is written with our blood, not with lead.
It is not a song of a free bird flying overhead.
Amid crumbling walls, a people sang this song
With grenades in their hands.

So, never say the road now ends for you,
Although skies of lead block out days of blue.
Our longed-for hour will yet come—
Our step will beat out—we are here!

http://hebrewsongs.com/?song=zognitkeynmol

# Chapter 10

## Save My Yakov

*Uzbekistan—December 1945*

Mama, Papa, Chaim, and I moved into one tiny, smelly room in a small house in Uzbekistan. I was a big girl now. I was over four years old!

The house was also home to several other desperately poor Russians and refugee families. Each family, most with small children, had only one small room.

Chaim was a sweet little boy. We loved each other and loved playing together. I didn't have any dolls or other toys. Chaim was my first living doll. I was very tall and thin. I could walk, talk, and run very fast, and I could help with Chaim.

Soon after our arrival, Mama, with the help of a midwife, gave birth to my new little brother, Yakov, in this dark and dingy room. Now we were five.

Our room had one big, dirty window that let in very little light—we could hardly see through it. Mama said if she didn't clean it, then no one could see into our lives.

The door led into a dark hallway where the lightbulb never worked. Even when both the window and door were open, we couldn't get the stink out of our room. Everyone in the house cooked cabbage, onions, and potatoes almost every day, and the smell was always there. Those three vegetables were cheap enough to buy.

Eight days after Yakov was born, a few people came to our room to visit. I thought all the people came for a happy occasion. They brought some food. There was a celebration, but I did not understand what they were celebrating.

There was some herring and black bread and some vodka to drink, which the men enjoyed very much. They acted funny and talked loud afterward, and they walked a little strange. Some bumped into each other and even the doorway as they were leaving. Mama was afraid they would break the only bed we had.

One of the visitors must have been a bad man—he made Yakov cry. I saw a little bit of blood, and I didn't know what terrible thing he had done to my poor brother, but I saw something sharp, like a knife. Mama didn't want this man to come back to our house.

Yakov was truly a beautiful child. His hair was a pale blond color, just like mine, and he had big, beautiful light-brown eyes. He was like an angel, a cherub—very pudgy and adorable. Where he got the pudgy stuff, I had no idea. Everyone around him was skinny and starving. He was so adorable and beautiful that I made the decision that he was going to be *my* baby.

Several days after the visitors came to the party at our one-room home, I could see something was very wrong with Yakov. Poor little Yakov's pink cheeks were now red, and he was very hot. Mama told me his head was burning to the touch, and she said his lungs were also burning. The sound was different when he cried.

Then his rosy cheeks began to get whiter and whiter. He wasn't breathing properly, and now he was coughing. Then his face got very red, and he was coughing even more and barely breathing. Mama said, "I must save my little Yakov! I am going to the hospital."

"Mama, I want to go with you," I cried.

Ignoring me, Papa said, "He's dying. Leave him alone. We can do nothing for him. It's the price of war."

Mama wouldn't listen. "I am going to the hospital!" she declared. "I will find a Jewish doctor to save my little Yakov! I must get help, or he will die." *There was that word again! Why must she always talk about dying?*

Mama wrapped Yakov in a blanket and put him inside her coat, holding him with one arm. She took me by the hand and said, "Volfe, take care of Chaim till I come back home." We walked out of our room, leaving Papa and Chaim behind. Mama never looked back.

I did not know where we were going. Mama said we were going to the hospital, but I don't think she knew where to go. We walked in the snow for a long time, and she stopped several times to ask people for directions. Mama now held Yakov tightly with her arms and told me to hold onto her coat so I wouldn't get lost.

After a long time, I looked at Mama. Her eyes looked as if they were burning. I was very cold in my thin cloth coat, and my legs were tired.

Finally, we came to a large area with many tents. There was a big red cross on each one. Many army trucks and some cars were coming and going in all directions. People in army uniforms hurried all over the place.

"What is this place?" I asked. "Mama, is this the hospital?"

Mama started walking faster, and I ran after her, holding onto the hem of her coat. With tears of relief and exhaustion in her eyes, she said, "Yes, this is where they will help your little brother."

Then we saw the very big building. Many people were rushing around outside—people with blood on their clothing, and doctors and nurses went from one person to another to help. Some sick people were on the ground, and some had parts of their bodies missing. Mama took hold of my hand to pull me along with her toward the hospital.

She said, "Never let go." I knew the rest of the words she didn't say: *If you let go, you will get lost and die.* Mama and Papa had been telling me that for a very long time now.

Mama pushed her way closer to the building, past the trucks and the strange beds without legs that some soldiers were carrying. We went inside. Mama stopped for nothing and no one. She tried to speak to the men who were busy working in the hallways. She asked repeatedly, "Are you a doctor? Save my baby!"

Some of the men pushed her aside. One yelled at her, "This is a military hospital. Get out of this place; you are underfoot."

Doctors and nurses hurried from room to room. Some of them had blood on their white clothes and on their hands. They yelled at Mama to go away and leave the hospital, but they didn't have time to throw her out. One man—I think he was a doctor—stopped in front of us, took a quick look, and hollered, "Your baby is as good as dead; just leave it with us and go home. We can't help the child!"

Mama lifted Yakov in front of her and pleaded with the doctor. "Please! Save this Jewish child! Thousands of our children are being murdered all over Europe."

The man didn't look at her. He just ran away without saying another word.

Mama didn't look like herself. Her eyes looked wild, and her face was burning. Her beautiful black hair was uncombed. She didn't care anything about herself. She just walked about, repeating, "Save my baby. Save my baby!"

She grabbed hold of another man, and this time she would not let go. All her life she seemed to have a sixth sense. She just *knew* this man was the one who could help. She pleaded with him. "Save a Jewish child. They are dying all over Europe. Save this Jewish child!"

He threw her arm away and vehemently said, "There are no Jewish children left. They are all dead!"

"*No! This* one is alive!"

"Then he is not a Jew!" he snapped.

My mother, visibly upset, pushed Yakov in front of him as she cried, "Yes, he is! I'll show you!" Tearing back the blanket and the rags wrapped around my brother, she exposed Yakov's bare little peepee.

The stunned doctor looked at this newly circumcised Jewish baby and tenderly took him from Mama. "Yes, this is a Jewish child, and I will do all I can to save him!"

He started yelling orders. People came running from all directions. They took Yakov into a room, and Mama and I hurried after them. They began with an examination of poor little Yakov, listening to his lungs and checking him all over. There were needles and more needles; then they bathed him and put him in bed with Mama and me on either side. They covered the three of us with many blankets, and for once, I was warm and soon fell asleep.

Some while later after we had a good sleep, the doctor gave more injections to my baby brother and instructed someone to bring Mama and me some food. She received a glass of milk—the first time in a year that Mama had had milk. They also gave Mama and me some white bread, not the coarse brown bread we usually had. And they brought a bottle for Yakov.

Papa was at home with Chaim. When he had to go to work, the old Russian woman who lived in the room next door came in every hour to check on Chaim and to give him a bottle.

Mama and I had slept only one night in that clean hospital bed with Yakov when Papa came with Chaim to take me away from Mama. He said to my mother, "Leave this poor baby to die in the hospital. You have a husband and two other small children who need you. You must take care of those who still have a life and have a chance to survive."

"I am not leaving my Yanke'le behind to die. I will stay with him until he lives."

"Well, we may not be there when you come back." He warned that one way or another, he was going back to Poland and would take Chaim and me with him. Papa gave my mother three days.

My mother didn't blink; she would not leave Yakov to die. With that, Papa, Chaim, and I went back to our one-room home.

Now I took care of Chaim when Papa went to work. On the second day, when Papa came home from work, Mama still had not returned. He told me Mama was still in the big hospital, and we must go bring her back. Papa picked up Chaim and carried him. He took my hand' and we left the room to go find our mama. We walked for a very long time, because we didn't have money to ride the trolley. Papa carried me too sometimes when I got too tired.

Papa looked very worried and asked me what I thought might be the best way to find my mama in that big hospital. I suggested to Papa,

"Let's just scream her name, *Mama!* She will hear us and come to us." So that is what we did.

Papa called loudly, "Devorah! Dora!"

I called out, "Mama! *Mama'le!*" We walked all over the building looking for Mama. How could it be that with so many people all around, no one saw us? Everyone seemed to be running in different directions, bumping into us, yelling for us to get out of the way, or they would call the military police.

One of the men told Papa it was not possible for Mama to be here, because this hospital was only for the military; only soldiers could be taken care of in this place.

Papa answered that his wife was in this hospital with his baby. Papa whispered to me, "They don't know your Mama! We know she's here, because this is where she brought your brother."

After a long time looking all around, we saw Mama standing at the far end of a big hallway with Yakov in her arms. He was very still.

Papa whispered to me, "I am afraid our little Yakov is dead. They can't help him now. Why did your mama not just leave him with the doctors? She cannot help him now."

We went to Mama. "Devorah, give the dead boy to them and come home with us. We need you," Papa pleaded. "You look sick. If the doctors can't help him, you must leave him with them and come home with us. Did you forget you have two other children and a husband? We also need you."

Mama just looked at him in silence. Now Papa sounded angry. "Devorah, you must come home with us right now and forget about Yakov. He has been sick too long. No one can help him now."

My Mama's eyes had fire in them. She glared at Papa. "By bringing him here, I have saved this son of mine! I lost my twins, my two little boys, to the Nazi murderers, and I will not lose another child of mine ever again! Yanke'le is getting better, and he will live! Look at him; he's resting. His fever is almost gone!"

Mama hissed at Papa, "You wanted me to leave him to die. I will never forgive you for this!"

Hearing this, I felt fear for my own future. *Would Mama forgive me if I were to make a bad mistake?*

Then she announced, "I have medication for him, and he will be better soon. Now we'll take our family home."

Several days later, when Yakov was much improved, Mama was finally willing to talk about this very scary time in our family's life. She told me Yakov had had a lung sickness called pneumonia and had been on the verge of death when the doctor began to do all he could to save his little Jewish life.

Yakov was alive! His cheeks were pink again, and I could see his dimples when he smiled at me.

What saved Yakov's life? Did G-d help Mama recognize the doctor as a Jew? Was it just a lucky guess, or did Mama's sixth sense work? I don't know.

Or was it Yakov himself, newly circumcised, who gave the most important clue of all? When the doctor saw evidence that Yakov was indeed a Jewish child, he took a chance with his very own life by using the military hospital facilities and medicine to treat this Jewish baby.

My poor Papa lived all of his life with the guilt of almost leaving Yakov to die in that Russian hospital. He did not fully recover from the memory.

From that time onward, Papa favored Yakov over the rest of his children. Yakov received most of Papa's attention. Unfortunately, that caused some of us to resent his "darling."

Yakov, a gentle, loving, and innocent boy, had only love and smiles for everyone, and everyone he met loved him!

Our stay in Russia was short-lived. As word got out that we were Jews, Papa's jobs were in jeopardy. Papa, refusing to remain under the Communist hammer and sickle, made plans to leave Russia once again. This time, he hoped to meet up with partisans in Poland who might help us find refuge with the Americans, whom he hoped would save Europe from Hitler's madness. We became "wandering Jews" once again.

# Chapter 11

# The Great Escape

*Poland to Austria—1946*

Rumors that the war was over came from everywhere, but no one was sure the rumors were true. If so, would this be our last long trek? Father wanted us to be with the Americans to stay alive.

Mama and Papa could not locate any surviving family in Poland. The hatred they felt toward Poland for allowing and helping the Nazis to kill most of the Jews would never go away. It would only intensify over the years until the day they died. Once they left Europe, they never returned to Poland.

All members of our families who lived in Warsaw, Rogove, Brzezine, Lublin, Levov, Lodz, Krakow, and surrounding cities, towns, and villages had been taken to Auschwitz, Birkenau, Dachau, Majdanek, Treblinka, Bergen-Belsen, and Buchenwald. After the war, some survivors helped us put some pieces together as to where all the others had been murdered.

Mama told me, "Into these camps were taken most of our men, women, and children. From my side of the family, you will never have grandparents, aunts, uncles, or any other family. We are all alone! All of you, my children, will have to start all over again. You will create a new Jewish family, and some day, a Jewish Nation! That is Papa's and my hope."

We were back in Poland yet again. We had left Russia just like Papa wanted. Now Mama kept saying this was all madness. We walked only at night, every night, all night long. We had been searching for a very long time for any family or for the "good people who would help us."

"They will take us to safety," Papa said. After a search lasting some days, Papa learned of two men who would help.

One very dark night, Papa found the two men. Two nights later, after lots of talking with these men, we joined a large group of other people also seeking to escape. Mama told me we would all run away from Poland together.

Papa agreed. "Yes, we will." This time, we would have help to escape from Poland, and we would go another direction.

Although the war had ended, not everyone believed it to be true. The killing continued, and the small remnant of Jews who still lived was still in great danger of being destroyed.

"We have to get out of Poland," Papa said. "We must get to Austria. The Americans have taken it. If only we can get to Austria, we will be safe."

Once more, we walked through the woods. We walked all night and slept in the daytime, hiding in the forests.

"Many people are in this group with us, and many languages are being spoken. We do not know if any of them are Jewish like us." Papa said I must not to talk to anyone. Only two of the eight people in charge were Jewish. They spoke Yiddish. Mama told me they were all partisans and that she and Papa had known one of them from Warsaw a long time ago, before the war started.

I don't clearly remember all the details as to what money or possessions changed hands to pay for this escape, but everyone had to part with many of their already meager belongings. The preferred currency was diamonds and gold. Everyone had to give the guides the shiny, precious stones. We used much of what little jewelry we had left as payment to go along on this big, long, and silent hike.

From what I could see, some of the people had only one child, and few family units had both parents present. Mama had three of us children with her and one very sick man. My poor papa! His feet were bleeding all the time. The man told Mama that children are always a big problem.

Mama declared, "I will pay you the extra diamonds you want; they are coming with me! None of them will be left behind!"

Mama promised the leader and his men she would keep her three small children silent. She then turned her back to them so they could not see what she was doing. She pretended to search in her bra for the hidden hankie that held a few small diamonds and some gold jewelry. "After this is all gone, it will be up to G-d alone to save and care for us," Mama said.

Then Mama put her hand inside the rags covering Yakov's diapers to search for the actual hiding place. The stink that came from them and him was very bad. Mama hadn't changed Yakov's diaper for two or more days. He was dirty, and he smelled. No one wanted to be near us. This was Mama's secret hiding place—inside the rags around my baby brother's bottom. That "weapon" kept everyone away from Mama's treasures. When she turned back to the men, she paid with the stones she had retrieved from Yakov's diaper.

The men took the pretty stones from Mama and told her if she couldn't keep her kids silent, he would leave all of us in the woods. And she better do something about the stink that came from her child. Mama said she hoped the bad stink would keep all the bad animals away from us.

It was very dark all around us. The woods were always dark and frightening to me, though I tried to be brave. The trees were very close to each other in many places, and we had to be careful as we walked through them so we didn't rip the few clothes we were wearing. They were all we had left to cover our bodies and keep us warm.

This particular group, led and protected by the partisans, grew bigger and bigger every few days. As we walked in the night, I could hear whistles, and then more people would join us. No coughing or crying allowed! If you had to cough, you had to put a rag in your mouth so no one could hear you. The demand for silence was fierce. There were so many of us. Mama told me we are G-d's children and that a new Moses was leading us out of hell. The first time was out of Egypt. However, the uncertainty of not knowing where we were, where we were going, or if we would survive this trek was quite similar, Mama said.

"The other time, G-d told them they would get to the Promised Land, and Moses led them. On this trip, we must trust the partisans to lead us. Maybe G-d will tell them what He is thinking."

I remember the trip we made through the forests. We walked all the time, all night long. Except when we heard trucks coming. Then everyone would drop to the ground, not moving and scarcely breathing. During the daytime, we would sleep. I didn't like that. Food? Water? We ate and drank what we had with us or gave away the last coat, shoes, dress, or even our underwear for something to eat. Mama was wearing several layers of everything. Mama said she was rich. People gave away anything they still had left in exchange for food and water, but if you didn't own anything anymore, you kept on walking until you fell, and you were immediately forgotten. Some people did just that, saying nothing. They just fell down as if to rest, and I never saw them again. The rest of us kept walking in silence, without stopping to pick anyone up. As we walked through the country, more people and guides joined us.

Something was very wrong with my father's feet. He did not have his shoes on, and he could not put them on. He had them hanging around his neck. His feet were wrapped in many dirty rags, and I always knew where my father was, because with each step he took I could hear the squishing sound of the rags and his blood.

I kept listening to that squishing sound to make sure Papa was still with us. Sometimes, if he stepped on underbrush, I could see lots of blood on it in the light of my friend the moon. Papa didn't say a word of his pain. He was carrying a large rag package that contained all we owned in the world. All of our belongings were in that bundle. He was holding it in one hand, over his back, and he carried a big stick in the other hand to help him walk.

Mama kept admonishing me that I was not holding on tight enough to her pocket. I had all but torn off the pockets, trying with all my might to hold on tightly. "Anna'le, if you let go, you will get lost and die." Every day she told me the same thing. "You will get lost and die." I heard those words, "you will die," more often in the first five years of my life than I ever have since.

It was a scary experience in the dark woods. I heard only my friends the wolves calling out at night. Papa told me the Polish wolves were only singing to the moon, just like my friends, the Russian wolves.

"Don't let go of my coat," Mama whispered every so often. "You'll get lost, and the wolves will eat you." I did not believe that. I loved my wolves.

Mama had Yakov on one arm and pulled me along with her other hand. Someone else in the group usually helped to carry Chaim, who was still quite small. Then one night, I didn't hear the squishing sounds of Papa's feet. I looked around as we continued walking, and I couldn't see my papa anywhere. We kept walking. I became very afraid. I pulled hard on Mama's coat. "Mama," I whispered, "Papa is gone! I can't see him anywhere."

"No, no. He is right here. You can't see him because it is dark."

"*No! No!* Mama! Papa is gone! I no longer hear the squishy sound of his feet!"

Mama started whispering, calling quietly at first and then more loudly, for one of the men in charge to come back to her. He was at the front of our group. A big, angry man came to see us after Mama called out. It was the same man who took the pretty stones from her. He warned that if she ever raised her voice again, they would leave her and all of us behind.

"My husband is missing," she insisted. "You must go back and get my husband!"

"No! You know the rules! Those who will not keep up, stay behind."

Those rules were not for her! "No, we will *not* keep quiet unless you go get my husband. You and another man can go, and all of us will remain silent."

He told Mama they were not going to do that. It would make all of us fall behind the schedule, and it was too dark this night to go looking for anyone.

"So you leave me no choice. My children and I will have to start screaming and crying."

"You want us all to be killed?"

"Well, what's the difference? If you leave my husband behind to die, I don't care what happens to us—or to all of you!"

So Mama pinched little Yakov. I saw her pinch him! She pinched him again and again, harder each time. He started whimpering. Yakov was a pretty baby who hardly ever cried and never complained. My sweet little brother was a good boy. My poor little Yakov was in pain. Mother told the man, "I will do it again and again until he shrieks, and he will wake up every dead or living person in all these woods. I will also tell my daughter to start screaming."

I don't think he believed she would do this. I looked up at Mama. "You want me to scream now?" I asked her.

"No, no, *Maide'le*. Wait a minute until I tell you; just wait. I will let you know the right time when you can start."

The big man whispered something to one man behind him, and two men came running. He ordered them to go look for my papa. They hurried back in the direction from where we had come. They were gone for a very long time. Then I could hear them returning. They had found my papa, and they were half dragging and carrying him with them. His arms were around their necks, because he could not stand alone on his feet. From there on, different people helped my father stay with the group. All the while, Papa hung on to our precious bundle.

Every once in a while, I asked Mama, "Do you want me to scream now?"

"No. As long as you see Papa anywhere near you, you don't have to scream. Just keep an eye on him; don't let him fall behind." I had to hold tight to Mama's coattails so I would not get lost and die, Mama said, and I kept an eye on Papa so he would not get lost and die.

I remember we were mostly hungry, and at night, we were very cold. The big man was angry if I had to stop to pee. He swore he would never again allow children on a march like that. No, never again! However, my mama had the best weapon in those last days of our journey—three very loud children. Papa never fell behind again, as we pressed on toward the Austrian border.

We rested for a short time. As we were resting, Papa said we were going to go to a place called Austria. When I think of this now, I do believe the war was all but over by then, and everyone was escaping from Poland, Czechoslovakia, Hungary, Romania, and Bulgaria—from all over Europe so they would not be under the Russian yoke.

I asked Papa, "Why Austria?" He said it was because there were American soldiers on the Austrian border. The Americans were there. "Really, Papa? What is an American?"

He was so excited; I was so excited with him. Papa had a big smile on his face. "Oh, they are very nice and good people."

"Are we going to be with them? Are we going to go with them? Will they give us food?"

"Yes, they will give us food, but no, we will not go with them."

Mama said yes, we would go with them out of this hell! My dear papa said no again. I looked at the two of them and said, "Well, we can't do 'no' and 'yes' at the same time. Are we going to be with the Americans, Mama?"

"Yes!"

"Papa?"

"No! We are going home. We are going to the Holy Land, so we can have a future for our children."

We had been on this journey for a long time. Then Papa saw the border with Austria. He pointed to a little booth with soldiers all around. American soldiers and some Austrian men were there who could interpret when needed. However, the Americans were in charge. Papa was so excited to see all those American uniforms. As sick as he was, as emaciated and sick as we all were, the fact we survived to get to that border was no small miracle, Mama said.

None of us spoke English. In our group a few of the guides tried to converse with the interpreters. My parents spoke German very well, but for some reason, they did not want the Austrians to know that fact, just in case we would be mistaken for Germans and not be allowed to cross the border.

Those Americans looked at our ragtag group of people and obviously decided we should be allowed to enter Austria.

Some people not in uniform spoke another language I had never heard before. I kept hearing the word *Yehudi, Yehudi* (Jew, Jew). I looked at my mother with surprise. I was taught all my life, by her and Papa, never to say that word or let anyone know I understood anything that was spoken around me, in any language, and to never, ever tell anyone that I was a *Yehudi*, a Jewish girl.

Mama looked at me and spoke quietly in Russian, "Do not say a word. Always remember you are a Jew but never tell anyone. If you tell anyone, you will die and not come to America with us!"

"Mama, did you hear the word? He said the word! Did you hear the word he just used?"

She answered, "Yes, but we don't know if it's in a good way or not in a good way. Don't say anything."

What we didn't know was that the young men who were dressed in light blue or khaki clothing, not uniforms, were neither German nor American. I thought they were very clean and handsome.

"They are clean; they are so clean! Do they look nice to you too, Mama?"

For the first time in a long time, Mama smiled at me and she said, "Yes, they look very nice to me as well."

"They are so very clean," I repeated.

"Yes, they are very clean. They must have lots of water."

"Will they give us a drink?" I wondered aloud.

They had strange shoes on their feet; I could see their toes. "Mama, I can see their toes. Look, their feet are also clean, and they are not bleeding like Papa's."

The clean men who helped us to enter Austria were using the word *Yehudi*. Then they went away and I couldn't see them. I later learned they were Zionists from Palestine, trying to identify the Jews among the group to separate us from the *Goyim* (Gentiles) so they could help us get to our homeland.

Someone told us to stand next to the small cabin. A black box kept ringing, and people would talk into it. Papa told me it was a telephone. I promised myself that someday I would have one just like it.

Then Papa's American soldiers told us and another group of women and children to move forward to one side of the road—women and children only. The men must stay on the other side of the road, to the right of the border. Then the soldiers began to rob the men, going into their pockets, turning them inside out and putting into their own pockets anything that fell out. They did this to all the men and bigger boys. They pointed to the wrist and said in German, *"Hast du zeyger, gelt, hast du schmuck?* Do you have a watch, money, jewelry?" They wanted any jewelry or valuables we had remaining. All the people stood in shock, not moving, watching them do this. They were unable to comprehend what was happening!

"America is rich country," Papa yelled. "You just liberated Europe; you saved the few Jews who remain alive. How can you do this? Is this why you save us? So that you can rob us of what little the Nazis didn't take?"

They ignored Papa. He was talking in German. They were going down the line from one man to the next, searching their pockets, and coming up with mostly bread crumbs, which they threw to the ground, much to the horror of the former owners. Those few crumbs of bread were all the food they had for the day.

Going through pockets—opening bundles to see if there might be anything of value—the soldiers continued to search. They pushed and shoved the men to the ground in disgust when they didn't find anything they wanted in their belongings.

Then they got to my father. I understood what they said. As before, it was in German: *"Hast du ein zeyge? Schmuck?"*

My Papa said, *"Neine.* No, I have nothing."

"The man is speaking German, Mama! Papa is talking the wrong language! They are going to kill him! What if they don't let us go on?"

Mama then screamed to my father in Polish. "Where did you learn those words?"

Papa was startled. He completely lost the color in his face. He realized the mistake he made in even understanding them. He shrugged it off. "These are Americans," he yelled back to her in Polish.

One of the soldiers started to go through my father's pockets and then inside his jacket. He tore the front of the pocket. I wanted to run to Papa, but Mama was holding on tight to all of us. "Stay next to me and don't do or say anything, or you may get your father killed."

My father was in horrible condition; his feet still had lots of blood on them, and he could barely stand up. He told the soldier to stop touching him, or he would fall. The man didn't stop, so Papa pushed the American man away. The soldier was furious and hit my father with a fist in his face. Papa lost his balance and fell to the ground, with blood coming out of his nose and mouth. Mama held on tight to all of us kids, but I tore myself away from her grip and ran to my papa.

As Papa's American man was about to kick him, I lay down on top of my papa and continued shrieking "No!" in every language I knew, again and again. "No! Don't touch my papa!" Two other soldiers came running and took this bad man away.

My father said to me in Yiddish, "I hope he and his kind die very soon, before we leave this cursed country for the Holy Land."

"Papa, you told me it is not nice to say that."

"Yes it is, when bad people deserve this blessing."

Those nice-looking men in the khaki and blue clothing came back again. I was lying there on top of Papa and crying. My papa was hurt; the blood still came from his nose. The clean men came to us, and one of them picked me up. He wiped the tears from my face and ruffled my hair. "Why are you crying, little girl? What's your name?"

I looked at him and said, "You didn't help my papa. They beat him up; they wanted his watch. Papa does not have a watch. We gave away everything so we could come here."

"Who beat him up?" the clean man asked.

I pointed at the man who beat up my father.

"He beat him up?"

"Yes, he beat him."

This man spoke a broken Yiddish, very strongly accented, but Yiddish nonetheless. I knew when someone was Polish; I knew when someone was Russian by the way he spoke Yiddish. I even knew if someone was German, but I didn't recognize this man's accent.

There was a loud argument, with fists waving in the air between the clean man, his friends, and the Americans. He came back, picked me up, and held me in his arms. He held me so very tight. For the first time in a very long time, I felt safe and defended. I felt so protected in his arms. Although he was a total stranger, I felt I could trust him. I knew he was a good man. Not only did he speak Yiddish, but there was also just something about him. He held me to his chest, as if I were his own. He behaved like a papa or a big brother. He held onto me, with his clean face next to my dirty face. He owned this child in his arms; I was that child!

I looked at him and told him, "My name is Anna." Then I asked him, "Who are you and your friends?"

For the first time in my life, I heard the most beautiful word I had ever heard. "Zionists. We are all Zionists. We've come to take you home."

"Take us home?" I asked. "Where is home? We don't have a home. Mama said all the Jewish homes are burned. Mama said the Nazis burned what they didn't want and stole everything else that belonged to the Jews. We don't have a home," I repeated.

"Oh yes, little one. Yes, you have a home. I know exactly where it is, where you will live someday soon, and I am going to make sure you and your family get there. You will grow and be happy there. In that new home of ours, we always have sunshine; it will be your home forever. Your new home is always beautiful, and you and your brothers will grow up to go to school and play. You will swim in the ocean; you will run on the beach and have fun." I didn't want him to know I didn't know the words *beach* or *ocean*, so I said nothing about that.

"Papa is sick; he can't walk."

My Zionist told me, "That will not be a problem for us. We will carry every last one of you in our arms to the trucks and then to safety if we must."

I told him I would not be going on the trucks.

"Why not? Why will you not go on the truck?"

"Because Mama said when they came with the trucks in Warsaw, bad people took my twin brothers away, and we never got them back. I am not going on the trucks. I want to be with my family."

"If I go with you onto the truck, will you go then? I will be right there with you all the time. You can sit in my lap on the truck all the way to the camp."

After a very long conversation, I finally agreed to trust him and go on the truck with him. That was one of a very few times in my life I agreed to trust someone.

We were loaded onto the trucks, and we drove off. I do not know how long we were on the road. They gave us canteens of water to drink—as much as we wanted! The water was so sweet and clean. It had been a long time since I'd had clean water to drink.

They gave us each a big piece of bread, and no one had to steal from each other. Everyone had his or her own big chunk, even each child. I did what Mama said. "Only take a few bites and then hide the rest for later, because you might not get more later."

My new Zionist friend kept telling me, "Eat your bread; eat now!"

"No, I have to hide some for later."

"No, don't do that! I will give you another big chunk later."

"No, I have to hide it for later."

He took out another big piece of bread and wrapped it in my skirt and said, "Hold onto this for later; eat this one—all of it—now!"

*Eat the whole thing?*

"I want to see you eat all of it," he repeated, as he wiped his eyes. They had tears in them. I was afraid he was crying because he gave me his last bread, but he told me he was crying because he was happy. After the first few bites, my stomach was full. A small amount of food was almost too much.

After a very long drive and a nap in the arms of my new Zionist friend, the trucks stopped. We now joined other trucks and became part of a convoy. Then we arrived, after several more nights on the trucks. The trucks stopped, and someone picked up the flap in the back of our truck. My friend was sitting right next to me, as was my papa, with our big bundle under his feet to keep his legs up to rest and to stop anyone from stealing it. Papa would be taken care of, my friend said, and they would fix his feet when we arrived at the new place. His blood had stained the bundle, but my papa never complained.

The pain he was in must have been terrible. Still, my papa never said a word. "Papa, your feet are still bleeding."

"Don't worry, my little Maide'le; it's nothing. It will soon stop; it will stop very soon."

With the canvas flap on the truck lifted, I looked outside. I was afraid we would be back in the forest once again, but it wasn't that at all. It was a very different sight. It looked nice. I saw many houses, big houses. Some were very broken from the bombs, Papa told me. Papa said we were now in a city called Salzburg. "The war is over, and we are now safe!"

Right in front of us was a very big place. I looked at my father. "Papa, look at this place! Look at the big house. What is this?"

Papa told me it looked like a palace. The person named Zionist said, "It *is* a palace."

"What is a palace, Papa?"

"A palace is a big, beautiful home like this one where kings or very rich people live."

"Rich? And what is rich, or king, Papa?"

"People who have lots of money, who have many ways of making money are rich." He told me a story about rich people. He said they live in big, beautiful houses and have everything. "Just like your Grandmama and Grandpapa."

I asked again, "Do they have lots of food?"

"All the food you can eat."

"And water?"

"All the water you can drink and for bathing. Yes, and all the fruit— apples and grapes and strawberries—you may wish."

He might as well have been speaking in another strange tongue. I had never heard those words before. I had never seen those fruits. Though that building fascinated me, I did not ask any more questions.

My father asked the Zionists, "Why are we stopping here? Who lives here? And can we get some food for the children? We are a convoy, just like the gypsies. We were hoping for some handouts and help."

The person named Zionist told us, "This is a Jewish palace. It belongs to the Rothschild family. This is where they lived before the war."

They helped us off the trucks and got us to stand in long lines to go inside. There was plenty of water. We needed plenty of water, not only to drink, but for washing. We had lice all over our bodies. Those lice were so huge. We did not merely suspect we were full of lice; we knew it. We could feel them moving inside our clothing, on our heads, and all over our arms.

Later, in the big house, some kids played a game to see whose lice were faster. As the insects walked from the top of our arms to our fingertips, we would sit and stare, watching for the winner of the race. We were fertile ground for them; we were filthy. I was filthy; everyone was filthy. Some people called us filthy Jews. Yes, we were filthy! What little water we received, somehow begged, or stole, we kept for drinking. We could not worry about bathing.

"We can survive many years without bathing," Mama said, "but we will not survive very long without drinking."

I learned at an early age that you must not ever waste water. The luxury of a bath was unheard of during our long travels.

We went into a very big room in the building. Desks and chairs were everywhere. People asked us questions: "Who are you? What are your names?"

I looked at my mama and said in Yiddish, "Don't tell them; don't tell them." The minute somebody knew your name, you might get in trouble and be taken away and never found again. "Mama, please do not tell them!" I begged.

The man behind me heard what I said, and he said to me in Yiddish, "Everyone here is a Jew! Listen to me, little one. *Everyone* here is a Jew!"

I looked at him and said, "Everybody? Everybody in this room is a Jew?" Then I remembered Mama saying never to admit I was Jewish, so I said to him, "Well, I'm not a Jew!"

Mama looked at me. "Yes, Maide'le, you are."

"Mama, don't say that!"

"It's not a secret anymore, Maide'le. It's all right now. You don't have to be afraid. Everybody here is a Jew." I looked all around the room. *So many Jews in one place? And everyone tells each other they are Jews? I do not understand any of this.*

After they got all the information from everybody, they told us: "You must talk to the Red Cross. If you give your name and all the information about yourself to them—where you were born and family history—then maybe they can see if somebody is looking for you, and maybe you can also find your family if someone is still alive." They were making lists of survivors.

My Papa told them, "I have two uncles in America. Can you find them? They live in New York, America. We must look for them, because my wife wants to go to America."

"Papa! You want to go to the Holy Land! I want to go with my friends the Zionists!"

Papa said, "It's going to be our way, don't worry. We will go with your friends the Zionists. They will help us."

Yes, my friend the Zionist did tell me he was taking all of us home. I wanted to go with him to our new home.

"We will go with him, don't worry. Soon we will be home forever."

Papa gave the Red Cross people his uncles' names; they both lived in New York. Papa said he wanted to know if the uncles were alive and if they could do anything to help our family. The Red Cross people promised they would give the information to the office in America; they would do the research and give the information to someone called CARE, pronounced in Polish *Carai*. I did not know what any of that meant.

Yes, they were alive, we found out much later. But no, they didn't wish to do anything for us.

I was very overwhelmed with this massive, magnificent house. I was in a palace, and my father was sitting on the floor, because he could not stand on his feet anymore. A man came to take us to the corner where we could sit. Papa looked at me and said, "Come here, Anna'le. Sit down next to me."

As I sat beside him, he said, "I always knew you were a princess."

"Papa, what is a princess?"

"That's a beautiful little girl who is dressed in a beautiful, clean blue satin dress. She lives like a very rich father's daughter and must live in a palace. See! You're in a palace! That makes you a princess."

"Papa, I am so dirty, and the lice are biting me."

Papa said, "Shush, be quiet now. No, you're not dirty, and you have no lice. Look into my eyes and see what I see. I see a beautiful girl with beautiful, blond curly hair and big brown eyes, and she's wearing a blue satin princess dress with a big sash and with gold and blue ribbons in her hair. You are so very lovely."

I looked into Papa's eyes. They were green with brown and gold specks, and I saw that princess too. "Papa, will I ever have a pretty blue dress like that?"

"Yes, and it will be made of shiny satin, and it will have a big, beautiful bow in the back and a nice ribbon for your hair in the exact same color."

That was so nice. It was my first happy dream, and I was not asleep. I was so happy. We sat there hugging each other and smiling as the lice traveled between our bodies. I was thinking of that beautiful, clean princess with the curly, blond hair and the pretty, blue dress made of satin. I didn't know what satin was, but it was shiny. Papa said so.

Then the Zionists came to take us. Mama and I walked, and they carried Papa, Chaim, and Yakov as well. We walked and walked in that palace for a very long time. There were hundreds of people, or was it thousands? To me, it looked like all the people who were left alive in the world were in one place. They brought us to a small section of the big room.

As we were walking, I looked all around, and the entire big room had nothing else in it except many, many beds against the walls and in the middle of the room for all of us to sleep on. As many beds as we had people were in that room. Three long pieces of wood just the width of a human—that was all you got. They were everywhere, from just off the floor, almost to the ceiling. All I could see were people climbing up and down just as if it were a big anthill. There were a few little planks put together that looked like ladders in front of every small group of these beds.

I said, "Papa, where are they going? Why are they climbing up to the ceiling?"

"Oh, these are bunk beds. The ladders help us to climb. These ones are for us; we have three beds."

"Why do we have three beds, Papa?"

"One for Mama, one for me, and one for you and your brothers."

"Are we going to fall out?"

"No, Maide'le, I'll make sure you don't fall out. We will put you kids on the bottom bed, which is not far off the ground, the two little boys on one side and you on the other. We will spread out our *schmatas* (bundles of our last worldly possessions) on those hard wooden planks to sleep on and some for your covers and protection so you will not fall out."

I was not about to go to sleep! I had to see everything. I had to know everything. I didn't trust anyone. I needed to know what was going on. I was frantic! *What do you mean lie down? Why? What's going on? What's about to happen?* Every time somebody told me to lie down or be quiet, something horrible happened. *I am not doing it again. I am a big girl now. I am older. I'm almost five!*

I must have fallen asleep. When I awoke, Papa was gone. I looked at my mother, and I cried, "I told you! You should not have given his name to anyone! Now my papa is gone. It's your fault they took him away! Where is my papa?"

"He'll be right back," Mama replied.

"No! I am going to find him! I will find my father and bring him back!"

I went storming through the palace, calling out, "Papa!" Again and again! I had to find my father. I was running around, and I was looking in all directions. All I could see was what looked like an army of ants going up and down on all the wall-ladders. They were mingling back and forth with each other. More people-ants were coming in and going out, nonstop all over the big room. Some were crying, and others, hearing bad news, started to scream and cry as well.

Many were sick with dysentery. Some were squatting just where they stood a moment ago. Someone else screamed. The noise got louder and louder. I could not breathe, and the stench was getting worse by the minute. It was terrible. It made me feel ill.

Somehow, I remembered how to get back to the place where Papa had given his name at the big desk. I would look for the right person and make him give me back my papa. If he had my father's name, then he must have taken him.

I ran around in a big circle, searching for Papa. As I circled about, the ceiling, the people, and the beds started going in a circle in the opposite direction. Then they started moving faster and faster and faster still. Everything became dark, and then black, and I did not know what happened. I fell.

I awoke to a loud, shrill scream. "Don't touch her! She's mine! She is mine; do not touch her!" It was my mother's voice. She came to me and, like a big bird, just swooped down on me with her body to protect me. She picked me up in her arms, holding me close. I felt warm and comforted.

Mama was sitting on the floor with me in her lap, rocking back and forth and talking to me very quietly. "Anna'le, all is well. Everything is in order. Papa came back. He is worried about you. Wake up, my little one. Papa came back, and he wants you to come back to him."

I looked at her face, and I did not believe her. I said, "I want to see my papa now. They took away my papa."

"No, he came back, and you were gone."

That was the first time I actually heard any words of concern about me from my mama. Mama always talked about the boys. For the first time, I felt loved and truly understood. *She does care! My mother does care for me!* I had heard her say, "Don't touch her; she's mine." Just as the man named Zionist had said I was his, and I had trusted and believed him, now I knew Mama cared for me too.

My poor mama could not pick me up. I was too heavy for her. She was so thin I could see her bones. Mama took me by the hand. "Come, I will show you your papa. He is where I told you he would be. If not, I will let you run off to look for him."

Hearing the commotion, my father left my little brothers with a stranger and was already half the way to us. My poor papa could barely walk; now he was running and calling my name, bandages falling off his feet, leaving his bloody footprints on the floor. If a light wind had blown on him, he would have fallen. He was so weak and sick, but Papa picked me up, held me tight to his chest, and said, "Don't ever run away again. You had given me a very terrible fright."

"Papa, I thought nothing frightens you."

"Yes, you frightened me. You must never leave Mama to come look for me."

"I promise, Papa. I will never run away again. I didn't run away this time, Papa. I was looking for you!"

The poor man could barely stand up, and two people caught him as he was about to fall. He put me down, and they took him to a first aid station to get his feet and legs bandaged again. This time I came along to protect my sick papa.

There they washed and put medicine on his feet and legs all the way up to his knees. Then they carefully swaddled them with some white cloth I had never seen before. When Papa and I came back to Mama, I was teasing him: "You look so clean! You look like all the men called Zionists."

Papa said, "Yes, I also had a bath at the time you ran away! I also found out a big secret!"

"What is it, Papa?"

"You're going to have a bath very soon as well. You will be cleaned up and smell nice! Just like your Zionist friends. It will make you very happy. And they will get rid of the lice too!"

My Papa knew everything; he was right again.

Did I remember being clean? No, not for a very long time. I didn't remember being clean since I had been in the church. I knew it was something very good, and the lice don't bite as much when you are clean.

"Well, if you're clean, the lice won't have anything to live on, and then they will stop biting you constantly. That should make you happy," Mama said.

*Yes, Mama, it would make me happy. A life without lice? That could make me very happy.* Constantly scratching and bleeding, with flies stopping for a meal all over me? It was very painful and annoying. It also made me look dirty all the time.

"Don't you want a bath?" Papa asked.

"Yes, I do, but how can we then drink the water, Papa?"

"You'll have all you need to drink and enough to get washed as well. Not everyone can have a bath now, but at least the children can."

*What is the sense of having a bath and then putting on dirty clothes?* I had no clean clothes. The lice were everywhere, and in this big, beautiful palace, we gave them back and forth to each other.

Mama said she would wash the clothes and me at the same time. Maybe my lice would drown.

I have no idea how long I was a princess in that big palace, perhaps a few weeks. Too soon, we had to go. We had just begun to settle into a routine when we were on our way again. The palace was a transit camp. From there, people went to different displaced persons' camps. Or, as I learned later in Germany, the *DP Lagers.*

We spent the best part of the next three years in several different DP camps.

The Americans and the Red Cross had set up camps all throughout Germany for the Jews who had survived and were flocking to the area by the thousands.

*Why people are coming to Germany only G-d knows, and I hope no one will ever stay or come back to this cursed country,* I said to myself. I didn't know the answer. I only knew Mama was right when she said, "Good people will never live in this country ever again!" Only those people my mama called "the cannibals" would live there.

The "Nazi cannibals" murdered Mama's mother, all of Mama's siblings, and the husbands and children of her married sisters. Most of

Mama's and many of Papa's cousins, nieces, and nephews also perished, as well as two of his siblings and their spouses.

No, I will never be in the same place with the cannibals ever again. I made this promise to Mama one week before she passed away.

In the early 1950s, my cousin Ami (Papa's sister Miriam's son) was celebrating his bar mitzvah, the first such happy occasion for our family since arriving in Israel. It felt like *my* special day. Mama and Papa gave me—the new Israeli princess—a beautiful light-blue satin dress. It had a big bow in the back, and there were blue ribbons for my hair.

# Chapter 12

# The Actress from America

*Molly Picon—1946*

On a warm day with the sun shining, I had a bit of freedom to run through the camp. That is, when I was able to get away from helping Mama with my two little brothers. I was happy; the birds were singing. I loved to watch them, and I always saved some bread crumbs in my dress pocket to feed them. That day, I looked for dogs, cats, or someone to play with.

I neared the small home of Mama's Uncle Chaim Schotland, his wife, and son who were in the same DP camp with us. Yosef, the son, had two young sons of his own—Baruch and Alexander. As I approached, I saw grandfather and grandsons pulling weeds in their small vegetable garden and asked if they needed my help, hoping secretly they did not.

"No, Anna, you run along and play. Here, take these sweet peas," said Uncle Chaim.

That morning I was very seriously looking for my furry friends. I planned to name them and bring one home to live with me.

Just then, a voice intruded on my thoughts. It was Papa calling for me. It seemed I could never get away by myself for very long.

My first thought was that Mama could not manage alone with the two little ones and needed my help. Papa approached and said Mama had something very important to tell me. I must come home right away. He said I must agree with her no matter what she asked of me.

Papa was behaving strangely. He did not look right at me. "Papa, what is wrong? Are the boys well?"

"Yes, they are well, but Mama has something on her mind, and she needs your help!"

I ran. Mama needs me!

I hurried into our small room. Mama and the kids looked well and nothing was out of place, but Mama's cheeks were red. Her eyes sparkled as they did whenever she got very excited or nervous.

"What is wrong, Mama? What do you need?"

"Anna'le, I must tell you; something wonderful is about to happen to us. Now you must listen to me and do exactly as I tell you!"

"Yes, Mama, anything you say."

"Well, *Anna'le*, let me tell you a short story. I know it will make you very happy! This morning some people stopped to talk not far from our door. They were talking about a famous young Jewish American actress. One of the men told the other that Molly Picon with her husband and a group of performers would be visiting some of the DP camps, singing, dancing, and entertaining us. We have heard that when she comes, she will bring gifts of lipstick and stockings for the women! She is looking for an orphaned child to adopt and take back to America to live with her and her husband. I intend this child to be you!"

As I stood in stunned silence before my mama, I saw her flushed face, and the only thing I understood was that Mama wanted to give me away again to some stranger and send me off with her to America.

I had to think quickly. I was Mama's only helper. *Even if she doesn't love me, how can she manage to look after the boys without me? Yet how can I refuse this order when she has made up her mind, and Papa has told me to do what she says?*

"Mama, Mama, please don't send me away! I will stop asking so many questions. I will do as you say for the little ones day or night. I will help you more. Please don't make me go!"

Mama stopped talking and focused her eyes on me, staring at me as if I had just thrown cold water in her face and spoiled her plans.

"I must get you to America, and Molly Picon is our only hope right now. After you have lived with her in America for a few years, you will bring all of us to live there with you! What is wrong with that?"

"I am not an orphan, Mama." *Or am I?* I thought to myself. "Can't Papa's uncles bring us to America? Do you have to sell me?"

Mama's expression changed from happy and excited to one of confused disbelief. "Silly you! Are you mad? I just want us all to go to America, and this is as good a way as any!"

"Mama, that woman wants a child who has no Mama or family. She is not looking for me. I have you and Papa and a family."

Now angry, Mamma declared, "No! You do not have anything! You will do as I tell you! You will not stand in the way of my plan!"

I ran outdoors away from Mama and collided with Papa who was standing near the door listening to every word. "Papa, do you also want to give me away to this American woman? Now I know Mama has no love for me, but you told me you loved me. Was that also a big lie?"

He turned away mute, and I followed him.

I continued. "I can promise you, Papa, the two of you will not succeed in doing this terrible thing to me. I will not be given away! Never see my little brothers again? No, I won't go!"

Thinking fast, I declared, "This is what I will do. I will pretend to agree with everything Mama tells me to do until the day when I meet that woman Picon. I will tell her the truth, but I'm not going to leave you all."

Papa quietly replied, "Go look for your cats and dogs. Go play with them. Let me talk with Mama; all will be well." And he back went into the house.

As I turned to go, I heard Papa's voice. "Have you lost your mind? Would you really give away your only daughter for a ticket to America?"

*Papa will protect me,* I thought to myself as I ran to look for the stray dogs and cats—my friends that no one else wanted either. They would understand.

In some deep grass, I found two kittens with orange and white patches and little pink noses. I gently picked them up and ran toward the little bombed-out house on the edge of the camp. This was my sanctuary. I crawled through a window into the basement where no one could see me. It was a refuge where I could escape the noise of my brothers. Sometimes I would even stay all day and sleep in its peaceful solitude.

The two little kittens curled up in my lap and fell asleep for a while. Then their pitiful crying sound made me cry with them. Nobody wanted any of us. I knew just how they felt.

I remembered Mama once said that G-d helps those who help themselves. *What can I do to help me?* I would have to go along with Mama's plan and do everything she told me to do till the day I would meet the American woman. That way I wouldn't get so many beatings. Then I could tell the Picon lady the truth and ask her to please not take me with her; that I would not be happy with her in America.

Later that day I reluctantly returned to our family's small cabin. For the next while, Mama taught me proper manners—how to walk, talk, eat, and behave like a lady. She rehearsed me in answering many questions. *So many lies to memorize.* How had I become an orphan? On and on. This was a new kind of hell for me, but I played along and there was a measure of peace in our home.

One day I returned from a visit to my small sanctuary and my collection of animals. I was dirty and very hungry, because I had given all my food to the animals. As I entered the room, I could see something was very wrong. Mama was sobbing uncontrollably.

I ran to her. "What is wrong, Mama? Are you sick? Are the boys sick? Where is Papa?" I hadn't noticed Papa standing in the back of the room behind me. "What's wrong, Papa? What happened?"

"Mama is very sad and disappointed; she is very unhappy right now. Let's go out for a walk and a talk."

*What could possibly make Mama so very unhappy? Who would dare hurt my mama like that?* "Please, Papa, tell me what is wrong with Mama."

It was a very short answer. "Molly Picon will not be coming to our camp to look for her new child. She will visit some other camps."

It took me a few moments to digest the news Papa had just given me. Then, I felt great joy! I would no longer have to live with the fear of being sent away, and I wouldn't have to rehearse all the lies.

True, I didn't get to see Molly Picon, star of Yiddish theater and film in person, but that summer she gave me back my freedom by *not* coming to our camp.

No, I do not hate my mama; I hate the war that made Mama try any method within her grasp to achieve her goals. I feel a great deal of pain, sympathy, and pity for her and for all of us who did what we did just to stay alive.

In the midsixties in New York City, I attended the Broadway musical *The Land of Milk and Honey* in which Molly Picon starred. I had composed a note to her that morning, and after the final curtain call, I sent it backstage with an usher:

*Dear Miss Picon,*

*We must meet this evening! In 1946, I almost became your daughter! So I feel I am entitled to a meeting with you! Please grant me a few moments of your time.*

*Respectfully almost your daughter,*
*Sahbra Anna Markus*

A few moments later, a young man asked me to follow him backstage. There in a dressing room full of flowers and people stood the small figure of a lovely smiling woman with beautiful big eyes.

"So you are my daughter?" she asked. I reached out my hand in greeting, but she quickly said, "So, come give your mother a hug! So who would believe you are my daughter? You're twice my height!"

We hugged, and she walked me to a chair. "Tell me the story. How, when, and where was I to become your Mother?"

I told her of the DP camp in Germany and all the excitement and rumors in the camps about the American entertainers, and that the star Molly Picon was going to adopt a child and take her back to America with her.

I told her about Mama's desperate wish to get to America and her willingness to give me up so at least I would have a good life in her America. I told Miss Picon I would have told her the truth that I did have a mama, papa, and two brothers and did not wish to go with her. We both laughed and had tears in our eyes.

My visit was short. She thanked me for sending her the note and telling her my story. We hugged again, and as we parted, she asked me to come again for a visit. I have seen her in films and other shows. Unfortunately, we did not meet again. However, I will always remember her warmth and kind words.

# Chapter 13

# Remembering Galena

*1947*

In a very small, bad-smelling, and musty cabin, we three children were all alone. Where was Mama? Where did she go? She was very fat again when she left.

Just before Mama left, she said, "You will be the little mama for your brothers, Chaim and Yakov. Make sure Papa is well. You are the mama now until I come back." Whenever she left the cabin, she would say, "Always make sure Papa is well."

So my work as a Mama'le began when I was six.

We didn't have much to eat in our cabin. Papa told me he would go out to look for more food, and so he left. I was all alone with two hungry little boys until Papa came back in the evening with some bread and milk.

Then several days after Mama left, Papa went to bring her back. I was very happy to know Mama would return to us. Nobody ever came back after having been gone for days. This time, my mama *did* come back to us.

Mama entered our little cabin carrying a moving bundle in her arms. It was a new little boy. "Mama, why do we need another one?" She didn't answer. "Mama," I protested, "you and I know we don't need another one! We already have two boys and me, and we can't get enough food for any of us; we do not need another one!"

Mama brought this new one into our cabin anyway. I did not know where she went to get it, but I told her she must go back to that place and give back the new little boy. We couldn't keep him! She told me we had to keep him. I thought it very strange that he looked just like Yakov with pink cheeks and light-blond hair. He was a pretty baby.

"We don't have enough food for all of us; my two little brothers come first! We already have them. We must send this new one back!" I insisted.

Mama ignored my protests; she sat down and took her empty breast from her dress to feed this new one. My brother Yakov was hungry too. This new baby wanted to eat all day. Mama didn't have milk for everyone. Chaim and I didn't take the breast milk anymore, but my little brother Yakov still needed the breast. Now Mama would not have enough for him with this new little one wanting food all the time. *He will only make things worse for all of us,* I knew. He was only quiet when he had a breast in his mouth. All day and all night, he cried.

Unbeknownst to all of us, poor new little brother Yitzhak had colic. How can a six-year-old understand something like this? That poor boy cried almost nonstop for months. We were all exhausted and desperately needed some rest, some sleep. I begged Mama to let me use the pillow to make him be quiet. Mama said, "We don't have a pillow. And no, you may not do that!"

We didn't have pillows. We slept on some rags tied together, and we rested our heads on bundles of some of our extra clothing. Mama wanted to know how I knew the word pillow when I had never owned or seen one.

"I *did* have a pillow, and so did *he!*" I declared.

"And who is the 'he' with the pillow?" When I didn't answer, Mama asked me again. "Who had the pillow?"

I repeated, "He had the pillow!" I would not tell her who "he" was.

"Anna'le, please tell me what happened. Who had the pillow?"

I blurted out, "It was the *priest* in that church where you put me; *he* had the pillow! The bad priest had the pillow."

Although I did not fully understand at that time why Galena had stopped screaming, I knew it was all so simple—the pillow would make someone quiet. My golden-haired Galena didn't say anything or move ever again. She was dead. He had put the pillow on her face. *That* is how I knew how to make someone quiet. Now I knew why I wanted a pillow for this new crying baby boy.

Galena was not the only one to suffer in that place. Every night, I saw children disappear from the big hall. I saw them come back with big and small burns. In time, I learned to tell how old the scars were. Some had formed scabs. They were not as visibly red and scary. Some marks were turning dark brown, meaning they had started to heal. When we changed nightshirts, we could see the burns or the marks of whips on each other's bodies—all over the small bodies of boys and girls alike. For the boys, it was mainly on their backs. For girls, mostly on the front.

Now, years later, I know cigarettes or cigars had made those burns. Those men burned us while they were raping us. At times, there was more than one person in the room with us, doing bad things to us. Yes, I know all this to be true. I saw it all, and I felt it on my body as well. I still carry those scars that remind me every day of the hell I lived through.

A pretty little boy slept in one of the beds down from mine, a boy whose name I don't remember. He was bigger than I was; he must have been at least five or six years old. The boy had big blue eyes, just like my Galena, and black hair with pretty curls. One day, the bad priest did a very bad thing to him. The priest got on top of the boy and made all the bad noises again. At first, the boy was lying on his back, with his face up, and the priest was pushing on the boy's face with the pillow. The boy kicked him in the face as he struggled to get away, and he scratched the bad priest on the right side of his face, on his cheek. A toenail scratched him, and the man was hurt. I know, because I saw blood jump out of his cheek. I saw it jump, and then I saw blood on his face and neck. The priest turned the boy over onto his stomach. After a short while, with the boy screaming, that bad man put a pillow on his face again—to make sure he was quiet—just as he had done to my Galena.

Several of us children saw this, but not my Galena. She was dead.

I slept in Galena's empty bed one night, and I got a beating for it. After that, I thought I had better stay in my own bed, so he wouldn't put a pillow on my face as well. A few times, I slept under the bed and took my pillow with me. I watched him all the time. Everywhere he went, I was near him. One of the priests made a joke about us, saying to him, "You've grown a tail! Wherever you are, this little one is right at your backside. She looks quite attached to you." He acknowledged it did look like he'd grown a tail. "Yes, we think this little one really likes you."

Above the headboard of each little bed was a framed picture. The nice priest had told me it was the face of G-d, and I should pray to him every day. *No! That is the G-d of the bad priest. He put the pillow on my Galena's face! His G-d is a bad G-d!*

As soon as the nice priest left, I spat at that face on the wall. The priest who killed my Galena kept saying if I didn't kiss his G-d and pray to him, nothing good would ever happen to me. But *he* was a bad man; I saw him kill my Galena. He took her away! He took my Galena away. I spat on that picture of the poor, bloodied man with long blond hair. When no one was watching, I spat on it again and again. That is what I thought of the priest and his G-d. I did that for as long as I was in that church.

# Chapter 14

# Aunt Fela

Almost two years went into the long search. From our first day in the first German DP camp, Mama and Papa were continually looking for family members who had survived.

They were in touch with American and other authorities—the Red Cross and Jewish organizations—always carefully reading survivors' lists as soon as they were printed and inquiring of any witness who might have information.

One day when Papa paid a visit to the camp office, he received some good news. His youngest sister Fela had survived Auschwitz. She was alive and living in Munich with her husband and their young son. There was even a home address listed for her.

We were to learn Aunt Fela had met and married Stacheck (Sol) Gelnic just before the end of the war. Many years later, when we were in Israel, I learned from my father that Sol had been married before the war. In fact, he and his first wife had had a son, both of whom perished in Auschwitz. To my knowledge, he never spoke of this history, and I understand his offspring (my cousins) have only lately learned of their father's first family.

Papa soon asked for permission to leave the camp to go visit his sister in Munich. In fact, he made several such visits before the day he invited me to go along with him. I was very happy and eager to go with my papa that morning. I would get to see a big city and meet his sister.

So much of what I had seen throughout many countries of Europe was only rubble and broken houses. I thought nothing had happened to

Germany or its cities, so I was surprised and happy that they also had many broken houses and that some of the people in the streets looked very sad.

We finally arrived at a nice street, which was so very clean. Nothing was broken, all the houses were tall, and they had windows that sparkled in the morning sunlight. I told Papa it was not right they should have so much after what they did to rest of the people of Europe. Papa just nodded his head in agreement.

We walked up the steps, and Papa knocked on the big, fancy door. A woman in a black dress and white apron came to the door.

"I am here to visit my sister," Papa said, and the woman retreated into the house.

"Who is she, Papa?" He answered that she was a maid.

"What is a maid?"

"She cleans and cooks and cares for the family," he whispered.

*Why do they need one?* I thought to myself. *They must be very rich.*

Just then, a short, black-haired woman came from another room. My mind whirled. *More than one room for this small family?*

Father's sister extended her hand to shake mine. Papa said, "Give your Aunt Fela a big hug!"

I looked at her eyes. They were cold. I didn't want to hug her, and she did not wish to have a hug from me. She just held out her hand, but I did not take it. Her look told me what she thought of me. I did not like her either.

The moment passed, and Aunt Fela gave orders to the servant. We soon joined Uncle Sol in the dining room. I liked him immediately; his eyes smiled. He came to me, picked me up, and gave me a big hug and kiss. Yes, I liked him from the start.

The noontime meal was about to be served at a big table with a fancy cloth on it. I had never seen a tablecloth before, and I didn't know what to do with the utensils. Fela seemed very disappointed that I did not know the proper use of a fork and knife. I had never been the proud owner of such implements, and before that day, I didn't know you needed to use a fork and knife together at the same time. That was far too much work just to get food to your mouth.

The table was loaded with great quantities of food. I was excited and wanted to taste many things I had not seen before. I was in for a surprise. My first mouthful was so terrible I spat it out into my hand and put it under the table. Much of the meal did not taste good to me. Some of the food was overcooked, some not cooked enough, and all of it was very salty. All I could eat was the bread, sardines, some cheese, and fruit I had never seen before. Fela told Papa I was much too fussy and ungrateful for someone who had nothing, and I should eat whatever was put before me. To this day I remember it to be the worst meal I had ever been served. I am sure most of the food was thrown away by the next morning.

I later heard Papa tell Mama that Uncle Sol was a "wheeler-dealer" on the black market and did very well for himself, so Aunt Fela and her little family lived quite comfortably. Everyone in the large apartment had his or her own room, even their young son, Yitzhak, who was three years younger than I was, and the two German servants. There was also a guest room for Papa and me. Fela seemed very proud of her privileged status in life.

The following day after a quiet breakfast, Papa and his brother-in-law planned to go out and do some business. First, Papa suggested, we should all go for a nice, long walk.

Aunt Fela looked disapprovingly at me and remarked so Papa could not hear, "You look terrible dressed in that ugly old dress. You look like a dirty little mouse!"

She was right. I was in rags. I did not have a nice new dress, hat or coat to wear for this special occasion. I knew Mama had washed me well before we left the camp, and my clothes were clean. Mama had said, "I wish I could give you more, but thank G-d we even have this much." I loved my mama for doing the best she could for my brothers and me. We had very little of anything, so we did not worry much about how we were dressed.

However, it apparently mattered very much to Aunt Fela. I was not good enough for my papa's dear sister.

So one of the maids was instructed to clean me again as she had done the previous day before bedtime. Fela had remarked then, "You did not bring anything good to wear. We will have to do something with you tomorrow!"

To Papa and Sol, she announced, "This morning we will go out, and I will get her some decent clothing." She thought making jokes at my expense was funny; Papa and I did not smile. I did not want anything from her. I wanted to go back to the DP camp where people were not ugly and did not laugh at our misfortune.

So instead of a nice walk with Papa, Fela took me to a children's clothing store. She had me try on lots of coats, and she picked out one she liked that had a matching muff. It was a lovely set in maroon and cream-colored wool with a small herringbone pattern. The sleeves, collar, and pockets had soft maroon velvet trim. It was a beautiful little coat. I had never owned or even seen a coat like that before. I remember I was so very happy. Looking into a big mirror for the first time in my life, I could see a clean, nice-looking little girl.

Fela didn't seem to be concerned about my old shoes that had big holes in them. I guess if something was not visible, then it was not a problem. "The exterior must be presentable at all costs," she said.

Now with my new coat, Aunt Fela would not be embarrassed to be seen with me in public. She was so proud of her generosity that she had a photographer take a picture of me in the coat and muff. I saw that photo in her New Jersey home many years later.

Unfortunately, underneath the lovely coat, I was still in rags.

This was my first and last visit to my papa's sister. It would be many years before I saw her again, this time in 1962 at my mother's funeral in New York City. She had not changed, and I still did not like her.

A few years after that visit, Uncle Sol, Aunt Fela, and their son, Yitzhak (Ira), arrived in America, where their daughter, Helen, was born. Fela died three months before my father's passing in 1997. Papa, to the last day of his life, still loved her dearly. Sol passed away several years before his wife.

Helen died at the young age of fifty-seven. Her husband, Jacob, and two daughters, Dina and Sherri, survive her. My cousin Ira, married to Sima, is the last survivor of his generation. With their family of five children, they lived in New Jersey and now in Israel. Their loving son and many loving grandchildren survive Uncle Sol and Aunt Fela.

# Chapter 15

# The Inoculations

*Displaced Persons' Camp, Vilseck, Germany—1947*

R ed Cross officials finally realized almost everyone in the camp was sick. We had all sorts of skin rashes, lung ailments and assorted diseases. For us, the lice covering our dirty hair and bodies were the biggest problem. They liked us and they were not going to leave, even when we bathed in benzene.

Officials were also very concerned because none of the Jewish children in the camp and few of the adults had been inoculated to protect against serious contagious diseases. I kept overhearing the words *cholera* and *typhus*. The risk was great, given the lack of proper sanitation in the camp. They wanted to give all of us something so we would not get those horrible diseases.

The small administration building had long lists of names tacked onto the office doors. All residents must go and look on the lists to find out when they must come back to the infirmary to receive their inoculations. I went along with Papa. We found our names there, with the time for our appointment the next day. A boy told me the inoculation was very painful, so I was trying to think of some way to get out of going back to the clinic.

However, we returned and found long lines forming in front of the office. Standing in line, I listened to everybody talking. The adults argued with each other about whether the inoculations would really help. Most were more concerned about the scarce food for themselves and their children. Poor nutrition and awful camp conditions were of more immediate concern.

I did not understand why people complained this way. Just a few weeks ago, we didn't have any food at all to eat, good or bad. Not even a proper place to live, to sleep, or to call "home." Many of us had been sleeping out in the open under the stars.

Soon they called my name over the loudspeaker, and a nurse with a red cross on her white headscarf took me into the infirmary. It was time for my smallpox inoculation. I heard people say *pocken* was very bad. This inoculation would protect me from getting that kind of sick.

Papa came with me. The nurse picked up a piece of glass and took hold of my left arm. I became very afraid, and I yelled to my papa.

Papa was a hero, but he could not look at his poor child being hurt. He became very white, turned his head away, and then quickly left the room.

I looked at that square chunk of glass. It was not a needle for an injection as I had expected. It was just like the broken glass Mama used when she cut me over my eye on our way to the church. So I got very scared!

I screamed for Papa, but he didn't come back. Someone held my arms and said, "It will be over in a second." I stopped struggling and yelling for Papa. I watched as the nurse dunked the sharp glass into some yellow stuff. Then she took my arm to scratch it very hard a few times near my shoulder, making me bleed. The blood came out and she gently mixed it with the serum.

Wiping up the liquid that ran down my arm, she gently caressed my hair and my cheek, saying, "You're such a brave little girl. It will stop hurting very soon." And she kissed me on my forehead.

I was still very upset. Papa once told me he would never let anyone hurt me again, but he did. He told me it would not hurt, but it did hurt—a lot! Papa never lied to me before, but on that day, he did. I was very angry with him. I didn't scream now; I was brave. I was also angry.

For several days, I was sick. I had a high fever and felt cold and hot all at the same time. I promised myself I would never forgive Papa for lying. Never would I forgive him, because it all hurt so badly, and I felt so sick.

When I got well, the loudspeaker was still calling for many people who had not yet come for their inoculations. "You must *all* show up before the medical staff leaves. We must inoculate every last one of you!" Then they started calling out names, and one of them was again a "Markus." *Did they say Volfe?*

Father took my hand and said, "Come, Maide'le. We have to go back to the office."

"Papa, I was already there! I had my inoculation!"

"Do what you are told."

"Papa! I was already there, and I got very sick! I don't want to go again!"

Papa would not listen. He said if one was good, then two would be much better. Off we went to the infirmary again. He pushed me toward the nurse, saying, "Here is the last Markus who did not have the inoculation."

"Papa!" I protested.

"It's okay," Papa said softly. "You don't have to say another word, my dear little girl. Don't say a word."

To myself I said, *Papa, you are lying! I already had mine, and you didn't have any. Without it, Papa, you will get sick!*

I tried to tell the nurse. I kept showing her my arm. "See! The first inoculation is already crusting and healing now. I have one already." That nurse was not very smart. She only knew English, so she didn't understand me or my Russian or Yiddish speech at all.

The nurse asked how I got that mark, and my father quickly answered in German, "I will explain all this to you later; just take care of her now, and I will send her back to her mother." She didn't understand him or me, so she just took me by the arm and got ready for the inoculation.

"But, Papa!"

"Please don't interrupt."

"Papa!"

Nothing I said helped. I was inoculated yet again. I was now so thoroughly vaccinated that I couldn't catch smallpox or anything else that year or for the rest of my life. Again, I became sick with a high fever that lasted even longer than the first.

So twice, I was not going to trust him for the rest of his life. Twice he lied to me about the same thing! I will tell you that it gave me material to tease him with for the next fifty years.

Papa, the brave partisan warrior, the survivor of so much hell, the man who escaped the Warsaw ghetto, my big hero who survived hard labor in the Russian coal mines, was just a big, scared little girl. The man could not take a scratch from a piece of glass with some medicine on it. Was my papa really a coward?

His only answer to that question was, "You are right! When it comes to needles—or glass—I am the biggest, frightened little boy in the world."

I accused, "Papa, I was sick! You made me have it twice!"

"So now you will be twice as healthy later."

Thanks to my father's cowardice, I have *two* smallpox vaccination scars on my left arm.

# Chapter 16

# Atonement for Our Sins

*1947*

It was becoming cooler each day, and the leaves on the few big trees in the town were changing from green to yellow, gold, and orange. Until now, I only knew summer and winter, so it was fascinating to me to notice for the first time the colors of autumn.

Mama said *Rosh Hashanah* and then *Yom Kippur* were quickly approaching, and she was nervous. She was very concerned she might not have all she needed for the proper rituals for these very important holy days. Papa, she said, had lost interest in all things religious. Since G-d did not protect his sons and all our families from Hitler and his demons of death, Mama said Papa wanted very little to do with our G-d anymore. However, I did still hear him call on G-d whenever we had problems. *So much to think about and try to understand!*

"Mama, what do we need to have in order to make this a holiday the way you want it to be?" I asked.

Mama was sitting down, looking very sad. She reached out to me, and with tears in her eyes, she pulled me between her knees, holding me tight.

"How will I teach you all you need to know about being a good Jewish girl when I have all these obstacles in my way?"

She told me that at this time of year, her papa would have ordered from a farmer or the *shochet* (slaughterer) all the chickens or other winged creatures their family needed for the *Yom Kippur* ritual and the meal following the fast. On the morning before the holy day, her papa would bring the fowl to the family's home for the blessing and ritual and then take them to the *shochet* for slaughtering. They would say more prayers and blessings, and then all the sins of the family and all of Israel would be placed on the chickens before they were killed in the prescribed manner. All the good Jewish people would do this for their own families and on behalf of all the people.

Mama told me her mama would cook the chickens for their evening meal well before sundown and the start of the one-day fast. There would be prayer services all day long, and after nightfall, they would have another holiday dinner to break the fast. The children did not have to fast.

Mama's family always had dairy foods with which to break the fast. If we could get some dairy products, that would be great, Mama said. The extra chicken was on standby, so we would not go hungry.

"Why do we have to fast, Mama?" I asked. "Are we not hungry most of the time anyway?" It did not make any sense to set aside a day to be even hungrier! *What fool made up this rule?* I wondered.

"Refraining from eating for one whole day—from sunset till late the following night—we learn to dedicate ourselves with an open heart to G-d and give special time for prayer and confession of sins," she said. "This is what the Jewish people do on *Yom Kippur*, Anna'le. You must learn all about our faith and practices."

When Papa came home that evening, I asked him if he knew where to get a chicken. Papa said yes he did, but wanted to know why I needed a chicken.

I told Papa about Mama's tears and that she needed to have a live chicken for a sacrifice.

"Oh, that!" Papa said with a smile on his face. "Well, if this is so important to your mama, I will get a chicken for her. However, I will not participate in this religious ritual. I am no longer the man she married in 1937. I do not have the *payos* or the beard, and though I am still a good Jew, I no longer want any part of the rituals. I want nothing to do with your mama's way of worshipping G-d. He has shown no mercy for millions of His Jewish people, including so many of our children! The temple in Jerusalem has been destroyed. Because of that, all the sacrifices are no longer necessary. Only Mama's *Chasidim* still make the sacrifices. I will not be home when Mama performs this ritual!"

The following afternoon when Papa came home, he had a big, fat chicken under his arm. The joy on Mama's face was wonderful to see. She now had a live creature for the sacrifice and food for the days to follow.

Mama had wanted a pure white chicken, but this fat bird was the best Papa could get. She was mostly white, with some colorful feathers around her neck. She was a pretty chicken, but she must die for Mama's G-d, for our sins, and for our dinner!

Mama took the chicken and tied a long rope around one of its legs. Then she put it outside, tied the rope to a loose board on our little house and sprinkled leftover breadcrumbs nearby for the chicken to eat.

"First thing tomorrow morning, we will all have to get well-washed before this ritual takes place. Oh, what a very special day it will be for all of us," Mama said. "By doing the rituals, we will be closer to G-d than all the people who do not worship Him this way!"

My Mama was so very happy. I saw her smile several times that day. How pretty she was when she had a smile on her face. Mama opened one of her bundles and took out a small prayer book. She said this book would show her how to perform the ritual.

Morning came, and water was heating on the primus stove. It would soon fill the washtub for our bath. Our baby Yitzhak was first to be washed, then Yakov, then Chaim and then me. I had to help Mama with the kids. I was now six years old. Though very thin, I was strong and could carry Yitzhak in my arms while Mama had her sponge bath.

After she had bathed herself in the second full tub of water, Mama washed all our clothing and her only other dress. She went outside to hang all the wet clothes on the fence and small tree branches to dry in the breeze. We would wear our one clean set of clothing for Mama's ceremony and prayers. Now it was time to go into our little room for Mama to do the ritual blessings.

Mama took the long rope off the chicken and then wrapped a smaller one around both of the chicken's legs. The chicken was not happy to be on the ground with its legs tied together. It started to jump up and down, and from side to the side, complaining, squawking, and flapping its wings.

Mama lifted the chicken and tucked it under her arm to bring it into our little cabin. Then Mama took her little book and opened it to the right page. She started to say words in a language I did not understand. I know now she spoke Hebrew.

Chaim, Yakov, and I stood before Mama, as I held baby Yitzhak in my arms. Then we came to the most important part, Mama said, where she would have to lift the live chicken high in the air, holding it by its legs and swinging it several times around and around in a full circle over all our heads while repeating the blessings.

The chicken was much too heavy for my happy Mama to lift by its legs only, and she struggled with the chicken to keep its wings together. The chicken was stronger than Mama and soon got its wings loose. Now it was squawking, screaming, and flapping its wings.

As it did so, the chicken let loose a shower of lice—a torrent of lice all over our heads. Mama just heard the noise of the squawking, and she was not going to let the chicken have the last word on this. She raised her voice, and her prayers became much louder and then louder still. It became a contest of who could scream the loudest, Mama or the chicken. I think the chicken had more to lose.

Chaim and I could hardly keep from squealing and laughing at the sight of it all. Mama's angry look hushed us. She was still having trouble holding on to the chicken. Whenever she lifted it over her head, the wings opened up wide, flapping in the air as if to take off and fly away. Each time, another shower of lice came down on our heads. Now Mama's attempt to keep the lice out of her own eyes and ours became impossible.

That chicken wanted to fly away. It did not want to hover over our heads. I thought the chicken must have known Mama's plans, and it was fighting for its life. Now Mama held this rebellious chicken with both hands, swinging it in big circles over our heads. With each pass, hundreds of lice showered down on our heads and bodies.

We scratched and itched all over our bodies and knew we would have to wash all over again. Mama would have to wash everything we now wore. I wondered if she could drown so many lice in one tub of water. Then we would have to sit in the bed for hours, until the first set of clothing would be dry.

Blissfully, Mama finally came to the end of this part of the very holy ritual and was now angry at the chicken for not cooperating. We stormed off to the *shochet,* leaving Yitzhak with Papa.

The *shochet's* yard was just at the edge of the camp, and it smelled of blood. I could see a very big crowd of mostly men gathered there waiting to hand over their chickens or other livestock for slaughtering. Each time a new person came into the yard, they elbowed their way with some ease toward the front of the line. Mama had complete control over the chicken now, holding it tightly under her arm, and she ordered me to follow her the best way I could.

Carrying Yakov, with Chaim holding on to the hem of my dress, I advanced through the crowd yelling, "Baby falling." I easily followed Mama. People quickly moved aside, concerned, lest they step on a child. Then they looked angry that one as young and small as I would be carrying a child in her arms, dragging another along, and pushing her way ahead of them. Mama was surprised to see me in front so soon.

The *shochet* came to Mama and relieved her of the lousy chicken. He had his hand out, and Mama put some coins in it.

I was confused; I did not know you had to pay for killing something. What a terrible job to have! *How much were the Nazis paid per person to kill the Jewish people, and by whom? Was there a special price for small children?* Mama said they had killed my two little twin brothers before

I was born. She cried for them every day. *How much money did they get for killing my brothers?*

Jostled by the crowd, I almost lost Yakov out of my arms. Mama, now free of the chicken, snatched him up. Still holding onto Chaim, I could now look around the yard and see what the slaughterer was doing. What was happening to all the animals that came into his hands? A sweet little lamb was next in line.

Mama said, "Look away! You will not like to see this."

I had to know everything, and I continued to look. Then, just as the man was bringing the knife to the lamb's throat, Mama yelled my name. Something in her urgent tone of voice made me look at her, and I missed seeing the lamb killed. Mama had succeeded in distracting me, and I could see she was happy about that.

Then, loudly for all to hear, the *shochet* said a prayer. In one hand, he held a chicken, and in the other, he had sharp knife! Mama distracted me again just in time, and I missed the killing of the chicken as well. I did not miss seeing it jump out of his hands and run around headless until he caught it and put it into a bucket with the neck down and feet up in the air.

I told myself that next year at this same time when Mama wanted to do this ritual again, I would be joining Papa far away from the killings. I don't think I want to be Mama's kind of Jewish girl. I want to be more like my papa, a Zionist with love for our G-d, my Jewish people, and our new homeland and much less interest in the rituals.

And so it is still.

# Chapter 17

# The Apple

*Giebelstadt near Wurzburg, Germany—1947*

We were having our evening bread and milk. Papa told me that the next day I would go with him to visit Wurzburg. He said I would really like this nice city. It would be a good change from the DP camp of Giebelstadt where we lived.

All night long, I tossed and turned, looking forward to the trip. We got up very early in the morning, even before the birds started to sing. Papa helped me wash up and gave me some bread to eat. He said we would eat a good lunch in the city.

Papa had a Zax motorcycle that he had purchased in Munich after working for a long time to pay for it. He put me on the seat behind him and said, "Put your arms around me and hold on tight."

Mama came running outside. "Volfe! You are teaching her bad things. It is very dangerous to take her like that without a sidecar!"

"Don't worry, Devorah! She is my daughter; she is not afraid. She will be all right!"

We drove off fast, like my friend the wind. Papa called out every so often, "Are you still with me? Are you having fun?" Papa had promised this trip would be fun.

"Are you enjoying the ride on the motorcycle?" I know he said it with a big smile on his face! I was just holding on tight, nodding my head and laughing as Papa and I rode as fast as the wind.

I remember very little of the trip—only that I had my papa all to myself.

We arrived in the big city of Wurzburg while it was still morning. People were sweeping and cleaning the streets. I had never seen people clean streets before. Everywhere I looked, everything was so clean. People were walking about; no one was running, and no one was frightened. They all walked slowly and tipped their hats or heads to each other, saying, "Good morning." Everyone was very polite to each other. *What is wrong with all of them?*

Was I in a strange dream? *Why are the people not getting off the streets? If a plane comes and drops bombs on them, they will all be killed, and it will be too late to run away after the airplanes come! Why do they look so different? How is it that they are all so clean and dressed so nice?*

The men and the women had hats and gloves; they all had shoes and socks on their feet. Their shoes were not torn or dirty. They had a shine, and some shoes even sparkled. Papa said it was patent leather and that someday I would have pretty, red shoes just like those on a little girl we passed.

I tugged on my father's scuffed brown leather jacket and asked him to stop the motorcycle. "Papa, I have to ask you some questions."

Papa stopped the motorcycle. "I will park it here, and we will go for a walk before we go on. Would you like that?" Papa asked.

"Yes, Papa, I would like to look around, but I have to ask you some questions!"

Papa took my hand, and as we started to walk, I could feel the pavement through my torn shoes.

"Papa, I need to know some things," I said.

"I will do my best to answer everything you want to know."

"Papa," I asked, "all the people walking by in the street right now, are they Germans?"

"Yes, my little one, they are."

"And, Papa, are they not the people who killed all of Mama's and most of your family?"

"Yes, many of them did."

"Then are they the ones who also killed my two brothers when they were still very little?"

"Yes, they are."

"Then why are you and they being so nice and polite to each other and saying good morning to everyone? Why are you not killing them?"

"My child, the war is over now. They lost the war, so now the time has come for all people to learn to live with each other in peace. If I kill them now, I would be a murderer. Is that what you want?"

"Yes!" I screamed. "They killed my two brothers; they killed most of our family!" I would not—could not—let it go. "Papa, if they did this to all of us, the Jewish people, and as you told me also to people who were not Jewish, then how do we know if we let them live now, they will not do this to us again?"

My poor papa's face was very sad as he answered that we don't know what the future will bring, and we hope they have learned from their big mistake and will not do this again to anyone. That answer was not good enough for me.

"Papa," I started again, "no one stopped them from killing the Jewish people. If they make a war on us again, we will not have anyone left to fight them!"

"My dear little one, this walk was to have been a fun time for you. You have so many things on your mind that you mustn't worry about. Please, just look around at all the pretty houses and store windows and all the pretty clothing. I will take care of everything else for you."

"Papa, will you not kill all these Nazi Germans for me?"

"No, I will not. No more killing by anyone. Far too many millions have lost their lives in this war."

I didn't like my papa very much at that moment. He was talking to me as if I were a child! I was over seven years old. I was not a baby! We walked in silence down the street.

We stopped in front of a shop that had a display in boxes outside and many pretty, colorful things in the window. Some of the things were round, and some were other shapes and sizes. I knew some of the things were onions and potatoes. There were other things I had never seen before.

Some of them smelled very nice. Papa asked if I would like to have an apple. I didn't know what it was, but if Papa said that he wanted me to have it, then it must be something good. I did not know Papa had money or where he got the money. Although I had not seen German money before, I knew you used money to get things.

Papa took some coins from his pocket, gave them to the store lady, and then picked out the prettiest, reddest, almost perfectly round thing. He wiped it on his jacket, handed it to me, and said, "Eat."

*Eat? How do you eat this thing? What do you do with it? Do you just bite?* I had never seen anything so pretty before and so red. *How and where do I start to eat this thing?*

"You don't know what to do with an apple?" Papa asked. "You do not have to be a genius to know how to eat an apple."

Oh, so this is an apple! This pretty thing has a name. I did not know the word *apple*; I had not seen one before. Papa said it is *yabluskah* in Russian.

"I will show you how to eat it." Papa took the apple from my hand and bit into it. The juices sprayed onto my face and hand. I licked my hand; the juice was very sweet. Now I knew it was something good. From the look on Papa's face, I knew it was also delicious.

"Oh, you mean just bite?"

"Yes, just bite into it."

I took the apple back from my papa and took a very small bite at first. I chewed very slowly. It was a new experience and a sweet one. I wanted to make it last a long, long time. I promised myself to have many more of these apples someday soon.

Oh my, that apple was wonderful! It took me all day long to eat it. Just little bites—one tiny piece at a time. I was afraid to eat big bites. You see, each time I took a bite, the apple became smaller. It was going away. I couldn't have it go away, because then I would have nothing left. I must save some for later and some to give to my brother Chaim.

I put half of it into my pocket to show Mama. If I ate it all, there would be nothing left to show.

My poor papa's eyes filled with tears when I told him I didn't know how to eat an apple. I heard him whisper to himself in Yiddish, "A child seven years old doesn't know what to do with an apple! She has not even seen an apple before today! We call this world civilized. How can we live like this? Shame on us all!"

To me he said, "My little one, from now on we must all do better for you and for all of our children."

# Chapter 18

# The Gift from CARE

*Giebelstadt DP Camp—1947*

T he announcement came over the loudspeakers throughout the day. It promised: "This will be a great day that will remain in your memories forever!"

We had no idea what it could be. The announcer repeated that today would be a wonderful day for all of us.

"What can it possibly be?" I asked Papa. Papa didn't answer; maybe he didn't know.

"Ho ho!" Papa exclaimed. "This will have to be something fantastic if we are to remember it for the rest of our lives."

Some hours later, we learned that one adult from each family must go to the center of the camp to receive the good news. Everyone milled about; no one wanted to miss the big event.

From a distance, we could hear the rumbling of heavy trucks. "It sounds like a big convoy," Papa said. A convoy of trucks would be arriving very soon and would start unloading. *Will they have food for us?* I wondered.

As the trucks drove into the camp on that cool, late afternoon, everyone in the camp who was not in bed sick or dying came out to greet and cheer for them. There were many trucks, lots of noise, and dust.

"They have arrived at last!" some people were saying. Some of them knew what it was all about; they had happy smiles on their faces.

Mama said that written on the trucks was only the word *CARE*, pronounced in Yiddish *"Carai,"* not "care." My mother said, *"Carai packatin!* Care packages." They had arrived, and everyone was full of joy.

Papa was going to go to the center of the camp—but not without me! "I am going with my papa!" I told Mama. "I do not trust them; they may want to take Papa away. I don't want anyone hurting my papa or stealing our things from him."

Papa was not very strong yet. I was the protector of the Markus family. Papa said so all the time. I was a big girl now; I was seven years old, and I had to help with everything. I went along with my father to the trucks, while Mama stayed with my brothers.

Papa and the other men and women who came to the center of the camp all hoped for food. First, they had to give their names, and only as their names were crossed off the list did they receive a package.

"G-d forbid you should try to get a second package!" Papa said.

We hoped to find many marvellous things in those big cardboard boxes. We waited in line for a very long time, so we were getting cold and hungry. My father let me put my hand under the box. He told me I was helping him carry this heavy box to our little cabin. Papa and I hurried home as fast as we could.

Our home in this DP camp was a small, one-room cabin. Inside, very close to the ceiling, we had one very small lightbulb. Papa said it was naked. I have never seen one dressed! We were unable to turn the light on or off, and it did not matter; we could not see much inside even in the daytime. The camp had the main switch for the light in the office, and someone turned the lights on and off for all of us from there. It was only on for about three hours in the late evening.

In our small wooden cabin, we had one small window, only two feet by two feet in size. We had a strange-looking table leaning against the wall. One of its legs was against the wall with the other two in the front. It was a meter long and half as wide. We also had two small three-legged, backless wooden chairs. According to many people in the camp, we were very rich; we had things!

That was all that could fit into our little cabin if we wanted to be able to get to our bunks. We had four bunks, bigger and better than the bunks in Austria. The bunks in our little room were single beds, one above the other, with a set on each side of the room. Along the wall that did not have the window and door, Papa was able to place a small woodstove, which he had gotten in return for his working outside the camp. It was very nice not to be cold all the time.

Papa and I put the package down on our table, and it did not take long to discover its contents. Mama started to open one side of the box to get to all the good things her Americans had sent us. Papa said, "Please be careful."

Mama agreed she didn't want to hurt the box. *Yes, maybe we can use the box for something later.* All of a sudden, we had a new possession. My Mama was so happy that she had a box for later.

"Maybe you want to put some of your belongings in the box, and we can carry it on our heads, just like the people in Africa?" Papa said a funny thing.

The first item on top was a thick, folded piece of cloth. My mother's eyes lit up.

"She is a brilliant seamstress," Papa said. "She can make anything!"

Oh, she was going to take that large piece of wool cloth, and she would make things for the children. We would not be cold again. She would make a dress for me, Mama said, and pants and jackets for my three brothers.

My mother was so very happy to see that piece of cloth. "Nice wool," she said. "Very nice wool!" She took it out, and as she took it out of the box, she let it unfold to the ground. She found and held onto one corner and then the same on the other side, and she gave it a shake so it would unfold and come out nice and straight.

As she held the sides of the cloth, without looking at it, she said again, "Nice wool, nice wool." Oh, she was thrilled. "Oh my G-d, we are going to have some nice clothing without holes or patches!" Mama said.

*Mama will make clothing for all of us.* I was also happy.

As Mama shook out that cloth, her sudden scream frightened me. I looked at her face. I had not seen her face look like that in a long time. Her expression changed with such speed. I was seeing emotions I didn't fully understand and could not explain, even to myself. I looked at her and realized her heart had just died a little bit again from pain and disappointment. Many times Mama had told me a heart could die of pain; it really could happen with a great deal of pain.

That cloth had holes the size of my fist and bigger. "Moths have had a great meal for a very long time," Papa said.

The box also had a very bad smell. Mama said she could not guess how many years the cloth had been in that box and how many years that box had been in a warehouse. Mama screamed with inner anguish, threw the cloth on the floor, and stomped on it with her feet. Then she looked at me. I was very afraid for her. Mama looked sick, and her face was very red, her eyes blazing with fury.

Mama suddenly stopped her anger and yelling and spoke in a very quiet voice. "We have more things in the box; let's look again."

I was afraid to look again. *What if something else is wrong?*

Mama took out a small bag with a picture of eggs on it. I looked at my mother and asked, "They put eggs in a paper bag? The Americans, are they crazy?"

She said, "Let's hope they are not, my little one. Just wait; wait and let's see what's in there." Then she changed her mind. "Let's first take out all of the bags, put them all on the table and the box on the chair, and then we will open them one at a time."

There was writing on the bags, but we could not read American; we had no idea what it said, or what was in those bags. Mama opened the bag with the picture of eggs on it, and Papa opened the other bag. His was much bigger and was full of a white powder Papa said must be flour. Infesting those two bags were many different kinds of worms and G-d only knows what else, Papa said.

One was to be yellow powdered eggs, and the other was to have been full of flour, but that was a very long time ago, Papa said. He took the bags and the cloth in his arms, so Mama would not have to see or touch them again, and he hoped it would stop my mother from getting any more hysterical.

He hurried outside to the big empty gasoline drum that was the garbage place for our cabin as well as for three other cabins. He threw everything into that huge gasoline drum. Then he came back for the other bags and threw them away too. The only thing left was a large tin can with a picture of a chicken on it.

My Mama stopped her rage and looked at the tin and then at me with hope in her eyes. She never gave up. Still full of hope said, "Maybe there is something edible in this can."

Now where do people in a DP camp get something with which to open a tin can? "What are we supposed to do, use our teeth?" Mama asked me.

Well Mama did not have many teeth left. The Nazi soldiers who raped her on the road to the church had broken some of her teeth when one hit her in the face with his fist. I thought my mama was very pretty, even with teeth missing.

"Anna'le. You know, it could be a chicken in there!"

"Mama, you are being silly! How could a chicken get in there? How does a chicken get into a tin can? It is closed all over! How did it get into this thing? Why would it go in there? It will not be able to breathe!" I had never seen tinned goods before. I had never seen food in a can.

My father was so disappointed, even though it was Mama's Americans and not his and my Zionists who had done this to us.

Papa thought we were actually going to have a meal, the first decent meal for the children in many days, and there was nothing to eat.

Mama took the can outside, and I went with her. She found a rock, and after looking for a long time, I found a big rusty nail. First Mama rubbed the nail against the rock to remove as much rust as possible. Then she spat on the nail to clean it and wiped it on the bottom of her dress. "We will open this tin; you'll see!" she promised.

So Mama banged on the nail on top of the tin can, going in a circle, making holes a short distance apart from each other. As a teeny bit of liquid spilled out of the top, I put my finger on it and then put it into my mouth. I smiled and told Mama, "I think they are hiding a chicken in there! It somehow got in there; there *is* a chicken hiding in there!"

Mama asked, "Well, how is the taste?"

"Oh, Mama, it is very good. It tastes like chicken soup."

"Then I'd better be very careful and not let the chicken jump out," she teased.

Papa had been in Munich a few weeks prior to this day, and with the few German marks he got for some work he did, he had brought back with him from the city a set of cooking pots and a few utensils. Now my happy mama sent me to fetch the biggest pot. The big one would be large enough to get a small chicken in without overflowing, so I got the pot for Mama, while she opened the big can. Mama cut her finger on the can, but she was happy anyway. We had chicken!

She turned the can upside down, and there was broth and a whole, small chicken! It smelled wonderful. Mama was laughing and crying all at the same time. And she was doing arithmetic.

"Mama, what are you doing?" I asked her.

"If we eat this end, we will have that part left for the next day. And after that, if we only eat this ... and if we eat this part the day after that ... then I will have to save this one for the day after that, and then we have to save this...."

*How is she going to save any of this? It is only one small chicken, and there is no place to hide anything in this little cabin without a lock on the door.* Papa would get a lock the next time he went to the city, he'd told us a few days earlier. And it would have a key.

Anything you did not eat the same day turned to garbage overnight. There was no way to keep anything. Mama was about to put the pot with the chicken on the little stove when we heard a shout. It was my father yelling, "Devorah, come quick! Devorah, come now!" Well, if Mama was running, then I was running as well.

My father's voice sounded so strange. I had never heard a voice sounding so angry and full of pain, all at the same time. Never from my papa! We went running, Mama and I.

Father had lit a fire in the garbage drum so he could kill all the worms and the weevils and all the other horrible things that lived there in the bags. Papa was not alone. Everyone had brought their wormy parcels to burn in the big drums. Many other men had done exactly the same thing. Now Papa stood with his arm up, his finger pointing to show us something. He moved, slowly turning in a full circle with his hand and finger pointing all around us.

"Look all around you, Devorah. We are not alone in this." The entire camp looked as if it was on fire. All the drums had big flames! The CARE packages were all afire in the drums, the flames jumping up to the sky!

Those CARE packages were burning all evening, through the night, and well into the morning. All those trucks had come, with so many men who had worked very hard. Almost everything that came in the trucks was put to the flames. To think of all the money it had cost someone!

Some of us received a tin of chicken that day; many did not. Some people didn't like us; they didn't get a chicken. We were one of the few lucky families who had good food that night, and Mama said we would have to eat it quickly.

We made two meals out of it, maybe three; I don't remember. I know at least twice we had a meal of that small chicken. A morsel the size of a small finger would have been a big chicken meal for me. We were all skeletal; a very small amount of food filled our stomachs. We had to be very careful how much we ate and how quickly, lest we get sick and throw up. If we had even one bite too many, we might lose it all.

# Chapter 19

# The Doll

Papa often traveled to Wurzburg looking for work. One very special evening when he returned to our DP camp in Giebelestadt, he was carrying a package. With a big smile on his face, he handed it to me. *A gift for me?* I had never before received a gift from my papa.

Excitedly, I began to open the parcel. There were so many layers of newspaper and then pretty-colored paper. My heart was beating so fast I thought it would jump out of my chest. I opened the lid of the box. *Whatever could this be?* I lifted the last thin piece of paper that covered my surprise.

There before me lay the most beautiful thing I had ever seen in all my life—my very own doll! She had a beautiful smiling face and long, curly blond hair held back on each side with blue satin bows. She was wearing a pretty, blue satin dress with a pale blue top over the dress and white lace on the sleeves and hem. I had only ever seen one doll before now—in the church at Christmastime. She was small and not as pretty as my new doll.

My new doll had long black eyelashes, just like Mama and Chaim. She looked like she was sleeping. Then I picked her up, and she opened her eyes—big blue eyes! At the same time, she said "ma-ma" in the sweetest voice. I loved her from that moment. She was the first clean, pretty, smiling thing that ever belonged to me.

For the next few days, I played with my doll every moment I could, and she slept in my bed with me. She was mine, and I wouldn't let anyone else touch her.

One day as I was sitting on my bed playing with my baby doll, Chaim insisted he wanted to play with her. As before, I refused. I allowed no one to touch her.

Just then, Mama called. "Anna'le, come! I need you to help with Yakov. Take him outside while I cook our food."

"Mama, I can't leave my little baby doll. I must watch over her."

"Anna, come right now!" she ordered.

Reluctantly, I left my doll on the bed. It seemed like an eternity watching over Yakov—I was so anxious to get back to my doll. As soon as I could, I ran back to her.

Chaim was playing happily, but horror greeted me. My doll was everywhere! All that was left of my baby was dismembered parts! Chaim had pulled her arms out, untwisted her head, and torn her legs from her body. I stood in shock and anger, looking at what was left of my new doll. I could only think that I wanted to do to him what he had done to her.

Chaim was only four years old, and like a typical boy, he wanted to know how she worked—how it was that she talked, and opened and closed her eyes—how she was put together. In his examination, he had totally ruined her.

I had been so proud to have this doll, and now she was destroyed. Dead! Just like all the others. The dead children, adults, and animals I had seen. I had even stepped over some dead bodies to keep from squishing them. Now my baby doll was dead too!

I was furious. I slapped him hard on his shoulder and screamed, "I will hate you for as long as I live!"

I promised Chaim I would never forgive him for doing this, and I haven't! I have forgiven him for a million other bad things he has done to me, but not for killing my doll. She was my first real treasure that was mine alone, and she was gone!

Papa knew my pain. He tried to console me and said he would take me with him next time he went to Munich. We would have great fun together, he promised.

I felt broken, just like my doll.

# Chapter 20

# Only a Stone Should Be Alone

*Giebelstadt, Germany—1947*

E very morning Mama gave baby Yitzhak and young Yakov her breasts and then gave Chaim and me some breakfast of bread soaked in milk. Then Mama would ask me to look after my three little brothers so she could go to the DP camp office to read the lists posted there, which might have information about any family members who may have survived the war.

The walls of that big office room were papered with many lists of names of people, along with their cities and countries of origin— those who had survived the war and were looking for missing family members. The Red Cross and the Jewish Agency compiled lists and continually updated them in an attempt to reunite families separated by the confusion that was now Europe.

Every morning Mama left our small room, hopeful this might be the day she would find her Mama'le or her younger sister Bliema'le. Or perhaps she'd find her oldest sister Rachael Brown with her husband and their three daughters, Miriam, Esther, and Shifra. Or maybe learn that some uncles, aunts, cousins or friends had survived. Mama already knew her only brother, Aaron, had been murdered in the beginning of the war—the first Jew in their hometown of Brzezine to perish. She hoped fervently to find even one familiar name on the lists of survivors.

Each day Mama returned to our small room brokenhearted and sobbing.

I remember one particular day Mama returned from her mission and sat down on the small three-legged stool in our room. With elbows on her knees and her face hidden in her hands, she sobbed, "Why? Why have I survived? How can I go on all alone? I have been searching for over two years. I have read every list in every camp where we have lived. I have not found one family member on any of them! I don't know what else to do. G-d! You must help me find my family. I am much too weak and sick and tired to go on alone!"

Her plaintive cry continued. "My father said that 'only a stone should be alone.' He was only thirty-five when he died of a massive heart attack. Please, dear G-d, do not condemn me to a life of loneliness! Please give me back my family! At least one or two of them!"

I sat on the floor near Mama's feet, listening to every word, and I cried with her. My brothers were fast asleep. My poor mama was so lonely. I wondered how a person could feel alone like a stone. *Mama has Papa and the four of us children, so why is she lonely?*

I did not know how to help her. To her, we children were more of a burden than a joy, and it took lots of hard work just to keep all four of us alive. I could help with some of her work, but I was just a child and still needed her care myself.

Mama was never happy that I, a girl, was born after the Nazis killed her two boys. I was a very poor replacement; she had told me so many times.

Mama seemed not to notice me sitting there as she cried, talked, and prayed in great sorrow. I watched her silently while my mind held many questions.

Mama had told me many times that G-d lives in heaven and that He knows all and sees everything. *Well then, why can He not see the pain my mama is in? Where is He now?*

*Please G-d,* I prayed silently, *would you be willing to take me instead and give my mama back her family? That would make her so very happy!*

✡ ✡ ✡

As a young teenager in Brzezine, Mama was one of the prettiest Jewish girls in the city. Conversation ceased when she walked into a room, as her beauty captured people's attention. Beautiful, thick, wavy black hair flowed down one side of her forehead and over her shoulders. Her beautiful jet-black eyes set in her oval-shaped face never missed anything. She had lovely white teeth, and her smile captivated everyone. In spite of her strict religious upbringing, she would never give up her bright red lipstick, much to the displeasure of her mother.

Grandma was a businesswoman and didn't have much time for anyone. The servants and household staff needed supervision, and the two younger children needed loving care. So she expected Mama to shoulder much of the responsibility within the family and spend a considerable amount of time working in the family businesses as well. Mama also had to oversee the hardware store and the seamstresses at the tailor shops.

While my mama did her best, she often fell short of her mother's expectations, resulting in harsh physical punishment. Mama bore the brunt of her mother's hostility. The older daughters did not suffer the same treatment. Rachel, the eldest, left home when she married young.

Though Mama was resentful, she also learned to accept it as the normal way for a mother to treat the daughter she depended on, and it eventually became her way of relating to me.

In Israel, when I was in my midteens, Mama slowly came to life again with the prospect of her daughter beginning to meet people and date. However, she seemed to know very little of courting or of relationships between men and women. She took great delight in having me tell her about my friends, parties, and dates. Her eyes would light up as I answered her many questions. When I asked her why she didn't know of these things, she answered with a small joke, saying, "Isn't it lucky for us that your papa and I fell in love with each other, and we didn't have to keep looking for another partner?"

Mama's bright, intelligent eyes watched intently when someone spoke to her. No subject was off-limits. When my friends, male or female, came knocking, they were just as happy to stay for the evening to visit with my mama. They loved her quick wit, her laughter, her funny sense of humor, and the very wise advice she gave to them in their personal relationships.

I learned that many of my friends often arranged to come and spend time with my mother over a cup of tea and cookies. Many times, I came home from a date to find the living room full of my friends, who had spent the evening with my mother. At times like that, I was very proud she was able to move beyond the traumatic experiences of her own life and give encouragement to these young people.

Sometimes, as I stood unnoticed in the doorway to the living room, watching and listening, I felt sad. I wished I could be as at ease with my mother and she with me as Mama and my friends were with each other. It seemed she softened toward me because of her conversations with the other young people.

For years, I hadn't received any attention from her. Surely, I was deserving of some love and attention from my mother. *Do other children also feel this way?* I wondered.

The survivor's guilt that afflicted Mama all those years had a profound effect on her, preventing her from having a good, normal life, and it affected all those around her too. It took many years before my mother would sit and talk openly with me about my dreams or show interest in what I had to say.

On her deathbed, Mama finally acknowledged the thankless years I had endured, and she expressed her gratitude for all I had done and for the loving care I had given my brothers.

All through our childhood, I helped to raise my brothers, and I protected them from Mama's temper. They were never beaten. They have told me that their memories of childhood include a great deal of hugs and kisses from Mama and many fun times. To my knowledge, Mama's grandchildren have not experienced the kind of abusive punishment she and I both knew while growing up. I like to believe that the generational legacy of violence ended with me.

I am sure my mama is now in heaven! Our G-d is a merciful G-d, and I am sure He would not let her suffer any more after the hell she lived on earth. Now she is with her beloved twins and her entire family.

I have asked G-d many questions over the past sixty years. I am still waiting for most of the answers.

No one of Mama's immediate family survived the war. She did locate some extended family members: her uncle Chaim (her mom's brother) and his wife and one of their sons, Joseph, along with his wife and their two sons, Baruch and Alexander. She also found a few first and second cousins in Israel. Because we would never have aunts and uncles, we were to address these relatives as aunt or uncle.

Until the last days of her life, Mama and I continued to search for members of our family. We wrote letters and sent them all over the world, my mama refusing to believe they were all dead. While clinging to hope, she never stopped mourning her family who had perished.

For many years after Mama passed away, I continued her search. I discovered Aunt Gala, the daughter of Mama's Uncle Chaim, had survived with her husband Boris (Baruch) Kogen in the Siberian labor camps. Two of Gala's brothers also survived. Baruch Kogen was a World War II pilot with the Russian Air Force, having shot down thirty-two Nazi planes. Israel acknowledged him as a hero. When the doors of the Iron Curtain opened for a time, they all immigrated to Israel with their families.

Gala's parents had also survived. I remember her father (my great-uncle Chaim) and one of her brothers (Joseph) were in the same DP camp with us in Germany before they left for Holland and we went to Israel. The other two brothers and their families were in Russia. They also eventually moved to Israel. One brother later took his family and returned to Europe to live and work in Berlin, Germany.

# Chapter 21

# This Is My Flag

*2002—Israel*

*1948—Germany*

I returned from Israel in 2002, having participated in Sar-El (In Service for Israel), a volunteer army program founded in Israel in 1983 by Brig. Gen. Aharon Davidi. I was very excited to be on the army base for those three weeks with the young people of the IDF (Israel Defence Forces) who guard and keep our Jewish homeland safe.

The optimism of the soldiers, men and women alike, many of whom are only eighteen to twenty-one years young, was so inspiring. They talked of the day when their service in the army would be complete, and they could go back home to resume their lives. They spoke of their hopes and dreams. Some wished to further their education, while others wanted to travel, work, get married, and have children—conversations one would expect to hear from groups of teens in North America or in most free democracies in the world. The only difference was that these young kids were in the army, guarding six million Jewish people in the only country in the world where a Jew is free to be a Jew and to govern his own life and homeland.

I experienced many beautiful moments both on and off the base. I thought of my family and friends in Calgary and in the United States and wished they could have been with me to hear and see the things I saw, felt, and enjoyed. At no time was I concerned about my personal safety while visiting all over our small country. I had a sense of well-being and peace at all times. It was a sense of belonging to the place and the people. I have never felt this way in any other part of the world, through all the years of my travels in the Diaspora.

Our Jewish homeland Israel is an extraordinary land where there is equal passion for peace and willingness to work hard, to develop her potential, and to grow, not merely to survive.

I saw many groups of Jewish kids and Christian church groups that had ignored the naysayers, all the warnings from friends and family as well as their governments, and had come to support our homeland, our Holy Land, in her time of great need.

One particular morning, I went to the parade grounds after breakfast as we did each morning and stepped into formation for the flag-raising ceremony. Each of us waited in anticipation, hoping for the honor of raising the flag. This was to be my happy day.

As the commanding officer walked though the lines looking at everyone, he came to me and nodded his head—the signal I was to march forward to raise our flag.

On that cool early morning as I started my steady march to the flagpole to accept the honor of raising our flag, my eyes were riveted on the group of one hundred teenage soldiers and fifty-two of our volunteers from around the world. From seven different countries, they stood shoulder to shoulder, their common goal being the survival of our homeland.

Then as I looked up into the clear blue sky, I recalled another flag. It had been a cool morning without sunshine in a displaced persons' camp in Germany.

### A New Jewish Homeland—1948

I will never forget the morning Papa came running into our small wooden cabin. His face was red with excitement. He had blue and white strips of paper in his hands and a larger scrap of newspaper made into a cone. Papa said it was full of flour. He put the flour into a small pot, added some of our drinking water, and made a paste. He then put me on top of our little table next to the small window in our tiny cabin. Papa started to create a flag on the window glass with the paper and glue he had made. This was to be my first Jewish flag, the new flag of our soon-to-be home, Israel. It would be my first time seeing the beauty of the *Magen David,* the Jewish Star of David.

Papa used the paste on the back of six blue strips of paper and made them into a six-pointed blue star. Then he added more strips of paper in blue and white above and below the star. Papa said, "This is the Star of David, and this is our new flag. This will now be the new flag of our homeland."

"Papa, is that the new flag of Poland?"

"No, my little one. This is the new flag for our Jewish people and our new home Israel. We will soon be able to go there."

I had never seen my papa so happy before. Papa was sure we would have a new homeland very soon. "And no, we will never go back to Poland ever again!" Papa stated. "They did not help to save most of the Jewish citizens of their country."

Papa showed me how to make the same creation he had made and asked me to cover the window completely with flags in any sizes that would please me. It was a very small window—my papa was a big dreamer. Papa left our small cabin, while I stayed for the rest of the day, working on this marvel, our new flag. A flag for our people and for our new country. My papa was an optimist; he had a big dream of a homeland for Jews.

Mama told us that morning that the brown-skinned Nazis, the Arabs who were now in our Holy Land, would never allow the creation of a Jewish homeland to happen. She declared it would never be so, not even in her lifetime. *Could Mama be right? She is usually right.*

I knew from early childhood of the hatred shown toward my Jewish people and me. I was almost seven years old, and I hoped my Zionist friends were right—that I would have a home to go to very soon. Still, I wondered. *Could Mama be right again?*

Several days later, Papa said I had to come with him to be with our Zionist friends for a big event. We arrived at the center of the camp, and two of Papa's Zionist friends helped put me onto his shoulders so I could see everything that would happen on this important day. It was also to keep me from being trampled in the crowd.

Many people had worked for days to place loudspeakers all over the DP camp. As we stood at the very front, we could hear the speakers start to make crackling noises. Then the announcement came—the UN would start the voting in a few moments.

I could see, feel, and hear excitement spreading through the crowd. Some people looked fearful, some looked hopeful, and others just shook their heads as if to say no, it would never happen. Many hands pushed those people to the very back of the crowd for talking like that, and yet others said, "We will pay dearly for this, one way or another!" Papa said he hoped no one would start to fight at a time like this when we must be united.

I looked at the top of the little house in front of us. It had one of the bigger speakers, and it had a very long pole on top. Two men were on the roof with ropes, and they attached a flag to it. With a great cheer from the crowd, they raised our new flag up high. It was my new flag—just like the ones I had pasted on our little window. I looked at my papa's face. He had tears in his eyes, as did many of the people near us.

A light wind caught that beautiful new flag, and it began waving to us all and did not stop. No one said a word. We were all holding our breath. After what seemed like an eternity, the faceless, loud voice from the UN came to us from speakers high on the rooftops. The words were in English. The crowd was silent. I heard a dog bark, but no one dared to say anything.

"The vote will commence for the creation of the new Jewish state, the State of Israel." It was the speaker from the United Nations. As he continued, he said, "Australia—yes." The crowd erupted, screaming with joy.

The men standing on the roof motioned for everyone to be quiet again. "Afghanistan—no." Some screamed bad words, others started to cry, and I could hear the word *G-d* used by many. The next one was "Belgium—yes, for the creation of the new State of Israel." Now, no one said anything. Everyone was waiting to hear each country named by the speaker. Everyone, Papa too, kept score of the yes and no votes. The next country was "Canada—yes."

I looked at the faces around me. Some were still praying, while others were crying; still others had a very serious look on their faces, not daring to believe this was actually happening. That is when I knew this must be the most important day in our lives, not just for us here in the DP camp but also for every Jew in the world! It seemed like an eternity as the voting continued. Papa said in a whisper it was taking almost as long as the Jewish exile—only two thousand years.

Then another vote: "Venezuela—yes." It was in favor! It was the last yes vote. Then the last two countries: "Yemen—no. Yugoslavia—abstain." Papa said that was the same as no.

No one said a word. We were all holding our breath. Papa said they were counting the votes. After what seemed like an eternity, the voice came back from the speakers on the rooftops, and the UN representative spoke again: "In favor—thirty-three, against—thirteen, abstain—ten." The voting was over.

"We are the winners! We have won!" Papa exclaimed. "Our Israel is once again our home."

At the same moment, the camp erupted with shouts of joy. Now all the strangers became brothers. Many people were crying openly, laughing, and jumping with joy. Everyone was hugging and kissing each other. Papa took me off his shoulders to hug and kiss me many times, telling me, "My little one, we have our home Israel now. You and you brothers will finally live in your own homeland and be safe!"

Our Zionist friends took me out of my father's arms. They told me of the beautiful land that I would soon see and where I would be able to live. They hugged and kissed me as Papa did. Then many strangers also hugged me. They passed me along from one to another to be loved, hugged, and kissed—on and on, while my papa was running behind me, crying, laughing, and jumping for joy.

Many of these strangers had lost their children in the war, and they desperately needed a child to love at that moment. They took me into their arms, calling me by the names of the children they had lost to the murdering Nazis: Moishe'le, Sarah'le, Yose'le, and more. They laughed and cried as they hugged me. I could feel their tears on my face. I also wanted to cry with them. Papa said this was a happy time, so I just kissed them back and did not say a word. *For the first time in my life, I will also be happy.*

All at once, people started singing *HaTikva* (The Hope), the anthem that expresses the longing in the Jewish heart to return to their G-d-given land. As the last word, *Yerushalim*, fell reverently from their lips, the dancing began. I had never before heard Jews sing or seen my people dance. It was a wonderful sight. Papa and I joined in the dancing.

Papa said, "This is the *Horah*; it is our dance—a dance of joy. Learn to dance the *Horah*, my little girl, and dance it often for the rest of your life! We will soon be happy and at home in Israel."

We arrived in Israel nine months later with the hope of peace in our hearts.

As I walked to the flagpole on the IDF base that morning in June 2002, I knew I was not walking alone. I could feel my papa, the Zionist, walking proudly with me. We grasped the ropes together, and together we raised our flag high into our beautiful, blue Israeli sky. For another moment, we—Papa and I—stood saluting proudly before all the soldiers after we raised our flag to wave freely in the warm breezes of our Israeli homeland.

I am so very grateful to have been a witness to Israel's birth—to participate in the first dance of our freedom.

To those who were not yet born when I made that first paper flag, I say, "Keep our homeland safe and free for all future generations."

To all I say, "Next year in Jerusalem!"

# Chapter 22

# Papa, the Fire Marshal

*Windischbergerdorf*

Moving yet again! After hours of travel in a convoy of many trucks, we arrived with a large group of refugees at a village in a farming community in the heart of Germany. This small village seemed to be intact. I had not seen any place in our travels that was not partially or totally bombed to the ground. This place was completely quiet, deserted. No Germans were there—not even one person. An American base was a few miles away, but we did not see any soldiers.

This would now become an official new displaced persons' camp. It was not really a camp. It didn't have guards or barbed wire all around it. The new residents who arrived with us were all people who had survived the past few years of horror in Eastern Europe. There were a few small family groups, like us, but mostly it was people all alone.

All the little houses in this pretty village stood empty, their owners having fled in fear as the Americans advanced. All around us were fields planted with wheat that was starting to turn yellow.

"Mama, where are the people who live in these houses?"

"I hope they are all dead!" Mama replied. Her anger and hatred for all Germans knew no bounds, though I felt sorry for the families who had left their homes.

Then a man emerged from the first truck holding a long list in his hands. He called out our names and told everyone which houses we would occupy. One family per small house or several single people together. Some houses were for men only and others for women. He said anything left inside the homes was for us to use.

We had never lived in a house for our family alone, and I was now seven years old. I did not know anybody who lived in a real house. Certainly not Jews! This was a new experience. When the war started, we lived in cramped quarters in the Warsaw ghetto in Poland, Mama told me. In Russia, we lived in the street or in the woods, or in one small room if we could pay the rent. That is all I remember about our dwellings.

One day Mama told me every person in our village would be getting a job. The people in charge of our camp had assigned all the adults to special duties. Papa was going to be the fire marshal, the chief of the fire brigade.

This department had everything needed to fight a big fire. It must have had at least four buckets and one small ladder, Mama said. Papa was very proud to have been selected for such an important post. My papa, the fire chief!

Then Mama said, "Please G-d, help our village."

"Fire marshal, Mama? Is that bad?"

"No, Anna'le, it's not bad unless we actually have a fire. Your papa knows as much about putting out fires as you do!"

"Mama, I don't know anything about putting out fires!"

"I know," Mama said, "and your papa knows just as much as you do."

Life in our new town soon became routine. One day Papa announced that our village was going to have a big party that very evening. It was to be a big event, a *brit milah*, for a neighbor's new baby boy, the first to be born in our village and in time of peace.

Circumcision ceremonies are held on the eighth day after the birth of a boy. There would be a big party, and everyone was to bring food— whatever they could spare for the joyous occasion.

Mama could not go to that party. She had to stay home with us kids. She cooked a fat chicken for Papa to take with him. Anyway, she explained, it was mostly a party for the men.

"Mama, why is the party only for them? It was a woman who gave this baby life!" I protested.

Mama said they drink *l'chaim* (to life) with strong drinks that make them silly, and ladies do not do that.

"Mama, why does the lady not have a party for all her friends as well?"

"It just is not done, and no more questions. When you grow up, I am sure you will make up your own laws; right now, we will stay home!"

Papa was not home until very late that night, and I waited up for him. When he finally came home, he said most of the town was there, and only two women—the baby's mama and her sister.

Papa hugged me and told me to go to bed. He smelled funny, like cigarettes and something else. I didn't like it, and I told him he didn't smell nice and to not do that again.

He laughed and told me, "I will not do that again, till the next *simcha* (happy, festive occasion) or wedding or *brit milah*. He said he had had a couple of schnapps too many."

"Papa, will you not go to a party when a little girl is born?" I asked.

"Yes, Anna'le, I will go if you want me to. Now run to bed."

I know most Jews are not drinkers. When they drink, they get drunk, and then they are sick all night. The following morning they curse the day they were born for having been so stupid the night before. Then they promise never to do it again, and most do keep that promise.

I remember this particular night, because some time after we all went to bed, I heard noises from the ground floor. I came out from our upstairs bedroom to look down the stairs.

Papa had no clothes on, and from what I could see, he didn't look like Mama and I did. He was very white, and he looked sick. I have never seen my papa that kind of sick. Mama was helping him make it to the bathroom, and I could see he was sick all over himself. Mama helped him clean up.

I made sure my brother Chaim didn't wake up and see anything. After a while the house was quiet again—Mama and Papa, the chickens in the basement, the cats in the kitchen—all went back to sleep. I went back to bed in my room. I stayed awake for some time, wondering why nobody liked girls as much as they liked and wanted boys. Much too soon, the rooster in the basement told us it was morning.

The next day Papa was a bit better, but he did not do much all that day. I was very worried about him, but Papa promised me he would be well in a day or two.

That night we all had an early dinner and went off to bed to make up for the sleep we'd missed the night before. Again, I heard noises in the middle of the night, this time from the front door. First, a few fists banging and then more were pounding on the door!

"Wake up, Markus! Markus, wake up! Wake up your family! *Wake up, Markus!*"

The banging was getting worse, and more people yelled, "Markus, get up." Other voices joined in. It sounded like most of the villagers were now outside our front door screaming, "Markus, wake up!"

I ran down the stairs and pounded on my parents' bedroom door.

"Anna'le, what's wrong?" Mama asked as she tried to wake up.

"I don't know, Mama, but listen to all the people yelling for Papa to wake up."

Then we heard, "Markus, your house is on fire!" I looked around and saw smoke coming from the kitchen.

"Mama, there's smoke!"

She mumbled, "Where are the children? Oh, the children! Go! Go get them now!"

*Why should I go get them?* I thought to myself as I ran upstairs and pulled Yakov and Chaim out of bed. *I am a child as well! Who will care for me?*

We had to get out of the house quickly. The front room was now dark with smoke. Holding Chaim's hand and carrying Yakov, I went down the stairs as fast as I could. Papa was now out of bed. He ran to me, took Yakov from my arms, and lifted him out the window of their bedroom and into the hands of neighbors. Mama passed baby Yitzhak out the window. Then Papa he took Chaim, gave him to the men outside, and then lifted me out too. A woman put Yitzhak into my arms.

Papa helped Mama out the window, and he jumped out. Mama took baby Yitzhak from me, and Papa picked me up in his strong arms. He whispered in my ear, "Anna'le, don't be afraid; it is not a bad fire. We will be back in our little home again tomorrow or the next day, I promise."

Meanwhile, our neighbors started to put out the fire from the outside. Papa soon discovered the source of the smoky fire in the kitchen, and together, they put it out with buckets of water.

Papa leaned out of his bedroom window, laughed, and said to all the people gathered around, "Well, well! Did the first fire in our village have to be in the home of the fire chief?"

I wondered how Papa could laugh at such a serious time, and when I asked him later, he told me a story. Something about a Roman Caesar named Nero who laughed when his city was burning. Papa thought it was very funny, but I still didn't like the fire.

And I was still thinking about something else. *Why do I always have to go and do everything? Why does Mama want me to do all the grown-up chores? Why did she have all the other babies after me if she did not want to do all the work?*

When I was only six years old, I told Mama she had too many children, and she should give one of them to me. Mama told me to pick one. "Do you want Chaim?" she asked.

"No, I want the little angel, Yakov. I will teach him how to walk properly, Mama." He had been born with a deformity in his legs and had great difficulty walking.

Mama agreed I was to be the new mother for Yakov from that day on. However, she insisted I take charge of Chaim and bring him along with me anywhere I went.

"Mama, am I not a child—your child?"

"No, you're a big girl now, and you have to help with everything."

As of that day, I ceased being a child in her eyes. Working alongside her all day long or staying out in the yard supervising the kids, I no longer felt like a child. No longer was I allowed to *be* a child. I was now an equal, a female who was there to take care of everything that needed doing.

All the work with the children became my first responsibility. She had the babies, and I had the work. I didn't like Mama very much after that. Though I knew I was not a grown-up, I took on the responsibility of mothering my brothers.

We moved back into our little house three days after the fire.

# Chapter 23

# The New Rabbi

## 1948

It was a morning of great joy in Windischbergerdorf, the displaced persons' camp in Germany not far from the city of Straubing. Transferred to us from another camp was a young man who had been ordained as a rabbi before the war. Now we would have a teacher.

There was talk that school would open soon in one large room, and all children older than four were welcome. Mama was very excited, and Papa took a job to help make this dream come true. He was helping to locate and organize tables, chairs, pencils, and paper. He had even found some books in Yiddish and Hebrew. In less than a week, all was ready. My papa was wonderful.

Papa told his friends and helpers, "The one big room in the administration building should be taken for this purpose."

In spite of the protests of the camp committee, after two days of disagreement and arguing, Papa and his friends had won. They cleaned the floor, painted the room white, and hung a large blackboard on the wall. They washed the windows so the sun could come in and visit with us.

"Now this is a nice, bright, warm room for our children to learn in," Papa told everyone.

Chaim was four, and I was seven years old. *This will be my first chance to go to school,* I thought. I did not know why we needed to do this. *Why spend an entire day indoors when the sun is out and the birds are singing? No one is shooting, and we could play outside without any of us being killed*. I told Chaim this school idea must be a way to keep children from having fun and to keep us away from the adults while they think up another way to get us all into trouble.

Mama washed our few garments—rags, really—so we would be clean for our big first day in school. I had a short dress with a small cream-and-black houndstooth pattern. There was a small string bow at the top center of the dress bodice. My freshly washed socks had not been so white in a very long time, but no amount of spit and rubbing would ever make my ugly, scuffed brown shoes look any better. Chaim's wardrobe was not any better with his shirt, short pants, ugly socks, and shoes. Mama did her best. We were clean and so was everything we wore. That made us very happy, though Mama had used up most of our daily water for all the cleaning. *What will we do when we get thirsty?* Mama promised she would have more water by the time we came home.

Chaim and I could hardly sleep; morning would bring our first day of school. It couldn't come soon enough for us. Mama washed our faces, hands, and feet, and then we set off from the small wooden house where the six of us lived.

Papa took Chaim and me by the hand. We proudly walked out to our new adventure. It was a long walk through the length of the camp, and as we walked, we met with other children and one or more of their parents going the same way. If someone had both parents with him at an event, it meant he was an only child. One parent often missed an event to stay home and care for smaller children. When we arrived at the school, Papa made sure Chaim and I had a desk and two chairs in the very front row so Chaim could not go back to sleep.

The room was soon full with kids of all ages; some were going to study for their bar mitzvah. Most had never attended school before. We were all curious as to what would be happening for the next few hours. A short, slender man with a short black beard and glasses, dressed in a not-so-clean black suit, came into our big, bright schoolroom. As he stood in front of the class, he gave us his name: Rabbi Shmulik. (His last name I no longer remember.) He said he would be watching all of us very carefully. He wanted to make sure we would make him very proud.

For the first few days, Chaim and I were very happy. The rabbi started to teach us the Hebrew *aleph-bet* (ABCs) some words in Hebrew, and some new words in Yiddish. Chaim and I were very happy to go to school every morning.

As the weeks passed, we stopped running to the school. In the mornings, we walked slowly and enjoyed the blue sky and birds' songs. We hoped Papa might bring us some food during the day. In the early evenings, we had fun in the wheat fields and looked for fireflies.

One day after school, the rabbi asked me to stay after class. He told Chaim he could go and play outside and that I would be with him soon. I thought Rabbi Shmulik might ask me to clean the blackboard or put the chairs back in their place. Instead, he sat back down at his table in the front of the room and asked me to come to him.

*Does he have a new book he wants me to see?* I wondered. I was happy the rabbi was giving me extra attention. *I will be a great student and make him and my parents proud of me,* I thought as I walked to his desk.

When I reached him, he smiled and asked me if I wished to please him. I nodded yes; I wanted to be a good girl and a good student. He told me to come and sit on his lap. Mama and Papa were the only people who ever asked me to do this, so I was very confused. I told him, "No thank you, I am not allowed to do so with strangers." He told me that he was not a stranger and that he would tell my papa that I was a very special girl and a great student.

When I still said no, he pointed to his trousers and asked me if I knew what was in there. I said, "Yes; my brothers have the same, and I don't want to see it or talk about this."

He asked me to come closer, but I felt very uncomfortable and frightened. In shock, I looked at the rabbi's face, spat at him, and ran out of the schoolroom.

*This is not a good world; I don't want to live in this place.* First the Nazis and then priests in the church had abused all of us—the children given to them to hide and care for till the war was over—and now this rabbi, a man we were told we could learn from and trust? How can a Jew do this to the children of his own people? *Am I the only one, or did he do this to others? To whom do I tell this? Will anyone believe me? He is the rabbi, and I am just a little girl. If I tell Papa, he may come and kill him, and then my papa will go to jail.*

Chaim was waiting for me on the step, his beautiful black eyes and little face very serious. "Are you okay? Was the rabbi nice to you? What did he want?" Chaim asked all his questions at once.

I told Chaim I no longer liked the rabbi. I told him everything that had just happened, and that I would never go back to the school, even if our parents were angry with me.

"Not come back to school? But what will we tell Papa and Mama?" Chaim said. "If things are as bad as that, I will protect you. I will have to think of something to say to Papa, so we will not have to go to school anymore!"

I was hiding all the rest of the day. I would not eat or play with my brothers. I was very sad to learn that we, the Jewish people, had very bad people among us. Another "pig-face" man!

That evening at dinnertime, there wasn't much food. Mama was hoping soon to be able to sell the many chickens, ducks, and turkeys she was raising when they would be a little bigger. Then we would all have more food.

As we sat at the table, Papa asked how we did in school and if we were still happy with our new rabbi. Chaim, with a very serious and sad face, said he had very bad news to tell us. "The rabbi is dead, and we cannot go to school anymore."

Mama and Papa were shocked. "But he was so young!" Papa said.

Mama, with a tear in her eye, said, "What a terrible thing to happen now that the war is over."

Papa wanted to know when the funeral would take place. Chaim promised to try to find out. My dear brother Chaim! What a wonderful little actor. But I knew this was not a permanent solution.

For the next couple of weeks, life was wonderful. We played in wheat fields or herded Mama's flocks of turkeys, ducks, and geese, keeping them out of the wheat fields and deep puddles and from getting lost—or eaten by our neighbors! In the evenings, we filled matchboxes with fireflies. Mama made all the living creatures in our basement or attic sit on their eggs and hatch, and they did. Yes, life was wonderful. I almost forgot how much I loved and missed going to school.

After some days of fun, Papa came home early one evening. I could not interpret the expression on his face. Was he doing his best not to laugh? Or was he very, very angry and something was very funny as well?

As we sat down to our dinner of soup and bread, Papa told us the great day had come at last. "For two thousand years, Jews have been waiting for this great miracle, and it has finally happened! The Messiah has arrived!"

Mama and I looked at him with disbelief. Mama asked if he had had a drink at the *bris* (circumcision).

"Yes," Papa said, "I did have a drink in honor of the new little boy, but no, I am far from drunk on one small glass of wine."

Mama was hiding a smile from Chaim and me. She said she was sure poor Papa had lost his mind. Mama wanted to know if Papa was certain the Messiah had truly arrived. She was hiding that smile again! Papa said, "Yes, I am sure. According to the Bible, on the day the Messiah arrives, the earth will give up all her dead!"

Mama said she was sure poor Papa was not well. (What a great actress she was!) Chaim and I looked at each other with apprehension. *We are in trouble now!*

Papa continued his story. "I was walking not far from the place that was once our children's school and I almost fainted. Coming toward me was the poor young rabbi who passed away! He stopped to say 'good-day' and ask me how my children are. Well imagine my surprise at seeing and hearing him—a dead man walking and talking! I asked him how he felt and if he were much better now. He seemed a little confused but said he was well. I did not know what else to say.

"Will the children be back in school tomorrow?" he asked me.

"I told him, 'Well, now that you are much better, I will see to it. They will be with you tomorrow.'"

Papa ended the story, looked at Chaim and me, and asked if we had anything to say. Chaim said Papa was right—that this was truly a miracle!

That night I told my mama the truth. She took me to the school, without Chaim, to confront the rabbi, and I did. Mama invited two members of the camp committee to come along and hear what I had to say. They were very proud of me for telling what happened.

We had been so happy and thought ourselves to be lucky when the rabbi had arrived. Now we would be even happier to see him go. Had the other DP camp thrown him out for the same reason? In any case, that was the last we saw of the new rabbi in our camp.

# Chapter 24

# Cats, Turkeys, Geese, and Fireflies

The wheat field next to our house was very big. It went as far as my eyes could see. Mama warned us not to wander too far into it, because we might not find our way out again. I loved to lie on the ground in the field and listen to the whispers of the breeze rushing through the wheat as the wind moved it in great waves. The wheat was now yellow and very tall, much taller than my brother Chaim was at the age of four. I could stay there for hours, just looking up at the sky. No one could see me, and I felt safe and happy.

To me, our little house, our new home, was a very big house. It had a big, fenced-in yard. The ground floor of the house had a big living room, a large formal dining room, and an even bigger kitchen and breakfast dining area with lots of windows. A large entrance room led to stairs going up to a second floor with three small bedrooms. From there, another set of narrow stairs led to an attic with three very tiny rooms.

On the ground floor, Mama and Papa made the living room into a bedroom for themselves and our new baby brother, Yitzhak. My brothers, Chaim and Yakov, and I had the second floor just for us. We each had our own room. But Yakov came to be with me in my bedroom every night. He refused to go anywhere without me.

The basement was home for all manner of winged creatures. My Papa was not much of a handyman, but he made a kind of strange-looking, wide ladder-bridge so all the two-legged feathery friends could hop up to the small windows of the basement and out into the front yard. Mama was very happy now that she had a ready supply of fresh chickens, geese, and ducks for Shabbat dinner every week. She could also sell some of the birds and eggs and use the money to buy dairy products, fruit, vegetables, and any medicine we needed.

The attic was a great place to play, to hide, and to hatch chickens and turkeys and geese. Mama put a turkey into a big basket to sit on her eggs, and soon after that, a goose and a chicken were sitting on eggs in other little rooms up there. It became the official Markus Hatchery. And the birds all did as Mama told them. Soon, many new chicks were chirping around the attic and in the yard. Mama fed the chicks a special food she made by mixing hard-boiled eggs with green onions. I remember the smell of the onions on the little chicks. They loved the food, and Mama said it would make them grow big and strong.

One special goose was our watchdog. She was white with a small black mark like a flower on her back. That goose hated everyone except Mama and us kids. She would chase people and bite them on the seat of their pants. We thought it was very funny when she honked and flapped her wings at the man who was trying to steal one of our chickens. She grabbed onto him as he ran away screaming, but she held on tight. He kept yelling and threatening to tell Papa that we had made the goose attack him.

We loved that goose very much and named her Black Flower. She followed us everywhere on our walks. Whenever people we did not like came to our yard, we made sure the goose was outside to chase them. We thought it was a very funny and wonderful game to watch Black Flower run after them. We had never played games before and didn't have toys to play with, so this gave us lots of enjoyment. Life was very good now. For the first time I can remember, my mother and brothers laughed and smiled a lot. Mama had so much work to do that she did not sit all day, sad and weeping.

It was lucky for us that Mama Black Flower hatched nine baby geese. Our mama promised never to cook or sell our feathered friend.

We didn't have any pet animals—in fact, I didn't know people even kept pets to live with them at home. Mama told me that when we could afford to feed animals that do not work for their food, then we would know we were well-to-do, and then maybe we could have a pet.

I don't remember seeing any dogs in our village when we first arrived, though I did see cats. Some while later, I did see a few dogs. But Mama said we still couldn't have a pet. She was afraid they might eat our feathered friends.

Soon after we moved into the little house, two cats adopted us. One day as I sat alone in the shade of a tree in our yard, a large orange tabby jumped into my lap. She curled up and rubbed her face on my hand. I heard a soft, low rumbling sound coming from the cat. As I rubbed her ears and petted her, the pleasant, contented sound became even louder. I liked that sound, and I loved that cat. Mama told me that the cat was telling me that she loved me as well.

Another cat soon appeared in our yard, and Mama finally agreed that because they did do some work on our grounds—catching mice— she would allow them to sleep in the house if they wished. Thus began my lifelong love affair with cats and all animals. Even now, two of these purring creatures usually live with me.

Because Chaim, Yakov, and I did not have toys, we had to make our own fun. I wanted to do something to entertain my adventuresome younger brothers, so I would look for things to do in the wheat field next to our home. There I would catch little fireflies that sparkled on and off and put them into empty matchboxes—one for Chaim, one for Yakov, and one for me. Then we would put them all into a glass bottle so we could watch them sparkle. Those were some of our first playthings.

By gently shaking the glass bottle, we encouraged them to move and shine their little lights. Mama said we should give them as a treat to the mama duck to eat after we finished playing with them, but I always let them go back into the field so they could live and sparkle some more in the evening.

Little brother Yakov loved to toddle after the ducklings and goslings, wobbling from side to side on his little bowed legs. He would take a long, thin branch and gently guide them around the yard. Sometimes he would push the little birds toward their food or water. One morning while he was herding them along, one of the small goslings didn't want to move, and Yakov pushed a bit too hard. The little bird fell down, and Yakov pushed harder with his stick, trying to make it get up and go to the big basin for a drink of water. But it did not move. Of course, Chaim ran to tell Mama what Yakov had done.

Our Mama knew how to fix everything. I remember one day I noticed a chicken bumping into the fence and then into the house. It seemed to be looking for something. As I watched, I realized the chicken could not see. I ran for Mama and told her of that poor blind chicken. We easily captured the chicken and took her into the kitchen.

"No, Mama, don't cook her! She is just a little sick."

"No, my little one, I will not cook her. I will make her well. She gives delicious eggs and will stay with us for a long, long time."

Mama took some cotton and poured something from a bottle onto it. Then, while I held the chicken's head, Mama washed her eyes and put a bandage around the head. Now the chicken looked like one of the soldiers in the Russian hospital.

We put the chicken in the attic with plenty of food on the floor and several bowls of water. Mama repeated the eye washing for a few days, and then she returned the chicken to the yard. As Mama predicted, the hen happily clucked away for a very long time.

Now back to Yakov and the baby gosling. Sadly, not even Mama could bring the baby bird back to life. It was dead.

This was the first time for us kids to make a grave. Unfortunately, it was not the last. Poor Yakov! He was heartbroken for a long time, or at least until the birth of our first four kittens. Watching Yakov try to herd those kittens as they ran in four directions brought much delight to Chaim and me.

But many years later we still teased Yakov about the time he "murdered" the poor gosling.

# Chapter 25

# The Ice Factory

Papa's travels to Munich became more frequent, and when I would ask why he was away so often, his answer was always, "I am preparing a future for my children in the land of Israel."

Papa was working with his brother-in-law, Stacheck. My papa was very talented, but not so much in the black market ways of Uncle Stacheck. This uncle was involved in anything at all that could bring about a profit, whether legal or not. Papa, no stranger to the black market himself, soon became successfully involved on the fringes of some of Stacheck's businesses.

As time passed and Mama kept talking about going to America, Papa was quietly busy making arrangements with the Zionists to take the family to Israel. Papa did not tell Mama of all the work he was doing to bring about our *aliya*, our immigration to Israel.

The Zionists told Papa it was very hot in Israel for at least seven months of the year. However, they assured him if his wife did not like the heat, then we should all live in the north of the country where she would be happy with the cooler climate.

One day Papa came home very excited and happy. "Come, let's go for a walk," he whispered in my ear. "I have something to tell only you."

We left our little house, telling Mama we were going out for a short walk. When we were a good distance away, Papa said to me, "Do not fear. We will do great in Israel."

"What will we do, Papa? What will be great?"

"When your uncle and his family arrive in Israel to join us, Uncle Stacheck and I will build a big ice factory in Haifa! That will guarantee all of us a good life and lots of money!"

I had not seen Papa this happy before. "Papa, can you tell me more about this ice factory?" I asked, catching his excitement.

"Yes, I can, and it will all be good! Uncle Stacheck and I will soon have all the money we need to purchase the ice-making equipment for the factory and to ship it to Israel. We will send everything to Haifa in a few months. Our family will arrive in Israel about the same time as the crates arrive in Haifa. Uncle Stacheck and his family will come soon after, bringing the rest of the money necessary to construct the building of our ice factory. And we will be in operation, producing nice, cold ice in the very hot Holy Land."

I caught Papa's joy and gave him a big hug.

Then his face became very serious. "Anna'le, please don't tell Mama anything about this factory. Let it be our secret for a short time. We will tell her all about it very soon."

I promised Papa I would not tell anyone. *Yet another secret for me to keep!*

For several months, Papa traveled to Munich, staying for some days at a time. When he returned, Mama always had many questions, and he told her of his work with my uncle, but he still had not told her our secret.

Papa made up for being away so much by bringing home many gifts. We were excited to see the things he brought home for our family—pots, plates, utensils, cups, food, and clothing for us kids or for Mama. For himself, a big, black Borsalino hat, a fedora. Papa said it was like hats the mobsters wore in American movies. Papa looked so wonderful.

One evening Papa told us we would be on our way to France in a few days.

Mama was shocked. "France!" she exclaimed. "Why France? Is that where we will board a ship to America and go to be with your uncles in New York?"

Papa shook his head no. "We will wait in a small camp in France for a boat to take us all to Israel!"

Mama's face became white, and she started to shake as she screamed. "I will not go to a land full of murdering Arabs. They are nothing but brown-skinned Nazis. I will not live in the same land with them. I will not sacrifice any more of my children for any country or war. You can go to your precious Israel, but you will not take the children or me with you! I will not follow you, and I will not take the children to a land that eats its inhabitants. Now all this talk about Israel will stop. We are not going!"

In the camp, we had heard the news that all the neighboring Arab countries were attacking the newly proclaimed State of Israel, and Mama was terrified of being in the middle of another war.

Then Mama repeated to Papa his own words: "'I wish to have a future for my children in a land of peace and prosperity.' That place, my dear husband, is not Israel. The country is not yet stable; it is only a few months old, and Arabs attack daily! I will not stand by watching you go off again with a rifle in your hand while I spend sleepless nights with tears and fear you will never come back to us! If you must go to Israel, you will have to go alone! We—the children and I—are going to America!"

For the next few weeks, our home was not a happy one. Whenever Papa was home, he had great stories just for me. We would go for our long walks, which Mama began to resent. Papa told me of the glorious life we would all have in our new home and of the ice factory that would support our two families in great style.

I was fearful of the Arabs Mama talked about, but Papa assured me the small Israeli army was successfully fighting off the five Arab states that had attacked our small country. Victory was assured, and we would wait until the war was over before going there.

One night, Mama gave us our dinner before Papa came home and put us to bed early, announcing that she must talk to Papa. She planned to tell him he could neither say nor do anything that would make her want to go to Israel. "This must be settled tonight!" she declared.

I did all I could to stay awake and listen to them speak. I knew my poor Papa would be in trouble. Papa loved America very much, but he wanted the freedom of his own nation for his children's future.

So that evening while Papa was eating his supper, Mama asked, "Will your uncles help us get started when we arrive in New York?"

Papa answered, "I don't know. The last time I saw them was in Poland some years before the start of the war. We do not know the conditions they live in now. They may have families, and they may also be struggling."

"Well, do we know anyone else in America?" Mama wondered.

Papa shook his head no, but I peeked from under the covers and saw he was smiling at Mama as he took her hand. "We will have a great future in Israel without the help of my uncles in America. We will be completely independent. I have been working on a plan that will make you happy. Please listen to what I have to say. I know you will agree it is a good plan."

Mama listened without interrupting, as Papa told her all that I already knew about the ice factory we would build in Haifa. It would be a very big factory, and it would supply all the ice needed not only for the city of Haifa but also for surrounding cities and towns.

Mama's cheeks became flushed with excitement as she imagined the possibilities of a hopeful future. She waited until Papa stopped talking and asked one question. "If for some reason this new venture does not succeed, will you, without one word of argument, agree to emigrate from Israel to America?"

Papa answered, "I believe in the future of our new country and home and our children's freedom in their own homeland where they will never have to experience exile or anti-Semitism as we have!"

Mama persisted. "Will you agree to go to America if this dream of yours falls through?"

Papa promised. "Yes."

It did not take very long to get all our things together. We now owned two suitcases, and Mama filled them to the brim with our clothing. Several large blankets with the four corners tied together contained the rest of our belongings. Once again, trucks came to take some of us refugees across the border from the DP camp to another smaller transit camp in France.

It was a very long, difficult trip in the covered trucks. They were crammed with people of all ages along with their belongings. Mama had motion sickness all the time, even though Papa asked his friends the Zionists to tell the driver not to go so fast over the very bumpy roads.

It was late December 1948 and already very cold. Rain and snow fell heavily as we traveled, and we were all cold and wet. All around us bombs were bursting in loud explosion after explosion. Papa said the French army was still finding and blowing up mines and unexploded bombs to keep the population of the city of Marseille safe.

My little brothers were very frightened. Chaim asked me, "Anna'le is the war back again? You promised the war would not come back."

"No, my Chaim, the war is not back. I did tell you the truth."

When we finally arrived at the departure/transit camp in Marseille, France, we found the ship we were to board had left without us the day before we arrived. Mama was sure this was a sign—an omen that we should not go to Israel.

No ships! Papa was gone for some hours during the first day, trying to find some way for us to get to Israel. He returned to tell us we would have to wait for some time for another ship to take us home. Long, late-night talks with the Zionists told Papa it could take several weeks for another ship to arrive. More money would first have to be raised for this second ship and for the provisions for more than four hundred people who would board her. Papa, always optimistic, reassured us it would not be long, and we would all be home.

Meanwhile, our accommodation in that transit camp was a big, cold, leaky tent with two canvas cots, where we had been assigned a corner spot—meager shelter from the cold weather.

While we waited for another ship, Papa asked me if I would like to go with him to explore the beautiful city of Marseille. I asked if the people there had helped our people in the war. Did they save many of our people? Papa said he didn't think they did much to help the Jews.

"Then I will not go with you, Papa. They are not good people."

# Chapter 26

# *Caserta*—We Are Going Home

## 1949

The *Caserta* had arrived. The grand ship was an Italian passenger boat. When we all boarded, pushing and shoving, there were more than four hundred men, women, and children crowded together onboard. Mama's displeasure was very apparent.

"Are we sardines?" she demanded of Papa and some of the Zionists who traveled with us. "You cannot do this to all of us! We have no room to take a breath."

They herded us to the bowels of the ship where the walls were lined with bunk beds. Plank beds were mounted up the walls every two feet or so—four beds, one above the other. We were very lucky, as we had four bunks for the six of us. Mama kept the lowest one for Yakov and Yitzhak. The second one was for Chaim and me, and the other two for Mama and Papa, but they never both slept at the same time. One was always awake, keeping an eye on us kids and on our stuff, which was stowed on the very top of the fourth bunk. We all kept watch over our only earthly possessions.

We could hardly walk without stepping on someone. Children scurried about in all directions.

I wanted to watch our ship's departure, so I told Papa that Chaim needed to use the washroom on the upper deck, and I offered to take him.

"Well, Chaim, are you coming, or are you going to stay here with the babies?" I asked. As we pushed and shoved our way through the crowds of people, I yelled, "We need the bathroom; my brother needs the bathroom. Let us through!"

We finally made it to the railing at the very front of the upper deck of our big ship. The ship reminded me of a large anthill, crowded with people milling about on deck. It was very noisy and stinky, with the odors of many unwashed bodies. Some people were already nauseated and vomiting over the rail and even on the deck. It was almost as unpleasant topside as in the bottom of the boat.

Some people just wanted fresh air, others were smoking, and still others complained of the late departure. I heard someone say there might be a food shortage on the ship. I listened and made sure to remember everything so I could tell Papa.

As Chaim and I watched from the rail, a huge crane was loading crates of cargo from the dock onto our boat. A box fell out of the big net and smashed on the deck, narrowly missing the people swarming about. Orange-colored balls, freed from the box, were rolling in every direction, as people scrambled to capture the prized toys. Chaim stopped one with his foot as it rolled past. He picked it up, and we examined it. It even smelled good. Suddenly, a big mean man snatched it away and put it in his pocket.

"Don't worry, Chaim," I said. "I promise I'll get us another one very soon."

The loud blast of the ship's horn recaptured our attention. Sailors were pulling and throwing ropes all over, getting ready to push off from the shore. Just then, one of the sailors passed by and handed me a small, dark loaf of bread. Immediately, I hid it under my dress, grabbed Chaim's hand and pulled him along after me. I didn't want that ugly, mean man to take away my bread.

Pushing, shoving, and kicking, I made my way through the crowd, holding onto the bread under my dress with one hand and dragging Chaim with the other. He kept asking, "Why are you holding onto your tummy?"

"Later. I'll tell you later. Just hurry!"

When we finally reached our place below deck, Mama was sitting on a lower bunk and breastfeeding Yitzhak. I went to her and lifted my dress so just Mama could see what I was hiding.

"How? Where?" Her look of surprise and gratitude is with me still. "*Velvel!* Come see!" She called for Papa, using the Yiddish pronunciation of his Russian name. The look of surprise on his face was my reward.

I told Papa that one of the nice sailors gave me the bread and that he might give me more if I ask. Papa warned me not to go near him again.

With another blast of the horn and a big jolt, the *Caserta* was underway.

"Papa, is a ship a girl?"

"Yes, Anna. That's because everyone who loves ships thinks they are pretty!" I didn't understand this, but I promised me to see for myself.

Allowing the strong current of moving people to take me with them, I again climbed the stairs to go up to the top deck, this time by myself. This time, as I listened to all the voices around me, I realized I did not understand most of them. I did not know there were so many languages in Europe.

Reaching the same rail again, I sat down in a large coil of rope where I could see everything around me. I saw that the plank walkway from ship to shore had been raised, and some of the refugees on shore were not able to board this ship. There was simply no more room. They stood there with tears in their eyes, holding onto their children, and with all their worldly possessions in bundles at their feet.

As I watched from the safety of "my ship," I remembered our family waiting on the train platform in Russia as train after train left without taking us. I remembered Papa and Mama's fearless determination, their desperation, their absolute need to get out of Russia.

A great roar brought me back to the present. Most of the people on deck surged to the left side of the ship, yelling what I assumed to be the same thing in many languages: "We are moving!" The rumble of the ship's engines and the vibration of the ship confirmed their declarations.

Joy, tears, and dancing erupted everywhere. Some people were jumping up and down; others were hugging each other. Over it all, the strains of *HaTikva* rose to the skies in Yiddish and Hebrew.

I sat on the deck for some time, watching as we slowly pulled away from the shore. It was good to be leaving Europe behind. The fog began to lift, and as the excitement quieted down, I started to shiver in the cold air.

I could not stop thinking. *Is Papa right? Will we have a good, safe, and happy life and home in his new Jewish homeland Israel? Or should we be going to America as Mama wants?* My knowledge in my short life was that up to that time, Mama was usually right.

I believed—I knew—Mama would see to it that life would be good for us, even in Israel. I also knew if the ice factory did not happen, she would eventually take us to America, even if Papa would not come with us. She had told me so. Mama came along on this voyage to Israel against her will and better judgment. This would be the last time Mama would submit to the will of anyone else when it came to her family's survival and safety.

I did not wish to go back below deck just yet. Whenever Mama looked at me, her accusing eyes told me how disappointed she was with me for agreeing with Papa and the Zionists in getting us all onto this boat bound for Israel. I did agree with Papa, but now I wondered if our overloaded ship would make it as far as Israel. However, everyone on board seemed filled with hope for a better future in our new homeland.

Within a few hours, a vile stench descended like a cloud on the ship, as most people became seasick on the rocking boat. You could walk very few places without stepping in all that vomit or worse! Many people were sick with dysentery, and the deck was now covered with people's poop. Mama became very green; both she and I were sick, but Papa, Chaim, and the small kids were okay.

When we finally did feel well enough to eat, the small amount of rations given to each family was not much to live on. One day I took Chaim, and we went up on deck to look for the good sailor in hopes of getting another loaf of bread, but I did not see him. All I could see was a filthy, neglected, smelly, small ship. No, she did not look like a pretty girl. We were far too many people on this little boat.

The ship's crew was too busy with their duties to keep everything clean when so many passengers were sick, so I think they gave up on that job. Our problems on board were many, but we would just have to live with them for the duration of the journey.

Sitting in the sunshine on my favorite coil of rope, a shadow fell across us. I looked up to see my kind sailor man. He was back again, and he smiled at me. With his back to the others, he stretched out his hand with a small loaf of bread, which I quickly took from him. I was about to bolt when he grabbed my arm and turned me about. Now he held a large orange ball, which he handed to Chaim. My brother took it and quickly stuffed the orange ball under his shirt. Holding our precious gifts against our tummies did not even make us conspicuous, because many people walked about or were on the floor holding onto their upset stomachs.

The sailorman chuckled at our eagerness. I covered myself the best way I could with my little coat and scrambled to leave the deck with Chaim. Soon we made it safely back to our bunks. Papa was washing Mama's face with water.

"Papa, look what we got for us!"

"Not now, Anna'le. Mama is very sick!"

"But, Papa, maybe she needs some of this."

Papa glanced up as we dropped the bread and the orange ball onto the bed. "Yes, the orange might help!" Papa took out a small knife and started to peel the ball. I stared in amazement. The wonderful smell was new to me, but I knew I would always love this new fruit. Papa broke off a small section and gave it to me first. The sweet juice was like nothing I had ever tasted. Papa gave one to my Chaim. He also loved it, and then Yakov's eyes lit up with pleasure as well. Papa picked up Mama's head and gave her a small section, encouraging her to eat.

The next day the same nice sailor gave Chaim another orange. When Chaim gave it to Papa, Papa told us the story of the many thousands of orange trees growing all over Israel. He said most Jews in Europe had a dream of having one wonderful Jaffa orange from Israel before they died! "And you," Papa said, "have had a section from two of them. Soon you will each have one all to yourself every day, and many more as soon as we arrive home."

Life became a daily routine of hunger, thirst, stench, and daily nightmares. Each time I fell asleep, I was awakened throughout the night by frightening screams from everywhere on the ship.

Each day I stayed up on deck for as long as I could, though it was very cold. That way I could be alone, and my parents would not pester me. I usually took Chaim with me so that he could also have some fresh air and would not be underfoot.

"Anna'le, tell me another story about our new home in Israel," Chaim asked. I had been repeating to him all the wonderful stories the Zionists told me of a glorious land full of hope and sunshine, where we would pick the flowers on Mount Carmel. I included many things I had hoped for, like lots of food, comfortable beds for each of us, and new warm clothing—more than we could need or put on all at one time.

In spite of the cold, we sat on deck hiding among all the large coils of ropes, hugging each other to stay warm, and sometimes we even slept in the clean, cold air.

"In a few more days we will be home in Israel," I whispered to Chaim as the rocking boat lulled us to sleep.

# Chapter 27

# My First Passover in Israel
*1949*

In the shivery cold of an early February morning in 1949, the crowded Italian boat *Caserta* neared our homeland, Israel. Peering through the wintry morning mist, Papa and I, standing on the deck, searched for the city lights of Haifa and the mountain Papa called Carmel. I could feel his excitement, but I couldn't see anything. It seemed such a long time before we finally docked in the beautiful port city.

"This will be our home, and now we will be safe from all who may wish to harm us. Israel is the only place where all Jewish people should wish to live," he told me.

It was mass confusion when we docked—everyone pushing, wanting to be the first to touch the soil of our new/old holy homeland. Families became separated; I heard mothers calling out the names of their children. Others searched for family on shore. Finally, we were all off the *Caserta* and gathering our meager belongings together. By late afternoon, men on shore directed us with our bundles and suitcases toward some open trucks.

Trucks carried the four hundred fifty passengers to relocation camps throughout Israel. Our family went to Kiryat Motzkin near the city of Haifa. After a long wait in line and a long talk with administrators of the camp, Mama persuaded them to assign our large family of six to one of a very limited number of small, one-room wooden cabins instead of sharing a large tent with other families, as most others were required to do.

Though tiny, the cabin was clean and furnished with a small table, three backless chairs, and two sets of three bunk beds—one for each of us. With the beds lining two walls, and the furniture and our personal possessions taking up all the other space, it didn't leave us much room to move. Mama and I did not like being confined in small places, but at least we were alone as a family.

"Our first home in the land of freedom!" Papa proclaimed. My dear Papa was very happy his friends the Zionists had kept their promises and brought us all to the Jewish homeland Israel. "Where we and all Jews belong!" Papa often repeated.

Mama, ever wary and worried about an inevitable Arab attack on the city and camp, declared, "They hate us. They will come and keep coming forever! They will never stop coming against us. This is a big mistake to come to Israel only to be killed by the brown-skinned Nazis!"

Conversations between my parents were often heated. Mama's only wish was to go to America. Papa's heart was in Israel. Mama believed America to be the golden land of opportunity and prosperity for her children. She feared staying in Israel. Papa, with his Zionist heart, was finally in Israel and told her he would never want to leave. He was determined to do whatever necessary to protect Mama and the children. He even joined the Israeli army as required and gave one month of service each year as a reservist. He participated in the 1956 Sinai Campaign.

As for me, I was happy to be off the ship and not see snow on the ground, only rain. I learned the rain would stop before Passover *(Pesach)*, and then we would have sunshine for many months—the country with eternal sunshine, where diapers would dry in seconds. Papa said this wonderful rain would grow beautiful flowers on Mount Carmel, and we would soon be able to go and pick some for Mama.

Soon Papa began looking for an apartment in Haifa. His sister Miriam and her husband, Ze'ev Touri, who had arrived in Israel during the British Mandate, told us that before long we would have our own place to live. "For now, just be happy where you are in the safety of the camp. We will help you, and in no time, you will start your independent life in Haifa, Israel."

I awoke to the sound of the rain drumming on our tin roof. What a lovely sound. I wanted to sleep longer, but then the sound brought back memories of the camp in France where rain poured through the holes in the big tent we shared with many others. We had all been very sick from the cold, damp weather.

Mama noticed I was awake, so she came and sat down on my bed. "Are you happy to be here in this country?"

"Yes, Mama, I am." I said that the stories the young Zionists had told us about Israel made me very happy, and now I would be able to see it all for myself. "This is our land of freedom, the historic land of the Jews, and hopefully now we can have peace. Mama this is a great land! No one will hurt you and me again. No one will rape us again! I am older now, and I know what I want. I understand a great deal more! I want to live where we do not have to be ashamed to be Jews!"

Mama's eyes filled with tears. "Will you never be my ally?" she asked. "Will you always mimic what your father and the Zionists say?"

"Mama, for as long as I live, I will be a Zionist and fight for a free land where our people can live safely! Whether I live in Israel or in America, I will never change."

(Though this conversation took place when I was almost eight years old, and much has changed in my life, I am today—as I was at the age of seven and nine—still a Zionist.)

"Well, get up and out of bed, my little 'old' girl. Passover will be with us in two days. We need to wash and clean everything we have, including the children and this little house, and see if Papa will take you to Haifa for some new ribbons for your hair. Would you like that?"

*To see the beautiful city of Haifa where we will soon live! The tall buildings, the shops! Maybe a pretty apple for me!* "Do we have money?" I asked Mama.

"Don't worry," she said. "Papa will get you at least one apple!"

Officials kept a careful watch on the new arrivals of the camp, so they could account for everybody while we awaited Government of Israel identity cards. Because none of us knew the Hebrew language, it would be easy to get lost in our new country. Papa had to ask for and received a special pass to leave the camp for the day so he could travel to Haifa.

I don't know how Papa knew where he was going, but he did, and we took a bus to Hertzel Street in the center of Haifa. The city was so very clean. No bombed-out buildings, broken windows, or broken glass on the ground. It was so beautiful.

Papa stopped to look in a men's store window with clothing that would look very nice on him. *If only we could get him some,* I thought. His face was like a child looking at delicious, sweet candies. I thought it was very sad that he could not go in and shop for himself. I liked to see Papa happy. His hazel green eyes had dancing sparkles in them when he was happy!

Papa said that for the holiday of Passover, it is customary to have something new and white to wear, so we must go shopping. "All my kids will get a new pair of socks!" We got white socks for all of us, even for Mama and Papa, though Papa knew Mama would be angry that white socks would not stay white very long.

"For you, my little 'big' girl, we will get some pretty blue and white ribbons and then an apple! Someday, Anna'le, we will buy you a pretty blue satin dress and shirts for the boys, but not this year."

My pretty, little coat from Aunt Fela no longer fit me well, but the muff still kept my hands warm. Drizzling on and off, the day was cool. But as chilly as I felt, I still insisted I must have a vanilla ice cream cone, even if it was only one scoop for Papa and me to share. Papa could not say no to me, and I licked my ice cream with joy. I looked up to see the sun peeping through the clouds as if he too were happy for me.

Papa took the long way back to our camp at Kiryat Motzkin. He knew I needed more time to taste this newfound freedom, and he did all he could to help me. He told me of the wonderful, happy days we would enjoy for the rest of our lives. "We will have lots of food and a warm, clean home, and plenty of clothing for all of us."

We returned to the camp just as it was getting dark. Mama was angry I had not been there to help in the preparations for Passover. I didn't know a thing about Passover. My first time to celebrate this wonderful festival of freedom would be in the free Jewish state, the land of Israel.

Right now, she needed my help to wash the kids. On the small table, Mama had set up a big pot of water to heat on the one-burner primus stove. On the floor was the laundry washtub three-quarters full of warm water, waiting for us to add more hot water. Chaim stood naked, waiting to jump into the water for his bath. After him would be the two younger boys, and then clean, fresh water would be poured for me and Mama and Papa. The whole procedure would take most of the evening.

Earlier, Mama had scrubbed our best special occasion outfits, and they now hung on ropes all over the little cabin. To me it looked like flags in a parade.

At first, Mama was happy with all the new socks, but then she said, "Why did you get white socks? They will be dirty in minutes!" She didn't wait for an answer.

Papa and I looked at each other, but we didn't dare say a word.

Mama continued her mumbling. "I hope these clothes will all be dry by morning, or no one will be able to go out till lunch time. Don't forget that tomorrow evening is *Pesach* (Passover) and our first *Seder* in Israel. I hope all the kids will enjoy this festival of freedom now that we are here in Israel, thanks to your Papa." (*Seder* in Hebrew means "order" and pertains to the religious ceremonial rituals done before the special dinner on the first night of Passover, or two nights in the Diaspora, Jews not residing in their G-d-given land.)

By now, Chaim was bathed, and I washed my beloved little brother Yakov. Then Mama washed Yitzhak. Finally, the bathing was completed, and we were all in our beds.

It was a very long night. I was so excited about having my first matzah the next day. Papa said it was tasteless and more like cardboard than food. Mama said I would learn to love this bread of our people, a symbol of our long history. She reminded me we would not have bread in our home for at least the eight days of Passover, so it would be best for me to learn to like the matzah.

The next day was also very long, getting us all ready for the early evening Passover Seder. Our clothes were finally dry, we were washed and dressed and combed and wearing our new white socks. They sparkled in the late afternoon sun. I thought we all looked wonderful. Mama and Papa looked very pretty, and they looked at us children with pride.

Papa was right again. Passover was with us, and it was no longer cold. The evening was warm with a cool, gentle breeze blowing from the Mediterranean. Chaim and I walked in front, holding hands. Mama and Papa held the two small boys in their arms. We walked proudly to the big tent for our Passover celebration.

It was the beginning of a wonderful new experience. Many people had already taken seats at the long tables. Papa and Yakov sat across the table from Mama, Chaim, Yitzhak, and me. I looked all around and saw everyone, clean and dressed in his or her best clothes. This was very exciting.

Mama leaned over to me and said, "Do not touch anything on the plates. First let me make sure it is good to eat." She was always on guard to protect us.

I saw people reaching and eating some things I had not seen before. I also wanted to taste all the new things, but Mama sternly told me to wait.

She looked carefully at the food on the plate before us. There was one egg, a bunch of some strange, oval-shaped black things, some fish, and one matzah.

"Oh my G-d," she suddenly exclaimed, "the economic situation in Israel is much worse than I thought. Look at what they are feeding us!"

I had never seen the black things before. I noticed most of the people were eating them with their fingers, and then licking the juice off their fingers. When Mama was looking the other way, I took one and quickly put it in my mouth. It was very salty, but good!

Papa leaned over and whispered to Mama, "What do you think they are?"

Mama responded that the only thing she had ever seen that looked like that was goat droppings. No child of hers would ever touch such an abomination!

I was eating my fourth one when Mama looked at me. Her horrified expression said it all. "Spit it out," she demanded.

"But, Mama, I like it. It's good. Eat one."

Then Papa reached out and took one.

Mama declared, "This is the last straw. We will not stay in this country another day. Right after Passover, we will be on our way to America where children are not served pickled animal droppings!"

Papa, with his eyes full of mischief, smiled at Mama. "I don't know what it is, but I like it. Try one, Devorah. You'll like it too."

Mama watched us in disbelief and then carefully picked up one little black thing, smelled it, and took a tiny nibble. Her face changed as she exclaimed, "*Maslines!*"

Papa nodded in agreement.

"Mama, what is it? Is it goat droppings?"

"No, it is not. I did not know these also come in black! They are olives. I thought they only came in green. I'm sure that is what they are, and your new land must have many of them growing all over the country."

The rest of the evening was magical. The people leading the Seder had many *Pesach* songs to sing. A man stood up and said a blessing on the matzah, the wine, and the meal.

It was time to eat the matzah for the first time. It was crunchier than I had expected and not easy to swallow. Yes, it tasted like I imagined cardboard would taste, but Chaim and I liked it.

Each person had a hard-boiled egg, several olives, a fish cake, a salad with many vegetables, and a small, deep bowl of chicken soup with one matzah ball. I had never eaten any of these before, and it was very tasty. Each of us also had a quarter of a chicken on our plate.

A woman sitting behind us whispered to Mama, "This may be the last time you will see chicken for a long, long time."

Mama promptly removed three pieces from our plates into a clean diaper. "For tomorrow," she whispered. Then, in a louder voice, she asked, "Where is the lamb? Why do we not have lamb?"

Papa quietly reminded Mama. "This is a poor country. It is absorbing hundreds of thousands in a short time. Be patient; give it time. I will see to it you have all the lamb you wish for our next *Pesach*."

Chaim and I ignored the conversation and shared one piece of the chicken. We had plenty. Before long, servers brought large baskets full of many wonderful, colorful fruits to the tables. Many I had never seen before. Mama loved all of them and made Chaim and me try a piece of each one.

We each received a small glass of Israeli wine to say the blessings. For the adults, the glass was filled four times. Chaim and I each had a full glass. Papa looked at us and smiled. "They will sleep well tonight."

I did sleep well and, for the first time, my dreams did not frighten me. I dreamed of colorful dancing fruit and of singing *Pesach* songs.

# Chapter 28

# Moving to Haifa

*1949*

Mama was up early that morning, and as I awoke, I sensed something was different.

"Anna'le, are you up?" Mama asked. "Get dressed. We are moving to our new home in Haifa today."

*Today!* I sat on the edge of the bed, unable to speak as thoughts raced in my head. I had lived most of my life in the camps. *Who will take care of us now? How will we survive on our own? Who will make sure we have food? Will Mama and Papa be able to take care of us all by themselves? Do they know how?*

This was a new fear. For most of my life, our family had depended on kind strangers for all we needed. It had seemed no one wanted us to stay in one place for very long. We only stayed long enough to get stronger and healthier, and then we moved to the next camp and the next—several DP camps in three years. As far as I knew, that was just the way everyone lived, except the people in Israel and America.

As I sat on the bunk, fear paralyzed me. Mama took one look at me and understood how I felt. She came to sit with me and put her arm around my shoulders. She began to talk to me for the first time as if I was old enough to understand.

"Your papa and I have always taken care of you and your brothers, and we will do so for as long as we live. Your only concerns from now on will be to go to school, study, grow, and be happy. Papa and I will take care of all the rest. We will be moving into an apartment with three rooms. One for you kids, one for Papa and me that will be our salon and dining room for entertaining guests who come to visit, and the big front room will be a kitchen for now, until we build another one soon. We can grow flowers on the two large balconies and sit outside in the evening. We will soon have an icebox with all the ice we need, and it will be full of food at all times! You and your brothers will not be hungry again. You will see; life will be great!"

I remembered Papa's plans for the ice factory. *I will help him make ice.*

"You and your brothers will be off to school and make Papa and me proud. You will have friends and be happy. Now come and let us get this all packed up for this move. We are going to our new home in the beautiful seaport city of Haifa!"

Mama's excitement calmed my fears. I quickly dressed and began to help her put our belongings into the large bedspread bundle.

"We must make sure to leave us all something to wear!" I said as Mama laughed with joy at my quick reaction to help get us ready to go.

By late afternoon, a small truck came to pick us up for the move to Haifa. On the truck were two other lucky families who would also be moving to new homes and lives. We sat on the floor of the truck, some seated on the bundles. We were less than an hour's drive from Haifa, and we were to be dropped off first.

The bright Israeli sun was very warm even at this hour. The trees were fresh and green, and flowers were everywhere. The houses, like the flowers, were painted in many colors—pink, blue, yellow. It almost looked like a circus. Arabs who had deserted some neighborhoods during the war loved to paint their houses in bright colors, inside and out.

*This is not a dream,* I told myself. *This is my pretty Israel.*

Then in the distance, we could see a very beautiful, tall, and long bridge. It was dark gray with white trim on top. As we came closer, the bridge seemed to grow bigger still. I shouted through the back window to ask the driver for the name of the bridge.

He yelled back, "This is the biggest bridge in Israel. It is the Wadi Rushmia Bridge, and your new home is right next to it, almost underneath. It is a good street with lots of children. I think you will like it here! The school is only a ten-minute walk away, so this is a very good location for all you kids."

Mama nodded with satisfaction to Papa. "Anna'le will walk the boys to school when the time comes. Chaim will start school in September this year, but maybe we can get him into the *yeshiva* (religious school) sooner."

Papa replied, "Torah study will not help him learn to defend himself and our homeland. Torah study did not save your brother from the hands of the Nazis. Most of the yeshiva students are dead. The only young men alive after the next war will be the ones who serve in the army and learn how to defend themselves and their homeland. My sons must know how to protect themselves and Israel. That can only be learned by first attending public school with all the other Israeli children and then by serving in the army."

"*No!*" Mama yelled in an angry voice. "No child of mine will ever serve in any man's army for as long as I live!"

And so it was, much to the distress of my Zionist heart.

Israel in May. Such a lovely time! The trees and bushes were in full bloom, and it was sunny most of the time. An occasional rain shower was a welcome reprieve for Mama—to cool us and clean the city of dust, she would say.

After getting the family settled into our new apartment, my parents registered me in second grade at the local public school for the last part of the school year. Though I was much too old for first or second grade, they decided to start me in the latter part of second grade because I didn't yet speak Hebrew.

Because of my earlier experience with the young rabbi in the DP camp school, I refused to attend the parochial Beth Ya'akov School for girls. Then, three years later, I insisted Mama take my brothers out of the yeshiva and enroll them in my school, where I could keep an eye out for their safety.

I knew Yiddish, Polish, Russian, and German, but that didn't help me to make friends with the other children. None befriended me, and I endured the two months until summer vacation without making a single friend.

# Chapter 29

# Haifa—Hope and Betrayal

*1950*

One Shabbat afternoon in July when Mama and Papa were resting at home with the two little boys, I took Chaim with me to go exploring. I could smell the salty breezes from the ocean, and I wanted to go there to run in the sand as I had seen in a picture book and then into the water to cool off. I loved to run!

I was surprised when a man spoke to us in Russian, asking us what we were looking for. "The ocean," I told him.

"It's not far from the next corner. Just cross the train tracks and walk that way through the industrial section."

Chaim and I memorized the route we were taking, using our big Rushmia Bridge as a landmark. After climbing some security fences, we were soon within sight of the ocean.

Before long, we were running through the shallow water in our underwear, laughing and happy together. The sand was warm as we lay down to listen to the waves and watch the seagulls soaring above us. It was so peaceful. In no time, we were fast asleep in the sunshine—my first good sleep in Israel.

I awoke to the gentle evening breeze and found Chaim sitting up watching me. "Mama will punish us for being gone so long," he whispered fearfully.

"I know," I replied, "but this day was better than all the hard work I would have had to do at home. Maybe the beating won't be too bad or last very long."

We arrived home to the sound of angry voices and one of the scariest sights I had ever seen. "*No,* they are *not* coming to Israel, and *no* they will *not* send us the money to get our ice factory crates from the port," Papa declared.

Doors slammed, and fists banged on the table. My mother's face was white, and her eyes were full of anger.

"There will be no ice factory!" Papa yelled. "My dear sister Fela has changed her mind; she and her family are going to America."

Mama's eyes blazed with fury. "I *told* you your sister Fela and her wretched husband could not be trusted!" She continued shouting. "They have condemned my children to starve in this G-d-forsaken land full of ugly Arabs! I will teach my children to hate your family. I will never forgive them for the hell they are putting us through. I *told* you I wanted to go to America!"

Chaim and I were very scared as we watched from the doorway. Our parents' rage and the frightening situation they were describing put great fear into our young hearts. With this news, I think Mama forgot we had been gone all day.

The more I listened, the more I believed that once again, my poor mama was right. *We should have done as she wanted and gone to America.* Now we had nothing and no way to support ourselves as a family. The fury and hatred in my mother's eyes were like nothing I had ever seen before.

Chaim and I followed Papa and Mama into their big bedroom. I asked, "What will happen to all the factory equipment? Will we not get it out of the port? Will we not build our ice factory to make Mama rich and cool?"

Mama looked at me as she spoke to Papa. "Look at her. She is still a skeleton, only skin and bones in your land of milk and honey. All my kids are starving!"

Still holding Chaim's hand, I pulled him with me to the bedroom where we four children slept. We sat down on the bed to await end of the heated discussion between our parents.

The last words in that argument were Mama's. "Tomorrow morning I will take all our documents and go with Anna to the American Consulate in Tel Aviv. She speaks Hebrew and is learning to speak English in school. She will help me fill out the necessary applications for immigration to America. I hope, for your sake, it will not take too long to get out of this Zionist land of yours! I wish for a future for my children in a country far away from this land and its neighbors. We are going to America!"

Mama and I left for Tel Aviv very early the next morning, leaving Papa to fend for himself and the boys. Mama had two slices of bread and marmalade, which was to be our food for the day, packed in a page of newspaper.

"Now this is my war," Mama proclaimed. "We are going to talk with the Americans and get us out of this country with its ugly Arabs and its burning hot sun!"

Our visit to the American embassy was a mad rush, running from one office to the next. We didn't have appointments. Mama just walked from office to office, expecting everyone to drop whatever he or she was doing to take care of her needs. And they did!

All day long, I watched Mama pleading our case—in Yiddish, Polish, German, and Russian—to one person after the next. Some, who spoke only English, would find a translator so they could understand her. Mama, flushed from anxiety and anger, just wanted someone to listen and care. The fire in her eyes did not go out all day.

"We will get us out of this land soon, or I will die trying!" she told me.

My heart was breaking as I watched her. I knew she would never stop until she succeeded. I feared for her well-being.

We needed many documents filled out and signed. The most important thing we needed was a guarantor, a person in America who would take on the responsibility to be our sponsor. Mama had not known we would need that kind of help, but still she was not defeated.

"Mama, let's go home. We do not have the necessary documents. We'll come back when we have everything we need, and then they will listen to you."

"Okay, Anna'le," she sighed, "we will go back home and talk to Papa. We'll see if his uncles in America will be our guarantors and get us out of here, even if we have to pay them for the help!"

Armed with a large envelope full of documents to be completed, Mama considered it a good day's work, and we returned to our home in Haifa.

Now that Mama had all her surviving children safely away from the Germans, her new obsession was to get us to a country where we would be safe and have food to eat. It became her new life's work. This obsession consumed her, and it would not stop until the day we stepped onto American soil.

Running almost daily from one government office to another and to lawyers' offices, she seemed to forget her home, her husband, and her kids. All we knew was Mama was now in charge of obtaining a future where we would no longer be hungry.

This betrayal by father's relatives condemned our family to many more years of hardship.

In 1952, following the ice factory fiasco, Mama no longer trusted Papa's sister Fela and her husband to be true their word about sponsoring us to go to America. Therefore, she went to the American Consulate in Tel Aviv to register our names on the American quota to immigrate to the United States. Though she knew this could take many years, it was a possible means of reaching her goal. Meanwhile, she continued to hope for Fela and Sol's sponsorship.

# Chapter 30

# Screaming

*Haifa, Israel—1951*

Our first home in Israel after arriving from the DP camps of Germany via the departure camp in France was a small, cold one-room cabin at the far end of the newcomers' Relocation and Placement Camp in Kiryat Motzkin. So we felt very fortunate when Papa was able to secure, through his brother-in-law Ze'ev, a small apartment in a three-story building in Haifa. The building had been deserted two years earlier by its former Arab tenants and now housed two other Jewish families who had also escaped the horrors of war-ravaged Europe. One family was from Poland and the other from Bulgaria.

Each residence had its own entrance from the street. We lived on the middle floor, safe from winter flooding. The other families lived above and below us.

Mama had hired builders to fashion a tiny kitchen beneath the very long outdoor staircase leading from the ground level to the third floor. She was delighted with that small room, which had a tiny window, a narrow counter, a small sink, and a table. Two little three-legged stools served many purposes throughout the house and allowed everyone to sit for Shabbat dinners. We even had a second-hand icebox that fit into the corner of this small space. Biweekly deliveries by the ice truck helped us keep our food from spoiling most of the time.

Papa called the builders again, and they sectioned off a space in one corner of the entrance room to build a bathroom. Now we would have a proper toilet with a seat instead of the hole in the floor used by the former owners. He even got a small hot water tank with a primus stove that burned a stinky fuel. Papa, Mama, or I would pump up the stove to heat the water so we could all have a Shabbat shower.

The entry room was large enough for us to play indoors in the winter. My parents' bedroom served as our living room, as well as a dining room for Shabbat meals and for entertaining our very few visitors. This room had the only good furniture in the house—a table with six chairs, a sofa, a large bed, and a beautiful wall unit where Mama displayed her new crystal collection and stored our good Shabbat clothing. All of us kids slept in one big bed in the other large bedroom that completed our home.

In the close quarters of this living arrangement, the neighbors above, below, and all around us soon knew the sound of my voice. Our neighbors heard me screaming loudly at least once a week.

Sometimes when they saw me outside, they looked at me with pity and asked if I was okay. Some even asked why I had been screaming and if they could get someone to help me. Who is beating you, and why? I was afraid to tell them the truth of why Mama was so angry, so I didn't answer their questions. I thought it was mostly my fault, and if I could only do what she wanted, she might be happy and stop hating and beating me.

I was not yet eight years old. I knew Mama would beat me severely if she found out I was telling my young brothers the story of what had happened to me during the war. However, I felt they needed to know the truth. Mama and Papa did not talk to anyone about the war, so once again, I risked Mama's displeasure and rage by talking to my brothers of my secret, dark past.

I had just finished telling them about the time I spent in the church and how horrible it all was when I heard Mama coming into our little home. I knew Chaim, being five years old, had understood me well. Yakov and Yitzhak were too young understand.

Chaim jumped up and ran from our bedroom yelling, "Mama! Mama! Come quick! Anna is scaring us! She's telling us those scary stories again about her time in the church and about the war!"

Mama stormed into our room, her face flushed an angry red. She screamed at me, "How many times have I told you to keep your stories to yourself? How many times? How many more times will I need to beat you to make you stop this once and for all?"

"Mama, they need to know the truth, and you and Papa do not talk about all the things that happened to us. Why?" I pleaded. "Why do you not tell anyone about what happened? I am not telling them about you and Papa. I am only talking about me in the church where you left me with the priests."

The first slap was a surprise, but the rest of the beating was not. Her unrestrained fists landed furiously on my head and then on the rest of my skeletal little body. When I fell to the floor from the blows and she could not reach me easily with her fists, she started to kick me, harder and harder. My brothers stood watching in shock, Yakov with tears in his eyes. I didn't see Chaim.

By now, I was feeling faint and could no longer scream—and she needed to hear me scream. She picked up the three-legged stool and slammed it down on my back. I heard my voice scream yet again, and I heard my ribs and the stool cracking. When the chair crashed on my back a second time and broke apart, I heard Chaim laugh with glee.

Gasping for breath, writhing in pain, and struggling to find safety for my small body under the bed, I looked up and saw she was reaching for the other stool. As she raised it to strike me again, Papa suddenly appeared and grabbed her arms, restraining her. By now, I was coughing and spitting up blood. My ribs hurt and felt like they were on fire.

Papa saw me and saw the blood on the floor. He was furious with Mama. "Are you mad? Have you lost your mind completely?" he demanded. "Are you trying to kill this poor child? She is almost dead!"

Still gripping Mama's arms, he dragged her out of our bedroom into the front room. All the while, she screamed, "She was telling the boys about the church where we left her! Oh, the guilt, the shame! We must stop her! If I have to kill her, I will do it; I will stop her! She will not talk about the war to anyone ever again!"

I heard Papa trying to hush her. He said, "As long as you and I never admit or talk about what happened, no one will believe her. She was very young, and in time, she will forget all about it. Or we can say she is just confused or dreaming."

Leaving Mama in their bedroom, Papa came back to find me coughing and bleeding under the bed. He gently pulled me out as I screamed out in pain. Cradling me gently in his strong arms, he carried me up the hill to Rushmia Bridge, where he stopped a car to take us to the hospital on Mount Carmel.

Papa's brother-in-law, Ze'ev Turi, had worked in that hospital for some years. I thought he was a doctor. I didn't know a man could be a nurse. I called him Doctor Turi, which embarrassed him and caused much laughter among his coworkers in the hospital.

My uncle, "Doctor" Turi, ordered x-rays be taken, and then wrapped me in strong bandages. In the hearing of others he said, "It is too bad she fell from that second-floor terrace! I will make note of this in the report."

Then quietly to my father he added, "Just make sure she keeps her mouth shut. Keep your wife away from her. This time she almost killed her! Next time she may succeed. I will take care of the rest, as I have in the past. This must not become known, or we will all go to prison!"

I knew then the reason for Papa taking me to Uncle Ze'ev's hospital. Papa did not want the police to know Mama had beaten me, and he knew his relative would help conceal the facts.

The x-rays showed I had some broken and cracked ribs and a punctured lung. I spent several days in the hospital.

Unfortunately, this was not the first time or the last that Mama's beatings left me physically injured, often requiring medical care, although I did not always receive the care I needed. Curiously, Uncle Ze'ev always tended to my injuries, though at the time I didn't question it.

I felt betrayed by Chaim, his tattling, and his laughter at my pain; I no longer trusted him with anything of real importance. Now I also felt betrayed by my own father and by Uncle Ze'ev, who were protecting my mother and not me. I couldn't understand Papa's actions, but I still loved him and would keep the questions to myself for another time.

As for my uncle, I could hate him and then forget him completely, as I did. We never had a conversation in all the years we lived in Haifa. After that day, when he tended to my injuries or when his family came to visit our home, I ignored him.

Something else had often puzzled me. Ze'ev's wife, Miriam, my papa's sister, always seemed to dislike my mama, and I could never understand why that was so. Years later, I realized this aunt, whom I loved very much, must have learned from her husband of Mama's violence toward me.

When it came to my young brothers, Mama was a good mother, and they probably have wonderful memories of their childhood. She showed them much love—hugging and kissing them, being generous toward them with the family's food, and tolerating their childish naughtiness and silly behavior.

For me, it was different. I was born shortly after the death of her firstborn twins, the two little boys murdered at the beginning of the war. I, a girl, was a disappointing replacement for her beloved sons, and she never forgave G-d for taking them away. She had little patience with me. When she was angry, she made sure I knew she did not want me, I was not important to her, and she was sorry I had ever been born. I was merely a servant to her and her sons.

One of the greatest accomplishments of my young life was learning to read. Trying to understand people, and why they were sometimes very cruel, I started reading every book I could get my hands on. Besides helping my search to understand human behavior, it was a respite from the hard work at home. Reading provided an escape into a world of fantasy far away from the pain and sadness in my life. I read many books from my school library and had a one-year membership at a private library as well. Without all my books, I may not have survived.

For some years after those beatings, I did not speak to anyone in the family about the war and the hell I lived through. Feeling quite alone with my inner pain, I even gave up on having much of a relationship with my brothers. The exception was Yakov for a few years. Chaim could not be trusted. Yitzhak, born after the war, was young, and Mama protected him well.

However, I still needed to talk, so I tried telling my friends from school about the things that had happened to me. Of course, they told my stories to their parents. The parents then asked me never to come back to visit their children again.

Esther Friedman was my friend. One day as we completed our homework in her room, her mother walked me outside and spoke to me. "Esther has told me your story, and she was very upset. As her mother, I am very concerned about her hearing any more of your stories. I would like my little Israeli-born Esther to have a good and happy childhood. You are much too old for my daughter. You have lived and seen too much!"

"Mrs. Friedman," I protested, "your daughter is six months older than I!"

"Yes, I know, but the life you've had has made you much older than your years. I am sorry for you, but please do not come back to my home again. Stop your friendship with my Esther."

I walked home, sobbing all the way. *Even in Israel, my people hate me. Where shall I go and find a friend? If not in a Jewish land, then where?*

The next day in school, I told Esther I no longer wished to be her friend, but I would not tell her why. One by one, I lost most of my friends the same way. I wanted, *needed* to tell my story, but no one would to listen to me. So I decided I no longer wanted or needed to have any friends, and I determined to do just fine without them.

Yes, I was "too old" even for children several years older than me. Many of them had happy homes and childhoods—two things I had never known. I did not wish to go back to their homes and see what a happy, normal life could be. With a very sick mother in our house, I knew I would never have any of that.

In the five years we lived in Haifa, Mama expected me to take the boys along wherever I went or to stay outside in the street and play with them. Caring for them was just too much for her. I certainly didn't want the job—I was still a child myself and wanted to have fun—but that's just the way it was.

As a result, I missed many after-school events and birthday parties. When I received an invitation to a birthday party, Mama insisted I take the three boys along. That made me unwelcome at the few parties to which I was invited and which I really wanted to attend. Most of the time, I was told, "You are welcome to come in, but not your brothers. They are small children, and only our daughter's classmates are invited."

It was very painful for me, but the only thing left for me to do was to leave the birthday house and take my brothers to our small playground and clubhouse near Rushmia Bridge. Inevitably, we got our only clean dress-up clothes soiled, and that evening my punishment would be another beating, more pain, and more screaming for our neighbors to hear, while they shook their heads in pity.

On Mama's birthday one year, she came up with a solution for how to silence her own torment and me.

"As a birthday gift for me and for your papa—for as long as we live—you must *never* tell anyone about what happened to you or to our family during the war. When we are no longer alive, then you may do as you wish."

Each year on Mama's and Papa's birthdays, she repeated the same request, and each year I promised. I kept that promise for many years, always fearing that when they were gone and no one could question them, no one would believe me. I have kept silent for much too long, and some of those fears have since come true.

Mama passed away on March 21, 1962, and one year later, I started writing down all I remembered. Some memories were not very clear at first due to so many years of silence. With many hours of hard and often painful work, most of them have come back. Sometimes a sound or a smell gives birth to a memory I had forgotten. So many memories!

# Chapter 31

# Kicking the Establishment

*Haifa*

I looked forward to the occasional time Papa would take me with him for a walk in the heart of the city. People walked about through the streets. I saw no fear in their faces.

*Is it true that a Jewish person can walk freely on any street in Haifa or anywhere in this land of Israel without fear? Am I now and forever at home in the land Mama said was promised to us by G-d?*

Mama didn't talk much about G-d. She said that since He let the Nazis kill her little boys, everyone in her family, and millions of other Jews, she was not yet ready to trust Him again.

"Papa, are we really free to do as we wish?" I asked.

"Yes, my Anna'le."

"Papa, if someone does something wrong in this country, what will happen to him? Will he be killed?"

This was to be the first time of many that Papa would recite the same answers. "You know for sure you are in a Jewish country when this happens: A Jewish thief or murderer will be caught by a Jewish policeman and brought to trial before a Jewish judge and jury. If found guilty, he or she would be punished and thrown into a Jewish prison guarded by Jewish guards."

"Would everyone be treated equally?"

"Yes," Papa said. "No one is or will be above the law in our Jewish land, including the prime minister!"

I believed every word Papa said, and looking at his very serious face, I *really* believed him. Still, I needed to prove his theory.

Standing near the men's clothing store was a well-dressed gentleman. I approached him, stood next to him for a moment, and then kicked him hard on his leg.

With a startled cry, he looked down and yelled at me, "*Lama?* Why?"

As I turned to run away, he grabbed my arm. Papa heard the commotion, saw the man holding onto me, and said, "What's wrong here?"

In Hebrew, the man asked, "Is this your little one?"

"Yiddish, Yiddish," Papa demanded.

Now in broken Yiddish, the man explained that without provocation I had just kicked his leg.

Realization dawned on Papa as he recalled our conversation from a few moments earlier. With a strange grin on his face, he explained that his daughter must have been testing his words that in Israel, nobody would be shot on sight for some crime without going before a judge and jury.

The man, rubbing his painful shin, looked at me and said in Hebrew, "*Miskena ketana.* Poor little girl. What a way to start a new life!"

Then to my father, he said, "Do you know who I am?"

Papa shook his head no.

With a gentle smile on his face, the man extended his hand to each of us in turn. "My name is Abba Hushi. I am the mayor of Haifa. Welcome to your new home in Israel."

We next met in 1952, when my schoolteacher invited him to our classroom. She asked the class if anyone knew our visitor.

I leaped to my feet. "I know! He is the mayor of Haifa, and his name is Abba Hushi."

Recognizing my face and voice, he smilingly replied, "Yes, we meet again, Anna. Your Hebrew is good. It's lovely to see you."

# Chapter 32

# Chaim, the Pigeon, and Zimmel's New Shoes

*Haifa, Israel—1952*

That day was just like all the other beautiful summer days in the coastal city of Haifa. The sky was bright blue and cloudless. An occasional gentle breeze from the Mediterranean Sea brought that lovely warm, salty smell of the ocean, which reminded me summer had arrived. I loved summertime.

We could not afford to go to summer camp every year, so I spent a lot of time playing with my brothers, as Mama insisted. Being the oldest child in the family was not always a good thing. I took care of them like a mother hen.

Eleven years old, and I knew everything about everything. My brothers thought so too, as long as I didn't interfere with their games. They didn't always want to listen to me and would soon get themselves into trouble.

With my great imagination and the knowledge I gained from books I had read, I invented games to play using things we found in our home or around the neighbourhood. Chaim and I made soccer balls from knotted rags. We played barefoot on the side of the road near the horse stable built into the hillside across the ravine from our house, or we went to the playground down the block near the big bridge.

Neighborhood kids had invented nicknames for the Markus children—we were "The Three Musketeers and the Hero." I was the hero, because I usually had to rescue my brothers from one problem or another.

Speaking of trouble, my oldest brother, Chaim, managed to find or create lots of it for us. With his very smart and active brain and his sweet tongue, he had a special genius for getting himself into and out of many problems all by himself.

Chaim, a handsome, clever eight-year-old, was tall, slim, smart, and athletic. He had a dark complexion, unruly curly black hair, and mischievous black eyes. His fun-loving nature and talent for excitement made him very popular with the other kids. They loved him and followed him around as if were some kind of general. They would do anything he asked just to please him and so they could be his friend. However, when I saw that special twinkle in his eyes, I knew he was up to no good. I could read his mind.

Chaim got away with his tricks and misbehavior most of the time. His idea of fun was to trick some innocent (or to him, stupid) boy to get into trouble and then take the blame for what Chaim had done. He called this his I'm-just-having-fun-and-no-one-gets-hurt game. He could create chaos out of nothing and then just stand aside laughing with triumphant joy at the outcome. Of course, the first rule of the game was that no one could tattle on Chaim. Still, he managed to convince his loyal followers that they were having great fun, even if it was at the expense of some innocent person. If the problem became too big for him to handle, he would run away or look to his big sister, me, to rescue him.

My two youngest brothers and I looked quite similar with our bright blond hair and fair complexions. Of course, playing outdoors all day long in the summertime made us very darkly tanned. Chaim had jet-black hair, like Mama and Papa. His eyes were black like Mama's, but Papa's eyes were hazel—brown with flecks of green.

The middle brother, Yakov, sometimes called *Yanke'le*, was six-and-a-half-years old. He was a happy, good-natured, more serious child. Handsome, blond, and fair-skinned with big brown eyes like a deer, he was a loving, caring boy and usually had a smile on his face. He didn't appreciate the shenanigans Chaim got away with and stayed near me for protection. We were very close. Maybe that was because I took care of him for some years when he was a small, sick baby.

Yakov was slow to learn to walk because his legs were what they call bowlegged. When he was born, his heels touched together, his legs forming a circle. I tried to make them grow straight with some exercises I did with him. I kept exercising him, stretching his muscles to strengthen and straighten the legs. What I didn't know at the time was that I happened to be doing all the right things to get him to where his legs would be almost as good as mine. Though they never became perfectly straight, they were perfectly useful, and he had full ability to walk, run, and even play soccer. When he was learning to walk, he often tripped on his own feet and fell to the ground on his face. He rarely cried or complained, and we all tried to help him get around. However, Chaim sometimes even picked on him and got him into trouble.

That summer, Yitzhak, my baby brother, was five years old. He looked a lot like Yakov; some people even asked if they were twins. Yitzhak followed big brother Chaim around like a shadow.

School had been out for more than a month, and some children were coming back from the first half of summer camp. Others would be leaving soon to go to the same camps for the next four weeks. For a few days, we would all be together playing in the narrow *wadi* (streambed) just below our homes.

Our houses were perched on one slope of the ravine overlooking a rocky dirt road. To get to the road and go to school in the warmer weather, we walked on or jumped over some rocks. In winter, the canal was always full of water. It ran very fast and cold and often overflowed, flooding the area. Then, to keep from getting wet or even drowning, we would have to go over the big Rushmia Bridge and walk the long way to school.

Two children had almost drowned in the canal trying to cross on their way to school. That prompted Mama to launch her own personal crusade, begging city bureaucrats to build two small pedestrian bridges so the children could safely cross over the water. After a couple years of Mama pressing the local government, they finally built the bridges, connecting our homes to the road.

So now, for winter fun, we could stand on the bridges just a few feet above the fast-moving water and watch the strange debris and garbage rushing down from the foothills of the big Carmel Mountains.

We lived about a hundred yards from the imposing Wadi Rushmia Bridge that spanned Wadi Rushmia. This bridge was the pride of two neighbourhoods, Chalisa and Neve Sh'anan, and connected the upper and lower parts of the city of Haifa. Now people didn't need to travel in a big circle to get to the upper part of the city and beyond to the top of the Carmel Mountains where the summer camps were located.

On this very bright morning, my brother Chaim was about to become a mighty hunter. A group of about a dozen children with nothing to do were in the clearing next to the small stable. Chaim said, "See that white pigeon up high in the sky? I can bring it down with one stone!" he bragged. None of us believed him.

Without a word, he bent to the ground and picked up a stone. He put it in his slingshot, looked in the direction the bird was flying, took aim, and fired. Up into the sky it went. We held our breath and then gasped as we heard the thump. The white pigeon froze in midair and plunged to earth. It landed almost at our feet.

Chaim was as shocked and as frightened as the rest of us, hardly daring to believe this had actually happened. No one looked at each other; we all stared at our feet. One well-aimed stone—one dead, pure-white pigeon.

Yakov, with tears in his eyes, broke the stunned silence. "We have to make a grave for this poor thing."

Chaim came to life and sprang into action. He had a project! He would arrange a funeral for the pigeon. Now we would no longer be bored. We could all help Chaim. He always had good ideas.

I knew one must bury dead bodies, but we had a dilemma as to what we should do for the ceremony. Some of the kids said it was very simple to make a cross and push it into the ground, just as we had seen in the movies.

"*No!*" Chaim yelled. "This is *my* pigeon. I killed it, and I will say how and what to do with it! We live in Israel, and that makes it a Jewish pigeon! One of you, get to work and make a Star of David. We need a box to bury the pigeon in!" Chaim looked at the boy standing next to him. Zimmel was about a year younger than Chaim. His hair was the color of a carrot. His face, usually pink and full of freckles, was now white with fear. It was his first time to see death. "Zimmel, do you have a shoe box at home?"

Zimmel nodded yes and then, finding his voice, announced that his mom and dad had just gotten him a new pair of shoes for the next school year. He took off for home to get the box. Suddenly, he felt very important to be part of this project. Zimmel came back not only with the shoe box—he was also wearing his shiny, brand-new, lace-up brown shoes to show off to us all. In his other hand, he waved a new handkerchief.

Chaim didn't like this boy very much and neither did most of the other kids. Jealousy was the reason. Zimmel, an only child, always had everything we needed and wanted, and we resented him for it.

Some of the kids had begun digging the hole. Chaim and I sat down on the side of the hill watching them work while he made plans for the rest of the project. I thought of something from a book I had been reading that he should consider—about Egypt and the ancient Pharaohs. It told of the night voyage of the dead to the afterlife on the other side. Chaim listened very carefully as I told him of the long night trip they took by boat and came back to life when they reached the other side in the morning.

"Is this not a great story?" I asked.

He looked at me with that certain mischievous look, his eyes sparkling. And I knew we were about to get into some big trouble.

"So what you are telling me is that by morning, the dead will come back to life and will be on the other side of the sea? And live again? Just like the kings of Egypt?"

I told Chaim it was only an old story I had read in a history book.

"Well," he said, "if it's okay for the Egyptians and all their royalty, why wouldn't it be just as good for our pigeon?"

"What are you thinking, Chaim?" I questioned suspiciously.

Laughing, he looked at me and said, "This is an excellent idea you have given me!"

"*Me?* I have only told you a story about the Egyptians. I didn't suggest anything. Chaim, what are you thinking? What are you up to?"

Whenever my mischievous brother had an idea, I could be sure that trouble would soon follow, and I would have to come to the rescue. However, this time, I was intrigued and wondered what fun we would have!

What was about to happen in the next few hours was not what took place in any of the books I had read.

Over the hill from the stable was a slew. It never dried up, winter or summer. Its still water was smelly and green with algae all summer long, a perfect breeding ground for billions of mosquitoes. To small children, it was a huge lake nestled into the side of the hill—a great place to play and get into trouble. It fit perfectly into Chaim's growing scheme.

Jumping up from our seat on the ground, Chaim called loudly, "Zimmel, come quick. I need you." Zimmel came running; he worshipped Chaim.

I looked at Chaim and whispered, "Zimmel? Why do you want him?" Chaim's eyes sparkled.

*Oh my G-d,* I thought. *When those jet-black eyes sparkle and twinkle like stars on fire, I know serious trouble is on the way.*

All of the kids gathered around, eager to know of Chaim's plan. By now, Chaim had tossed the shoebox on the ground by the stable and was holding the slowly stiffening pigeon in his hands, its feet curled toward the sky.

"Let's all go to the slew. Zimmel, do you wish for this pigeon to have a proper burial and a chance to come back to life?" Chaim asked.

Zimmel nodded enthusiastically, honored to be able to contribute his opinion on this most serious matter.

Chaim continued. "You know, according to a story from Egypt that my sister, Anna, told me, when the royalty and others in that country died, they crossed a big body of water like a lake. They floated, and when they got to the other side, they came back to life and went back to their families. Or, if it were a pigeon, it would then fly away and be happy again."

Zimmel looked mesmerized. "Yes, I think I know that story!"

"Well, we'll all need to contribute to the plan!" Chaim said, looking directly at Zimmel.

"Anything you say, Chaim. How can I help you?" Zimmel asked.

Chaim pondered aloud, "Hmm, what kind of contribution can you give us? We need something that would float like a small ship, so we could put the pigeon in it and float it to the other side of the slew."

We all looked at each other. We had nothing to contribute. Just then, Chaim seemed to get an idea as he looked down at Zimmel's feet. Zimmel was proudly wearing his brand-new shoes. Without so much as a blink, Chaim declared, "You should contribute a shoe so we can use it as a boat for the pigeon."

"Give you a shoe?" Zimmel shrieked. "My new shoes? I just got them! I am wearing them for only the fourth time, and I must have them for school next month!"

Speaking calmly in a reassuring voice, Chaim explained, "You do not understand what this is all about. We put the pigeon in the shoe, we send the shoe across the slew, and when it gets to other side, the pigeon will fly away! It will be back to life, and you get your shoe back. You will just wipe it off on the grass, and it will all be back as good as new! So what is the big deal?"

Zimmel calmed down, and with his limited intelligence, he agreed this was a very good idea. He took off a shoe and gave it to Chaim. Chaim wrapped the pigeon very carefully in the big new handkerchief he asked Zimmel to give him and put the pigeon inside the shoe. He then tied the shoelace around the pigeon to make sure the bird would not fall out during its voyage to the other side on its way back to life. Chaim then set the shoe on top of the slew and, with everyone watching, pushed it ever so gently away from the bank with a long stick.

Standing by Chaim, I whispered in his ear, "For this stunt, we are going to die—by the hands of his mother and ours. We are going to be killed for this one, I just know it."

He smiled his best, most confident smile at me and whispered back, "No! Nothing will happen to us. You always take care of us. You will fix this one as well."

It was too late now to stop! *I could have prevented this.* However, it was just too brilliant, too much fun and I simply couldn't make myself tell him to stop. I really didn't like this stupid rich boy either. He always made my brothers feel inferior. I figured he deserved what he got. I would enjoy the sport and deal with the disaster later. Besides, Zimmel actually gave Chaim his new shoe for the pigeon boat.

Chaim used the stick to keep nudging the shoe farther and farther into the deepest part of the slew. Zimmel stood watching proudly, knowing he had contributed greatly to this important event.

Now as the shoe reached almost halfway across the water, I heard the sounds. *Glug, glub, glub, glug, blub, blub.* The air slowly escaped the shoe. and it started to sink ever so slowly into the soupy sludge of the slew.

Zimmel became concerned. "What's happening, Chaim? What is happening? My shoe! It's going down!"

"Shush," Chaim whispered loudly. "Don't get excited. This must be done in silence. Shhhh! Don't you know the rules?"

Zimmel apologized but still looked perplexed. Immediately, all of the kids became very quiet, but I got the giggles. I tried to hide my hilarity behind a serious face so as not to give away the true disaster of what was happening before our eyes.

Chaim and I were having so much fun even though I knew we would have to pay dearly for this prank. *Zimmel's father will kill us for sure.* He will know the troublemaker Chaim was responsible for this great loss. New shoes are very valuable and must last for a couple of years before being passed along to a younger child.

In another moment, the shoe and the pigeon completely disappeared! Zimmel became frantic. "Chaim, the shoe is gone!"

Chaim whispered, "Will you just be quiet?! It's walking very slowly on the bottom of this lake to the other side."

We all waited and watched, the other kids expecting the shoe to reappear on the far bank. By now, some were getting tired of standing and began to sit down on the grass to wait for the Egyptian miracle. Twelve of us, kids of every age, sat staring at the slew without a sound, without one word.

Then Chaim spoke. "You know, Zimmel; I am getting very annoyed with this shoe of yours. If it is going to move one slow step at a time like this, it is going to take much too long a time to get to the other side! I am not going to sit here for the rest of the day waiting."

"So what can we do about this?" Zimmel asked innocently.

Chaim always had an answer. "We must give the first shoe his mate. You know, the other shoe, so they can walk together properly. I know this is the problem. No one can walk properly without having both shoes on. If the first shoe knows his mate is there with him, they will walk together happily to the other side, and come up on the other bank."

"Are you sure that's the reason it is taking so long?" the boy asked.

Chaim reassured him no one could walk fast on one foot. Zimmel saw the sense in that explanation, and so he took off his other shoe!

"Chaim!" I hissed. "Now you want the other shoe too?"

His eyes never stopped laughing into mine as he said solemnly, "Well the first one is not coming up if it doesn't have its mate!"

I just couldn't put a stop to his fun. Naughty as he was, I loved him too much. I just said, "You're absolutely right; it will never come up on the other side if it doesn't have its mate."

Our brother Yakov looked at me and asked, "Are you sure you want to let Chaim do this? This is too much even for him!"

"Well, do you think it will come up faster on the other side without its mate?"

Yakov just smiled and told me we will all pay for this one. Yitzhak declared, "I don't think it will ever come up!"

The other kids continued to stare at the "lake" in complete silence.

"I don't think we have a choice," I whispered.

Chaim agreed and put the other shoe into the water and pushed it carefully along the same green path as the first shoe. At exactly the same spot, we heard it again. *Glug, glub, glug.* The air bubbles came up as the second shoe joined its mate at the bottom of the slew.

Now we all just sat for another half hour. Zimmel looked despairingly at Chaim. Zimmel had dainty feet, not used to running all day over rocks and pebbles barefoot as we did. Our feet were tough and calloused from playing outdoors all summer without shoes.

Zimmel started to complain. "I need my shoes back."

I reminded him he still had his socks, which was better than we had. We only got one pair of socks in the winter, and then when they got holes, Mama would mend them over and over again until we could get another pair.

So we waited some more, but the shoes must have decided to go a different route. They did not want to come up on the other side as Chaim had promised. "Maybe they are halfway to Tel Aviv by now!" Chaim suggested.

As Zimmel looked up from the slew to Chaim's face, it finally dawned on him that he had been tricked. "I'm going to tell my parents!" he wailed. "And my father will punish all of you!"

"He'll have to catch us first," Chaim said.

I looked at Yitzhak and said, "Start now." That meant "run as fast as you can, because we will overtake you in minutes." Yitzhak was off and running, his tiny feet going as fast as they could.

I looked at Yakov and said, "Good-bye!" And he got up and left as well.

Then I looked at Chaim. "Fend for yourself, you fool! You had all the fun!"

I took off as he yelled, "Anna, don't leave me!"

My Chaim was very brave as long as I was with him. As brilliant as he was, he never had the stomach for a fight. He could talk his way out of almost anything. However, his courage failed him when he was faced with anything physical.

Yitzhak and Yakov ran home to hide under the bed. Chaim followed me to the playground down the street, farther down the ravine on the other side of the bridge.

We sat down on the swings next to each other, panting from the run. "Well," Chaim asked, "what is our life expectancy this time?"

"Chaim, I think this time you really did it!"

He was still laughing. "Yeah, but you always get us out of trouble."

"You destroyed the boy's shoes! Good, new shoes! We don't even own anything that good. The ones we have, Mama got at the flea market. And she puts in chunks of cardboard to cover the holes."

We didn't go home till well after dark. We were very hungry. When we went into the house, all Mama said was, "Eat now and go to bed! We will talk tomorrow."

I didn't get much sleep that night, anticipating the big beating that was sure to come. Chaim was fast asleep in no time.

Papa promised to replace Zimmel's lost shoes, and he did. However, because I didn't stop this terrible trick from happening, I didn't get any new shoes that winter and had many colds because my feet were often wet from my old torn shoes.

In some ways, it was all worth it. That was one of the best summer days we had had in a very long time.

# Chapter 33

# Waiting

*Haifa—1952*

M onths became years—three long years of corresponding with Fela, trying to convince her to help us get to America. Papa told Fela it was her fault that Mama and I were so sick. They had deserted us. Now if we should die of hunger or pneumonia and repeated lung infections, Papa would never forgive his sister nor speak to her again. He finally convinced her we would not survive in Israel, so at last we received from her the sponsorship documents necessary for applying to immigrate to America.

The immigration department put us on the Israeli Quota waiting list. During this time, we would have to pass many health checkups. The immigration quota meant it might take a few years before our number came up and we would be approved for departure to our new home in Mama's golden land—New York City, America.

Now the concern was to work hard and save as much money as possible so we would be able to book passage on a ship for all six of us when it came time to leave.

While we waited, life went on. Papa's expectations of a great life in his Israel had all but disappeared. Instead of working as a pastry chef making beautifully decorated cakes and tortes, poor Papa was lucky to get short-term jobs as a bread baker, a task usually filled by uneducated workers with little talent, and he felt shame to be included with them. This task did not suit Papa's creativity, and he was very unhappy. To Papa, it was a fate as good as death!

I asked Papa why his jobs did not last, and when he answered my question, I could see his heart was breaking. "Well, Anna'le, this is a very new country, and things are still being worked out."

"What things, Papa?"

I could hear the pain in Papa's voice and something else that was never there before when he talked about his beloved Israel—a sound of deep resentment. *Toward whom?* I wondered.

He continued. "We are a poor country, and the work is very hard. The wages are low, and the owners of the bakeries will hire anyone who will work long hours for very little money. Arab day laborers undercut us all the time, because they are willing to accept anything and be worked and treated like slaves. It makes me sick to listen and watch them all, but I am helpless to do anything. I am overworked and hungry and tired, and I am too weak to fight them all."

That was the longest speech I heard my papa give.

"What has happened to our Zionists, Papa? Will they not help us as they promised?"

"They did the job they promised. They brought us to our homeland, but they did not promise to feed us for the rest of our lives. That is our job. Mama and I will work, and eventually we will prevail. Life will get better, you will see, even if the Arabs are taking away the jobs the Jewish people need to survive."

"Papa, why is greed in charge? Don't they care we do not have food? Mama, the boys, and I are all sick with hunger! How can we build a new country on empty bellies? The Arabs should not be given one job as long as we have one Jew out of work and one hungry Jewish child!"

Papa gave me a weak hug and said, "Yes, my little Zionist, you are right. Unfortunately, the factory owners and shopkeepers are not of like mind with you. And remember, the Arab people also need work, and they have little ones to feed."

"I don't care," I said. "They are not Jews and do not belong in my country. They have many Arab countries where they could go! We should throw all the Arabs out of Israel and send them back to the Arab lands they came from. This land is for the Jewish people. Mama told me many times that G-d gave us this land, and we recently won the big war against all the Arabs. So why are they still here? We only have one Israel and have nowhere else to go!"

"We will talk another time, Anna'le. I have to go to sleep. I must be up at three in the morning to go to work."

We never came back to this subject again. I watched as my father's health and formerly good spirits faded away. He was a man with little hope for the future.

Mama was also losing hope, even as the dangers subsided in our new country. She felt she no longer had much to offer her little family, and she became increasingly lost to us. She would leave home first thing in the morning for many weeks and not come back for hours. We never knew where she was going.

One day she came home very happy. She had found a job she could do from home. Raincoats! She would make raincoats. Mama had many cutout parts in various sizes that would have be glued together to make the raincoats. Mama spread the parts for one coat on the large dining table after the boys were in bed. I helped Mama do her job.

We had to apply the glue carefully in a straight line along the very edge. After spreading the rubber gum (she called it *kauchuk*), we put the next matching part on top. Using a heavy, handheld roller with a handle, we would roll it back and forth until we pushed out all the extra glue. If some smears did occur, then we would need to use a rag dipped in benzene (purified gasoline) and wipe carefully so as not to damage the coat's fabric. They would deduct any damages from her meager profits. I learned quickly how to do the work. Some days, I pretended not to feel well so I would not have to go to school and could stay home to help Mama with her work.

Inhaling the awful fumes of the *kauchuk* and benzene made Mama and me sick, but we kept working, week after week. I only helped two or three hours in the evenings, because I had to go to school and then take care of the children, so Mama could work and Papa could sleep before getting up at three in the morning.

Saturday was the only day we spent any time at all with our papa. Weekdays when we came home from school in the late afternoon, Papa would be having a bit of food before going to sleep. Mama would make us go outside to play so as not to wake Papa. I hated Papa's night job, because it took him away from us most of the day and all night. That's how it was for the five years we lived in Haifa.

Mama made many wonderful raincoats in all sizes, but no one in our family had a raincoat because we could not afford them. Mama promised that if we finished a certain number of the coats, we might have one extra special meal for the week besides our Shabbat meal. Maybe even an additional small chicken!

In 1962 at the Columbia Presbyterian Hospital in the Bronx, doctors diagnosed Mama with stomach and colon cancer. Following extensive tests, one of the doctors asked if we had ever owned a gas station. It appeared the damage to Mama's body was the result of exposure to considerable quantities of gasoline.

"No," Papa and I said in unison, and Papa added, "We have never had anything to do with gasoline."

However, the next day, I sought out the same doctor to tell him what I suddenly remembered. For more than a year, Mama had worked on the raincoats and inhaled benzene and rubber glue fumes. The continued exposure was the likely cause of her cancer these many years later.

# Chapter 34

# The Donkeys of Haifa

*Summer 1952*

It was still summer all over Israel, and it would continue to be hot for another month. My brothers and I were running out of things to do or trouble to get into. School would not start for a few more weeks, and we were becoming desperate.

The pigeon fiasco had barely left the minds of everyone in the neighborhood. Every now and then we would see one of the more sensitive children come to visit the pigeon's grave. They would come to the slew and toss in a flower. The ground around the slew was becoming clean of all the little dandelions as the kids picked and sacrificed them as gifts to the pigeon.

Summers in Haifa were usually quite wonderful. We would go off to the beach and stay there for the day, or we would go up to the foothills of our Mount Carmel, just to the right of the ravine where we lived. Mama said, "Your white skin is becoming as brown as the Arabs'."

It was a long walk, a hard climb—a decent hike by any standard. And it was the only time we wore our shoes, because, of course, one can't climb or hike on hills or mountains without shoes. Mama warned us that if we destroyed our school shoes, she would punish us severely.

We especially liked one particular plateau a couple hours away. The yard around the house had many wonderful fruit trees—figs, huckleberries, and several citrus trees.

Sometimes we would see donkeys in the yard with ladders and large cans full of paint strapped to their backs. The animals would be standing patiently next to the small white house with the closed green shutters. We never saw anyone, and we did not care. We had no idea to whom the home, donkeys, or trees full of fruit belonged. We just came to visit the trees and taste all the delicious fruit they had to offer us, as we had been doing now for years.

Obviously, someone lived there; the small house was always nicely painted and very white. There were flowers planted all around, and they blended well with the natural environment and wildflowers that grew in the area. There were big, beautiful fig trees on either side of the house.

One of the fig trees grew green figs that became almost yellow in color when they ripened. Those figs would sometimes be as large as my fist. When the figs could not get any bigger, they would burst, and in the center were several drops of honey. It oozed from the fruit onto our fingers. It was so very sweet, and we always licked our fingers. To enjoy the fruit, all we had to do was climb up and sit on one of the big branches, or even lie down on one, and lick the honey from our hands and then eat only the heart of the fig.

The other fig tree also started out looking green as any fig, but by the late summertime, its big figs ripened into a deep, dark purple. We kids called them the black figs. The dark figs were just a little different and had a milder taste than the green figs. The honey in the center of the black figs also tasted different, and the skin was much thinner. We didn't even think of eating the peels, though they were delicious too. You had to give the rest of the fruit to the donkeys; that was my rule.

The fruit was so plentiful you could be very generous with yourself and the donkeys. They loved the figs as well. We split the fig right at the center with our fingers or our teeth and then ate the hearts of the figs, first one side and then the other. Then we just threw the rest of each fig to the donkeys while they waited patiently. They were very grateful to have them.

In time, we became friends with those donkeys. They spoke to us with that wonderful voice and sound to let us know they thought of us as friends: "Yee-haw, yee-haw!" They had us giggling with delight.

We all learned to speak to them in their language; it was great fun. Sometimes I would even mount one of them and just sit there. We never took them anywhere, and I helped my brothers to sit on them as well; they didn't even buck. "You should never be afraid of animals. They're good to get to know, and they work hard for you. They can be friends and helpful," I told my brothers.

There were two other trees in this small mountain plateau. Huckleberry trees. One grew big black berries and the other had huge snow-white berries—juicy, delicious, and sweet. The choice was ours as to what we wanted to eat that day, hour, or minute. The only thing we needed to do was to find a nice big branch and sprawl out, or even lie down and just barely move. Just as lazy as could be, we would reach out, pluck a fruit, and put it into our mouths. We didn't wash them. Mama always washed things. I never understood why, because we never got all the rain we needed in Israel. I always thought Mama was wasting water.

We would be up in our mountains, enjoying the fruit and enjoying the trees, the flowers, and our friends the donkeys. There was a well there, covered with thin wooden planks, sheets of wood, and then on top of all that some rocks. We would remove it all, send the bucket down to get some ice-cold water, and bring the bucket back up. Oh, it was the sweetest water in the world—*so* wonderful and very cold. We would drink the water and eat the fruit and, of course, get sick a few times and then go back to eating more fruit and drinking more water.

We spent many a happy summer day like that, never meeting the owners of the property. I have a feeling they may have known they had had visitors. I can't believe so many of us kids eating off their trees week after week during the summer would not have been noticed. We did make a dent in the fruit trees. But we never took any of the fruit home with us; we just picked what we could eat while on the trees.

One morning, Chaim was out on our bedroom terrace (the four of us shared the same bedroom) when he saw an Arab man coming down the road from the right side of the mountain slope, toward our valley and road. "Come, everyone, right now! That Arab man looks to be at least twenty years old, maybe older! Even thirty! An old man!" Chaim announced as the man walked along our ravine road.

"Hey! Here come our friends!" Chaim exclaimed.

"What friends, Chaim?" We all ran out onto the terrace that faced the front road beside the ravine.

"They are coming," he said. "I can hear the clicking of their hooves on the rocky dirt road. Do you hear them?"

The donkeys were coming.

There he was, a brown-skinned Arab man. He was dressed all in white and was riding one of the larger donkeys. I knew that painters dressed in white clothes so you could not see if they spilled some of the white paint. All the other donkeys were loaded down with paint buckets and brushes, and one of them carried several ladders. This was our first time to identify the owner of our friends the donkeys.

We could see the man was very proud to have a long caravan of donkeys jogging behind him. They were all very valuable, so we knew he was a wealthy man. I thought it was nice to know whose trees we were enjoying every summer.

"Chaim, maybe we should run down and say thank you."

Chaim snapped, "Are you crazy? He is an Arab! He could kill us for eating his fruit!"

"Yes, he is an Arab, but he lives here, and he is our neighbor."

"No! You don't understand. He is an Arab! I was told not to make friends with them!"

"We ate his fruit and drank his water. Don't you think we should go and say thank you?" I argued.

"Why? Do you want him to kill you?"

We watched silently as the proud Arab and his donkeys passed by.

Everyone was so afraid of everything; they were afraid of us, and we were afraid of them. What a life! *So much for freedom in our new homeland—this land we must share with people who hate us!*

A week or so later, my brothers were getting very restless; all the kids in the neighborhood were getting restless. We could only go to the beach so many times and stay there for just so long until we were burned to a crisp. A bit overcooked, we couldn't go back for several days, and Mama made us wear shirts so we wouldn't get any more sun. Some kids were even getting tired of my Tarzan stories, and I was too busy reading books to play with them or look after any of them.

I could not be bothered with any kids on that Saturday morning. I did not tell them anything about the books I was reading until I would finish each one. Only then could I condense the story so I did not have to spend hours talking with them about it.

My brothers had left earlier that morning seeking a new game or activity. My mother kept asking me where they were. Each time I would tell her they were just outside playing. I had no idea where they were, but I wasn't about to admit it or I would be sent out to look for them.

"Why aren't you with them?" she asked.

"Oh, I am going to be with them very soon. I just need to read two more chapters to finish the book and get a drink of water, and then I will go out to be with them."

The next time Mama came into our room she asked me again why I was not with my brothers. This time I said I needed to use the washroom. I came up with many excuses, but I had not seen them in several hours, and I had no idea where they were.

Just then, I heard someone from outside yelling. "Anna! Come see your brothers."

*Oh my G-d, what have they done now?* They always did something they weren't supposed to do. Of course, I was the one who would be punished by my mother for not having been there to see that it didn't happen.

I begged, *Oh please G-d, don't let this be anything I can't fix. This has got to be something I can fix!* I went out onto the terrace and looked to the big hills on the right. A thundering sound was coming from the road—a caravan of donkeys! They were running very fast. They were storming down our road, running as if (as Chaim put it hours later) someone had put a hot pepper in their bums! That is exactly how they were running.

Atop the big donkey in the very front was my brother Chaim, holding onto the mane and screaming, "Yahoo!"

We had seen the cavalry do that in a cowboy movie as they came to rescue some settlers. Mama gave us some money now and then, and we would see one or two films: either a Tarzan movie or cowboys and Indians. I always felt sorry for the poor Indians. Just like the Jewish people, someone took their land from them.

Chaim was riding on the first donkey, happily waving one arm. More kids from our neighborhood were on the other donkeys, and near the middle of the caravan was my poor brother Yakov. He was holding on tight and looking at me in silent terror. Yitzhak, white as a ghost, was clinging to the second-to-last donkey. He was scared out of his mind, lying on the neck of the animal and holding on with arms and legs.

The nice Arab man, this poor man, was running behind them. Nearing the last donkey, he grabbed its tail. Now he was chasing and running behind the animal and holding on for dear life. He looked as if he were waterskiing but was almost yanked off his feet. The animal kept looking back and making all kinds of angry noises, and I told myself, *We are all going to be killed!*

"Mama! Your sons; they're riding!"

"What are they doing? Are they having fun? Are they okay?" Mama asked. "Don't disturb me now. I want to finish the laundry before they come home."

"*Mama!* Come quick!" Something in my voice told Mama to come quick, so she came quick!

"I am going to faint" was the first thing out of her mouth.

"Mama, not now! This is no time to faint. What do I do?"

She ordered, "Go chase after them!"

"Chase after the donkeys, Mama? They are halfway down the street!"

"Go get my sons! You will get yours later!"

"Getting mine later" was a guarantee of punishment. As for me coming back later to get it, that was *not* guaranteed.

I started running, chasing after the donkeys and my brothers. Chaim was screaming with delight; the kids were all screaming with delight—or just screaming.

There was just one small problem with all this fun: if I didn't catch up to them in the next few minutes, the donkeys running down Wadi Rushmia Road would enter the intersection with Iraq Street, now known as Kibbutz Galuyot Street.

If the boys and donkeys were to get to the three-way intersection, they would surely die. It was one of the busiest thoroughfares in the lower part of the city of Haifa, full of buses and trucks, etc. Now I must outrun the donkeys. I had participated in running meets for my school. I was considered one of the very best sprinters—a very fast short-distance runner. I had even received commendations, and I was the fastest one in our school for my age, as well as the next few age groups.

To myself I said, *Well, if you are going to get any championship medals, you better win the gold today and save your brothers.* I started running, and I ran very fast. As I passed the Arab, he was still holding onto the tail of his donkey. He let go with one hand and waved his fist at me. He screamed that if he caught the one in the front, the leader whose name was "Chaiuum," he would kill him!

I told him, "You will not catch him; if anyone is going to kill him, it will be me!" Now I was running faster still. Next to the donkey that still carried my little brother Yitzhak, I grabbed hold of the mane, but the donkey kept yanking his head from me. I slapped him on his nose a few times, running and yanking and slapping all at the same time. That slowed him down sufficiently for me to grab Yitzhak from his back. I put him down and yelled, "Go home!"

Now I was chasing the other donkeys. As I caught up with Yakov and asked him if he was okay, he pleaded, "Please stop this thing!"

I told him I didn't know how, and he said, "Okay, I will see you later." I kept running toward the front of the donkey parade. If I could stop the first one, the others would come to a stop as well—at least, I hoped so!

I finally caught up to Chaim. He laughed as he looked at me. This monster, my dear brother Chaim, was laughing with delight. Then he said, "Hey, Anna'le, any idea how to stop this thing? I'm not having so much fun anymore."

I suggested, "How about if you use your knees and try to direct him into the hill or up the side of the mountain; he may stop."

Chaim grumbled, "The donkey will not go there. He won't do anything I say; donkeys are stupid."

"*You* are not stupid; just do as I say! You took him; *you* stop him! You don't even have a rope around his neck; you have nothing, not even a saddle—just a naked donkey."

By pulling his head to the side by his mane, I kept slapping the nose, and he kept yanking. We got him to slow down a bit. I said, "As soon as he slows enough and you think you can jump, tell me and I'll catch you."

After a few attempts, Chaim finally jumped off and a couple of the donkeys bumped into each other. In the chaos, Chaim and I pulled Yakov from his donkey. "Now," I said, "we better run ten times faster in the opposite direction to get away from that angry Arab man. What about the other kids?"

"Just tell them to jump and run," Chaim said.

So as we ran, I yelled to the other kids, "The minute you can jump off the donkeys, do so … and run! The Arab is very angry, and he is right behind us."

There was that poor man, running to keep his donkeys from being killed on the main road. Thank G-d they stopped just in time.

My brother Chaim, the hooligan, the instigator! Chaim the Great, the leader of the new Israel! I was certain he was the one responsible for this afternoon of trouble. I found out later that I was right. Chaim was bored and only wanted the donkeys for a fun joyride. Then he persuaded every child in our neighborhood to climb onto the donkeys, assuring them they would just be walking nice and slow.

Of course, no one told the donkeys of Chaim's plan. No one knew they were going to stampede; with Chaim yelling *"Yellaha! Yella!"* it didn't help. *"Yellah, yellah"* in Arabic means "get going" and "faster." *"Yellah Imshi"* meant "faster still," and he kept on yelling those words.

Those trusting kids imitating Chaim had come along for the ride. As more children chased after the kids on the donkeys, it had turned into a parade, a fun festival. Now we Markus kids took the longest, most roundabout way to get home.

Mama asked why we were all so sweaty. "Where were you for so many hours?"

"Oh, we were just playing in the playground, that's all." I knew my reward for not telling the truth would eventually come, because Mama had seen the boys on the donkeys.

"Mama, the donkeys didn't run; they were walking nice and slow, just for your sons."

"I saw them, Anna! They were galloping!"

"No, no, Mama. They only went a few feet like that, but farther down the street, when you stopped watching, they just walked slowly, and the kids jumped off. Then we went to the playground."

"How did they stop them?" Mama wanted to know.

"Oh, Mama, Chaim was so good! He just pulled on the donkey's neck, and it just stopped for him. I wish you could have seen it; it was wonderful!"

Mama looked first at Chaim and then back to me. "Is this true?"

I just nodded my head but didn't dare look at her or say a word. Chaim smiled at Mama with that special smile of his.

I knew I was in trouble, because I knew he would tell Mama the truth as soon as I left the room. Before dinner, I would be spanked for saving his life and would not get anything to eat. Chaim the Great had done it again.

Sometime later—I don't know how long—we were still peeking from the terrace or out the window every few minutes to see if the donkeys had survived the trip.

Then we saw the Arab man coming back with his donkeys; he had ropes around their necks. He had a long string of them, and he was shaking his fist in the air yelling. "Chaiuuum!" He walked by our house, staring at our terrace, looking right into our window. "Chaiuuum!" He called in fury, waving his fist in the air.

My mother said, "Chaim go out, someone is calling you."

He said, "It's not for me; it's okay, Mama. I don't feel like playing."

The man called out repeatedly, "Chaiuuum!"

Mama insisted. "Somebody wants to talk to you, so go out on the terrace; don't be rude." Chaim looked at me and asked me what he should do.

I suggested I could pretend I was him, and go out, but Chaim said, "He wants Chaiuuum!"

I went out instead. "He is busy; what do you want?"

"He stole my donkeys," the Arab accused.

"Not my brother," I replied sweetly.

"Of course he did; you saw him!"

I said, "I didn't see a thing."

"You saw him."

"No one stole them. They only borrowed your donkeys and went for a short ride."

"You were not on the donkey?" he asked.

"No," I answered. "It was just some of the neighborhood kids!"

"All your brothers were on the donkeys!" he insisted.

"Not *my* brothers! They are afraid of animals."

"Well they were not afraid today!" he said.

I finally nodded my head in agreement. "You are right. They were not afraid today." I hurried to add, "They will never do that again. I promise you—my word is good."

Chaim the Great was a magician. He could locate or conjure up a naughty situation to get into at least once a week.

# Chapter 35

# Shabbat Meals

Papa's sister Miriam, her husband Ze'ev, and their children lived in Haifa, about an hour's walk from our little home at the foot of Mount Carmel. Their son Ami was a little younger than I was, and their daughter Carmella was about the same age as Chaim.

Mama merely tolerated the adults; she loved the kids. I loved my aunt and her children, though Mama and I grew to hate their recurring "surprise" monthly visits. They would show up uninvited just in time for our one decent meal of the week, our Shabbat lunch—every month!

Mama always greeted the kids with smiles, hugs, and kisses and asked them all to come into the big living/dining room. They all sat at our big table, talking with my father about the politics of the month, while Mama dragged me out and told me privately that I must take my brothers to the playground yet again for two hours or more. She would serve them and Papa the food intended for our Shabbat meal.

Aunt Miriam would never get up to help my poor, sick mama with serving the meal. She and even my father ignored Mama and treated her like a servant whenever his relatives came to visit.

I could see what was happening, the injustice of it all, and I complained long and loudly to Mama.

"Do you plan on giving away all our food again? Shabbat lunch is the only good meal we have all week. What little food we have must last us for at least two days! Each time they show up, that family and Papa get to eat all the food! Mama, you don't even get a bite. You, my brothers, and I will have no food again for two days! Why don't you just serve them some tea and send them away? They never even do as much as that for us! Why do you do this every month? Why do you love them more than your own children?"

"No, I do not love them more. I do not love your aunt and uncle!" Mama said. "Your father and the laws of hospitality make me do this!"

"Mama, they are parasites, selfish opportunists," I protested. "They steal the food from my brothers' mouths! Aunt Miriam and her husband are taking our food. They both have good jobs and plenty of food to eat. You and Papa do not have as much as they do!

"Mama, when we visit them once every other month, why do they never allow my brothers and me upstairs to their apartment? We must always remain in the street to play. We are never given lunch at their home. Aunt Miriam just calls her two children to come up for lunch and tells us to wait in the street till they are finished, never offering us so much as a glass of water. She doesn't care we are very hungry. Only once did Carmella bring us each a slice of bread with jam on it."

I dreaded those visits and lost all affection for my Aunt Miriam. She and her husband continued that abuse of Mama's hospitality for five years. In all those years we lived in Haifa, they never invited our whole family to eat with them on Shabbat or any other time. They invited Papa alone to their house maybe three times for Shabbat. It seemed he loved these people, his "family," so much more than he loved us.

I felt that in Papa's need to appear successful and to accommodate his relatives, he allowed even his own wife, my brothers, and me to go hungry on many a Shabbat.

Sadly, I had started to lose love and respect for my father. On one of those occasions, as I waited hungry in the street, I yelled out for all to hear, "Papa, today I do not love you at all!"

# Chapter 36

# Superstitions and
# Sweet Lefkie

The long, fun-filled days of summer in Haifa lingered on and on, hot and humid. The Markus kids practically lived outdoors, running barefoot and wearing shorts and sleeveless tops. Our clothes, though old and shabby, were clean, as Mama or I washed them every night. Our skin was darkly tanned.

Always playing in the street, my brothers and I had a nickname that I hated. A shriveled, ugly old Romanian woman who often sat on a big rock by the bridge called us "the Gypsies." I didn't like her, and I kept thinking G-d should not have let this witch live for so long!

Then, after the death of the white pigeon, I began to hear rumors that something terrible would soon happen on our street. The source of the rumors was the old woman's young granddaughter, Anutzia. She was a pretty, blond woman and the mother of two small children—a baby and a blond boy named Lefkie. Four-year-old Lefkie was a very sweet, well-behaved little boy with big blue eyes. He sometimes played with my brother Yitzhak.

Talking to a small group of women, Anutzia declared, "He started it all! He killed the big white bird. That pigeon was high in the sky, and he brought her down with one stone!"

I knew she spoke of my brother Chaim.

The women stood with arms folded, muttering their contempt for such reckless behavior.

"You mark my words." Anutzia continued as she glared at me. "There will be a death on our street very soon—the death of a child—and it will all be the fault of those Gypsies!"

I ran home to my mother to tell her what Anutzia had said. "Mama, is our Chaim in danger? That woman said a child will be dead soon! And she called us Gypsies!"

Mama just laughed and told me the Romanians had even more superstitions than the people of Poland and Russia. They themselves were the real Gypsies—not the *Ashkenazim* (Eastern European Jews) of Poland! I was not to pay any attention at all to such nonsense.

"Nothing will happen to any of our children, Anna. She needs to worry about her own children! Just go to the kitchen and get the money for the iceman. He will be coming soon and our icebox is almost empty. Our food will spoil if you don't get the ice today."

My mama had made predictions in the past, and she was always correct. So I did not worry for our family.

As I ran to the kitchen for the money and the sharp, iron-clawed ice tongs, Mama called out a reminder. "Make sure you take your brothers with you to play. They must go along with you; it is your job to look after them."

Concerned for my brothers, I thought again of that old woman, the witch. I do remember I was not very frightened of her. However, I knew I needed to protect my three brothers. She seemed to want to be near them and the other children and even to touch them. So we did our best to stay far away. I told my brothers never to go near her or even talk with her.

No one knew her name. She was dark and ugly and talked to herself constantly, making predictions and calling people names. She was very old and small with a large hump on her back. She had a long nose with a big wart on top and two big warts on her chin. The one on her nose almost looked like a third eye. She smelled of the cigarettes she smoked nonstop. She called out the same warnings of doom that Anutzia had given.

Now I had work to do. The ice truck was coming.

Twice a week the kids and adults would run from all directions at the sound of the truck horn and little bell the driver rang. Long lines formed, with customers eager to get their ice. Children hoped to get some slivers of ice chips to suck on to cool themselves on a hot day.

When customers gave the iceman their orders, he would pierce the big block of ice with an ice pick and a hammer and cut off the size block that the person wanted. That was when we might get some small slivers of ice chips.

That day I only had enough money for a third of a block. It would not last very long in the heat of our small kitchen. When it was my turn, I paid my money, and the driver cut off a part of the big ice block for me. He pierced it with the tongs I gave him and handed it back to me. It was very heavy, and I had to take my time walking back home, being careful not to drop it. I wanted to hurry back to the iceman's truck to get some ice to eat. Because we could only have ice cream about once a year, the ice chips were a real treat.

I entered our little kitchen, calling Mama to come and help me lift the block of ice into the icebox.

Our icebox looked like a small fridge with a top compartment for the ice. In the very bottom was a large container that collected the water that melted from the ice. Each day Mama or I had to empty the container on the bottom so it would not overflow and flood Mama's prized kitchen floor.

As Mama was helping me with the ice, she asked, "Where are your brothers?" Her voice was strained.

"They are still by the truck, waiting for some ice."

"Go! Run and get them now!" Mama's eyes had a look that told me I must go quickly. I knew that look well. It was a prediction that disaster was on the way.

I ran back out to the road, just in time to get a small, leftover piece of ice. All was well there, but as we were licking our ice pieces, I remembered my mama's eyes and told my brothers we must run back home quickly. "Mama wants us now!"

I asked little Lefkie to come with us, but he wanted to stay behind and get more ice.

My three brothers and I ran across the little bridge over the ravine to our home. As we went up the stairs into the house, the sound of screaming children stopped me dead in my tracks.

I looked quickly toward the road. The ice truck driver ran from his truck as kids gathered around something on the road. Ordering my brothers into the house, I turned back.

Running as fast as I could toward the truck, I pushed some of the smaller kids out of the way. Lefkie was lying on the ground, not moving. He looked like he was just sleeping, but there was a big pool of black-red blood beneath his head.

I had not seen a dead body in some years now. I stood frozen, just staring. No one moved.

Then I heard my own screams, demanding the driver do something. He was the only adult with us. All the others had left with their ice.

He stammered incoherently. "It's too late. He is dead. I didn't see him. I asked all the kids to move back from the truck. I was leaving. I was going to my next stop. Oh, my G-d, what can I do now?"

"Put him into your truck and take him to the hospital," I screamed at him.

"Go get his family!" he yelled back at me.

*Lefkie! Sweet Lefkie! Anutzia! Oh, his poor mother!* My mind whirled.

Then my blood ran cold as I remembered Anutzia's prediction. It was coming true! At the same moment, I remembered my mother's words: "She better take care of her own kids." In the hot summer sun, I felt very cold.

As I ran behind our home in the direction of the small apartment where Anutzia and her family lived, I ran into her father. I blurted out the terrible news.

With barely a pause, he exclaimed, "It's your brother Chaim's fault! He killed the pigeon!"

"No," I screamed back. "It is not Chaim's fault. It's Anutzia's fault for making that terrible prediction."

He ran away with fear in his eyes, as I watched silently. A few minutes later, I heard the horrible screams of a heartbroken mother and then silence, as poor Anutzia must have fainted.

I hurried back to our home to tell Mama and my brothers what had just happened. Mama started to cry, her tears flowing quickly.

After a time, she spoke solemnly. "This is Anutzia's punishment from G-d for being a horrible gossip and for saying bad things about all of us—you kids as well as all the other people in the neighborhood. Poor little Lefkie has been punished for his mother's sins."

"Mama!" I protested. "This was a Jewish child!"

Lefkie was indeed a sweet little Jewish boy, but he had a very bad woman for a mother. Anutzia never foresaw her beloved Lefkie would be the fulfillment of her superstitious prediction. She never imagined her own little son would be lost to her.

We lived on that street for another two years after this tragic event. We never heard Anutzia speak another word of gossip.

Papa found a great new job in Tel Aviv, and in the summer of 1954, we were very happy to move to that vibrant and beautiful city by the Mediterranean where we lived for the next six years.

# Chapter 37

# Mama and the
# Sabbath Candles

*Tel Aviv—1955*

I can hear my mother's beautiful, soft operatic voice in prayer. Mama is standing in front of her family. Our lovely Sabbath table is set with the best silver, linen, and crystal, as well as with her tall silver candelabra with eight arms. Each candle represented a member of the family, as was tradition in the Ashkenazi community.

As Mama lights the candles to welcome the Sabbath, her voice is calm and her face transformed.

Her beautiful face shines with the fervor of the moment, but her tears begin to fall freely down her scarred cheek. Listening to my mama pray and cry every Friday evening for years was more than we could take one particular Friday evening.

After the Sabbath meal, after the songs and conversations, my brothers asked me to find out why Mama cried every time she kindled the Sabbath candles.

Yakov questioned me. "Is this not a happy time, the most important day of the week all throughout the year? Can Mama not be happy for just a few minutes? That is not too much to ask for one evening of the week. Can Mama not do this for us on the Sabbath before our special meal? No one is very hungry or wants to eat after so many tears. The Sabbath meal is the only good meal we have all week, and it is the only time we all sit together as a family."

I had been asking her these questions for many years but had never received an answer. In my heart, I promised myself this would be the last time I would raise the subject.

That evening after our meal, I went to the kitchen and asked Mama the same questions yet again. "Mama, why all this sadness, and why do you shed all these tears every Friday night just before dinner?"

I so very clearly remember Mama's face as she took my hand and walked me to her bedroom. We sat down on her bed, and for a very long time Mama didn't say anything. Her eyes were closed, and I thought she may have fallen asleep.

Just as I was about to get up and leave the room, I heard my mama's beautiful, soft voice whisper as if from a great distance, slowly overcoming great pain, and she began to speak. I don't believe Mama even noticed or remembered I was in the room. Her eyes looked beyond me into the past. She was as far away from me as Poland is from Israel.

I do not know what sights she was envisioning, but suddenly her voice changed to the voice of a much younger woman. Mama was describing a beautiful Sabbath table set for fourteen in anticipation of guests who might come home from the *schul* with her papa.

The eight in her immediate family were her mama, papa, their five daughters, and one young son. Mama's only brother, Aaron, was eighteen and the treasure of the family.

"You must know, my little child," Mama said, "that preparations for the Sabbath were not taken lightly. It was a great deal of work for us all, and even more so for all the servants."

*I didn't know they had had servants! When did the family have servants? How many servants were there, and for how many generations?* So many questions were running through my mind. The realization struck me that I knew so little about my own background, but I didn't dare interrupt her flow of speech with all my questions.

"So much water had to be boiled for all of the family's baths," she continued, "and all the bed linen had to be changed well before noon. The house had to shine, and all the heavy dark furniture had to be polished. I can still remember how our home smelled of honey from the beeswax we used for the polish. My sisters and I put much care, planning, and hard work into preparing the Sabbath table, set with the white lace tablecloth and matching napkins. The best silver had to be polished, and the crystal had to sparkle."

How proud Mama sounded as she saw once more in her mind her family's beautiful Sabbath table. "'You must not forget to fill all of the crystal vases with pretty flowers,' Mama said. 'You must never forget the flowers. You must have them everywhere, in all the rooms.'"

Mama continued. "Your grandmother would light the candles to welcome the Sabbath before anything else could happen at the table. The beautiful cover for the braided breads, the *challahs*, was made of white satin with a large menorah at the center. Delicately embroidered all around it were Stars of David with gold and blue threads. My youngest sister, Bliema'le, made it as a gift for our mother."

Mama's body started to sway slowly back and forth. She appeared to be listening and keeping time to the rhythms of melodies she alone could hear. As she continued to describe all the wonderful dishes the cook and her helpers had prepared, she talked about the food, describing one dish after another. Then she described all of the pretty, long colorful dresses her mama and sisters wore in honor of the Sabbath, dresses with long sleeves and ruffles around the necks, wrists, and hems. The lovely pieces of jewelry that accompanied their dresses were gifts from their parents. They would wait for Papa and their brother, Aaron, to come home from the Sabbath service at the big synagogue. Then the festivities would begin.

"My papa would bring home several guests from the synagogue, people who were travelers from other cities and towns. We always had guests for the Sabbath meal, at times as many as seven men. Some would stay until the end of the Sabbath and depart on Sunday morning after a good breakfast, but some would leave to sleep in other homes after the meal.

"Your grandmother never knew how many to expect until after they all arrived at our home. Then the big moment would come. All the men and then the women would wash their hands and come to the table, standing and waiting for my mama.

"As she walked to the far end of the table across from my papa, she stood for a moment, looking proud and lovely in her black satin high-necked dress with the triple strand of large pearls around her neck. Your grandfather had given her the pearls as a tenth wedding anniversary gift. He had purchased them on his trip to Paris some years before.

"My mother's wig was cleaned, combed, perfumed, and shining. Her delicate, snow-white lace scarf, which looked like a halo, hovered gently on her head and shoulders. As she reached for the matches, she paused for just a moment. She did the same thing every Friday night before striking the match and lighting the candles. She looked with love upon the faces and into the eyes of every one of her children. Then she glanced at her husband. She gently and shyly smiled to him, and he smiled back. She would politely nod to each guest and then adjust her snow-white shawl to cover her head, shoulders, and part of her face. Finally, she would strike the match, light the candles, and wave her hands three times in a circular motion over the top of the little flames, bringing the light and the holiness of this Sabbath evening deeper into our hearts and our home. She would then bring her hands up to cover her face."

As Mama's tale unfolded, I heard her, in a gentle singsong, begin to whisper the prayer over the Sabbath candles.

My mama continued. "Everyone in the dining room waited in silence while Mama prayed. The meal and the rest of the evening were festive, the food and wine very good and plentiful. All the men seated at the table sang the *Shabbos Zmireas*—the songs of joy for the Sabbath— and at times my mama and I joined in the singing. Most times, it was midnight before everyone in the family had gone off to their rooms, and all the guests to their beds.

"My mama and papa would stay in the dining room until the house was quiet. They would sit together to talk for a little while before going off to their suite of rooms in another wing of the big house. The family and the house would once again settle in for the Sabbath."

"Mama," I questioned, "why all the tears? Why all that sadness?"

Mama looked at me as if she was seeing me for the first time in her life. After a very long moment, she replied, "Don't you understand, my only little girl? I am alive! All the people at that table are dead. I am the only one of more than one hundred relatives in my family who is alive! I am the only one here!"

I put my arms around my poor little Mama'le's thin, shivering body. She was shaking even more than before. Mama's tears were now falling freely, covering her face. I put my face next to hers to comfort us both. My face became wet as well, as our tears mingled. I don't know how much time passed.

Mama spoke again. "Every time I stand before the candles, every Friday evening, just as I light the Sabbath candles, those faces from the past are again seated at the table as they were before Hitler and his army of hell's demons descended upon us. Then I hear one of you children say something to another or your papa's voice asking one of you to be good and wait until I finish the prayer for the Sabbath. All at once it all comes rushing back to me that all the faces I thought I saw just a moment ago are no longer among the living, and my heart breaks. My tears cannot and will not stop. I cannot believe I will be able to go on like this for much longer."

Every time she told me she could not go on like that much longer, I knew she was silently willing herself to die. Never accused of being speechless, I, Anna, felt as if I were the mother and she the child as I silently held my dear brokenhearted mother in my arms. Mama the child calmed down a little as I rocked her back and forth.

I had promised my brothers I would have the answers for them, but I still had many more questions I needed to ask. I also knew this might not be the right time for all of my questions. It was never the right time.

My poor, dear Mama'le didn't move. I hoped I was not overstepping some invisible line she had established years ago. Gently, I started asking again.

"I need to know, Mama. Do you ever stand before the Sabbath candles and see Papa, my three brothers, or me? Mama'le?" I could hear my voice pleading. "We are all alive! Can you hear me, Mama? We love and need you so much! We are so alone, and you don't see us. Do you not see *our* faces when you light the candles?

"You have not been raising us, Mama. Our home is lonely and empty without you. No one has much to say to each other. My poor papa loves you very much and misses you as well, Mama. You are so far away we do not know where or how to look for you, to find you and bring you back to us. This is very difficult for us, because even though you can't seem to see us, we can see you!"

I didn't know if Mama'le heard one word I had spoken to her, but I could feel her move very slowly in my arms. She looked at me, and for the first time in my life, I knew she really looked and saw only me. The look of love in her eyes and on her face was the same as the joy in my heart. For the first time in my life, she truly noticed me.

"Anna'le! You, my little *Ankah, Anushka*." These names of endearment she seldom used when speaking to me. "You have been a very good little mama'le to your brothers. Ever since you were six years old, I knew I could trust you to do the right thing for them for the rest of your life. You must; I cannot, and I will not."

Then once again, she was gone, deep in thought and smiling at her memories.

None of us had ever been able to get her to speak of her family and their life before the war. This heart-wrenching story acquainted me with Mama's family history in a way I had not understood until then.

At home as a young woman, Mama's escape after her chores were finished for the day was music, opera, and reading books in the company of her sisters. Family was her greatest love. In the evening, the sisters would gather by the piano, singing wonderful songs, harmonizing, writing, and creating new music and lyrics.

Eventually, Mama started to live with a dream of someday singing in the opera and then meeting a fine young man to marry so she might escape the environment of her mother's discipline.

In 1936, she met my papa, a very progressive young man who did not wear a beard and *payos*, and she fell in love with him. They married in 1937 and traveled from Brzezine to Warsaw, hoping to start a prosperous business and to raise a family. They worked together and were successful on both counts. The business grew, and one year later Mama gave birth to twin boys. Their early life together proved to be loving and prosperous. Unfortunately, the Second World War began, and Mama's joy was short-lived. The young family was confined to the ghetto for about two years. It was from there that the twins, not quite two years old, were taken away to Treblinka and murdered.

Now on this Shabbat evening, I understood that Mama's visits into the world of her ghosts was a condition I would have to accept in order for Mama to stay physically alive and not simply will herself to die. The only wish she had—the only thing that was important to her—was to be with her departed loved ones.

I looked at Mama in my arms in that bedroom and at what had once been a very beautiful face, now scarred by the lash of a Nazi whip. Her eyes were hollow and her cheeks sunken. The Nazi animals had broken or knocked out many of her teeth. They had also torn out her fingernails. I knew how some of that had happened—I was on the wagon with my mama that horrific afternoon.

Every year on the birthdays of Mama and Papa, she asked repeatedly, that as my birthday gift to them I would promise to say nothing to my brothers or anyone else about our family's history as long as she and Papa lived. No matter how hard I tried, I was unable to dissuade her.

Nothing I said or did could convince her it was the shame of the Nazis and not her personal shame. Most of the world had just stood by and watched, doing nothing to help our family, or the one and a half million Jewish children, including my twin brothers and several cousins who had perished. Six million Jews! Murdered in that horrible Holocaust!

"The shame is not ours, Mama! It is not yours or mine. We were not guilty of the horrors that happened to us and to our people!"

My beautiful mama'le put her head on my shoulder and her arms around my body in a warm embrace and then closed her eyes. Mama didn't wish to hear another word I said.

Soon her eyes opened, and once again, she was visiting a distant past. Her face relaxed with a gentle, loving smile as a faraway face or memory appeared in her mind's eye. My poor mama'le was lost to me yet again.

When this happened, I was fourteen years old, and we had been living in Tel Aviv for six months. I knew then that I was much older than my mama was; she never had time to grow up. The clock had stopped for her in the Warsaw ghetto when she learned of the murder of her brother Aaron.

Mama was a young wife with a young family when the war started. After the war, hers was mostly a tragic, unhappy life. Mama's family—her parents, four sisters, one brother, aunts and uncles, nieces, cousins—were all lost. Her suffering left her too traumatized and numb to experience much joy with her young family.

She came to life during a crisis, but the rest of the time she moved about in silence, ever ready to spring into action at the first sign of lurking danger, even as those dangers subsided in our new county. Keeping a home was of no interest to Mama. She often left the house without explanation, taking long walks so she would not have to cook or clean. Her family seemed to matter very little to her. My brothers and I were like orphans in our own home. We loved our mama, but she was only a shadow in our lives.

I will never forgive the Nazis and all the nations that stood by and allowed them to steal Mama's soul, robbing her of the joy she should have had from her four living children. When the Nazis marched into Poland, my mother's life and soul marched out. For her, as for many others, it felt as if it were the end of the world.

I began writing this chapter on March 21, 2002, the fortieth anniversary of my mother's death on March 21, 1962, at the young age of forty-nine. I completed the chapter June 7, 2002, the fifth anniversary of my father's death on June 7, 1997, in Miami Beach, Florida. May their memories be for a blessing.

# Chapter 38

# Betrayed Again

*Tel Aviv—1957*

W e moved to the beautiful city of Tel Aviv in 1954. We lived in a very nice apartment in a newer four-story walk-up building on Hertzel Street. Just down the street was the beautiful, big high school, the prestigious fortress-like Gymnasium Hertzelia where my brother Chaim attended classes.

My three brothers all attended school and were growing big and strong, though all were very thin. Almost every late afternoon and evening, the boys would play soccer. It was a priority to them, and they did very well in that sport. Years later, Chaim became a member of the American soccer team from New York City for the Maccabiah Jewish Olympic Games in Israel. That was his first time to return to Israel after we immigrated to America.

Mama worked when she could get a job. Chaim and I worked part-time while attending school. Papa had a very good job in Tel Aviv earning a great deal of money. He worked for the Israeli Army, making elegant wedding cakes and tortes for young soldiers who were getting married. We should have lived like kings! However, no matter how much money came into our home and life, we saw no improvement in our lifestyle. Mama kept putting the money away for the day we would have all the documents needed to "get out of this hellhole you call a homeland. Only then will we start living and not before!" she declared.

I had a full life. I enrolled in a two-year business college program where my favorite classes were Bible and journalism. I also took classes in ballet, drama, and opera, four to six hours each day and some evenings, as well as callisthenics. I even started dating boys. That was my life, and it was fun as long as I could pretend all was well.

On many a Shabbat, Papa would take me with him to soccer games at the stadium near Jaffa. It was one day during the week he and I could spend together.

Though we lived in a very nice apartment, it was not a happy place. If I was not in class, I was out on a date. I would do anything to escape from my sad, dysfunctional family environment. I despised listening to Mama's constant complaints: the timeline on the Israeli quota for America, the documents taking "longer than the Jewish exile," and "will our life expectancy be long enough to fulfill our dreams?"

Food was still not plentiful, and we wore secondhand clothing and shoes. Mama did all the shopping alone—usually at a flea market. I had started dating and was heartbroken each time I looked at my meager wardrobe. Some of my friends and dates stopped asking me out, because they were embarrassed to be seen with me. I did the best I could to look presentable, but slowly, more and more people stopped inviting me. I did not dare complain again, as Mama's fury was more than I could take.

One July day, I heard screams coming from the long stairway of our apartment. I rushed out to see Mama on the landing, halfway down the steep set of stairs. She looked like a rag doll, her body twisted unnaturally. Strewn all around were official-looking papers.

Mama moaned in pain. My screams for help were much louder than her cries. Neighbors came running, and someone called for an ambulance.

I sat down on the floor and cradled Mama's head in my lap, softly telling her all would be well. "A doctor is on his way to help."

Mama whispered, "If I do not recover from this, you must always remember and know for a fact that those two heartless bitches, your father's sisters, killed me. If I do recover, I will never again allow them into our home or lives. We will go to America soon, even if it is my very last accomplishment in life!"

"Mama, how did they hurt you again?" I asked.

"Read these papers, and you will know they have committed murder!"

I did my best to calm her down, but then she fainted, probably from the pain.

I picked up one of the scattered papers. It was from the American consulate. There, to my horror, I saw that Fela had taken her promised sponsorship for our family and given it to her sister Miriam and her family. Mama had been reading that news when she fainted and fell down the stairs.

Yes, that same family who came to eat all our food one Shabbat of every month for five years, all the while proclaiming they were good Zionists. Good Israelis who gave birth to two Israeli *sabras*, nativeborn children, Jews who would 'forever' live in the land of Israel. Hypocrites!

During those Shabbat lunches, as they stuffed themselves with the food my brothers and I did not get to eat, they pumped my father for detailed information about America and the best way to get there. Yet again, his sister Miriam and her husband, Ze'ev, had deceived my trusting, loving, gullible father. This time I feared it might just cost Mama her life. If my father had been an only child, how much better all our lives would have been! My mama would not have suffered so much for so many years from their selfish, sadistic handiwork.

Hearing the commotion, Chaim came running up the stairs from outside. At the sight of Mama in such a state, Chaim was panic-stricken. I immediately sent him to bring Papa home from work. It was best he have a job to do since his love and fear for Mama would only be an obstacle to helping her.

The ambulance came after a very long wait. They took Mama to the Beilinson Hospital near Petach Tikva. When Papa came home from the hospital, he told me Mama's spine was broken and she would need extensive surgery, but he tried to reassure me all would be well.

I knew Papa was not telling me everything, so I reminded him that I would be sixteen years old in a few days, and it was time for him to tell me the truth.

He began to cry with a hopeless sound I had not heard from him before. "Mama may not come home again," he sobbed, "and what will I do with all of us? The doctors said she will survive, but chances are she might not walk again."

As I stood watching him, I didn't share his hopelessness. I just *knew* Mama would be well again and take us all to America. Now my concern was for her to have the best doctors to save her life and help her to walk again. I promised myself that I would help as always and that she would walk.

Dr. Ashkenazi and Prof. Bachmaran would handle Mama's complicated case. Papa and I went to the hospital to talk with them. They told us Mama had several broken vertebrae in the center of her back, and it would be a very long and complicated surgery. They could not promise she would ever walk but were confident that in time she might recover fairly well.

I left Papa with the doctors. I needed to talk with Mama, to encourage her not to lose hope and tell her the doctors said she would be well again soon. As I entered her room, she was reading from the book of Psalms, and much to my surprise, she was in good spirits.

"Mama, are you well?"

"Oh do not worry, my sweet girl. All is going to be well! I had a dream last night about my uncle Chaim Schotland from Amsterdam, your grandma Rivkah's brother. You must remember him, Anna, from the DP camp in Germany. With his long, blond hair and beard and his sparkling blue eyes, I imagine he looks like our prophet Elijah. He came to me in my dream last night and told me not to worry and that I would continue to be a mother to my children for many years. Uncle Chaim asked G-d to take him if He really needed another soul to go home to heaven when they do my surgery. He asked G-d to take him instead of me! Uncle Chaim told me not to be worried and that he has taken care of everything for me!"

She looked so very happy that I did not have the heart to question it.

"Do you truly believe this, Mama?" I asked incredulously. All I could think was how amazing the story was and how it had lifted her spirits.

*Well, if that works for her, how can I argue?* I thought. I told Papa about it, and he agreed we should just go along with this superstitious belief. If it helped Mama, that was all that was important.

# Chapter 39

# Our Mama Golda

*July 1957*

I had not been feeling well for several days. The pain on the right side of my belly was getting worse every day. The doctor thought it was probably just a very bad "monthly" coming on. However, when the pain did not go away, I went to the doctor again, who now realized I must go to the hospital immediately for surgery before my appendix burst. I requested to go to the same hospital where Mama was waiting for her surgery.

On the morning of my birthday, July 14, I had an emergency appendectomy at the Beilinson Hospital. My poor papa was at his wits' end, with both Mama and me in the hospital at the same time. When he came to see me, he found that my bed was in a hallway because the hospital was so busy. He said he was sorry to see me there and that I might not get a room for another day or two. Then he went home to the children.

I was in a lot pain and felt forgotten by all. The stitches holding my incision together were causing me great pain. In my drowsy state, I thought if I could pull them out, the pain would go away, so I began to tug at my bandages and the stitches.

Just then, a woman's deep voice ordered me to stop my actions immediately. Something about that voice kept me from telling her to mind her own business. She continued. "You are no longer a child. You are a young woman now, and some day very soon you will join the army and make us all proud of you!"

I stopped what I was doing immediately. Even the pain seemed to stop at the sound of her voice.

"Do you know me?" she asked softly.

I turned my head to look at the woman with the familiar voice. "I *do* know you," I stammered. "You are the mother of all Israel! I love you. You are Golda Meir. Papa calls you 'our Golda,' the only sane Zionist voice in our government today!"

Her laughter was deep, wonderful, and infectious. I started to laugh with her and then abruptly remembered my sore belly. As I was about to call out in pain, she took my hand and said, "This future soldier of Israel must not be left and forgotten in the hallway! In our land of Israel, men and women are all equal, and we can all achieve anything we wish. You must remember that!"

I promised I would, and I remember her too.

I was to learn she had undergone surgery a few days earlier and wanted to lift the morale of all the sick. She made her way throughout most of the hospital, starting with the very young children and then continuing on to the rest of us. She did that for several days while she was in the hospital. As a great admirer of this fine stateswoman, I was very gratified to have met her.

Good to her word, I was moved from the hallway to a room that same day. As soon as I was able to get out of bed, I went to visit Mama who was still waiting for her operation.

Papa was beside himself with anxiety. Trying to spend as much time as possible with Mama and me at the hospital while still having to tend to the boys, he was taking too much time off work, and he feared he might lose his job. I told Papa I would get the doctor to release me early so I could take care of the kids.

They discharged me within a week, though I could not yet walk very well or do much work around the house. My brother Yakov, not yet twelve, helped me with the cooking and cleaning. He was always a good, helpful boy. My just being there made it easier for Papa to go to work.

Finally, the day came when Mama would have her surgery. Papa asked me to make sandwiches and put some fruit and water into a big bag to take with us to the hospital. We took the bus to Petah Tikva and arrived about nine o'clock in the morning. The surgery had started at six o'clock, and they told us it would take a few more hours. I took my brothers out to sit on the grass under a tree. They were very frightened, but I insisted on believing in Mama's dream about her uncle Chaim and his promise.

I did not dare ask, "What if?" No! Mama *would* survive, I was sure of that. She *had* to. She had not come all this way to be defeated before accomplishing her big dream of going to America.

# Chapter 40

# Mama's Surgery

Some hours later, I left my brothers under that tree on the hospital grounds and entered the large medical facility. I found my very pale papa in the basement near the operating room. As we stood there frightened and silent, Dr. Ashkenazi and Prof. Bachmaran came out of the surgery suite, their surgeons' coats stained with blood.

"Oh my G-d, is my mama alive?" I yelled out.

The two of them looked at us. One spoke. "Yes, your mama will be coming through this door on her way to the recovery room. Do not expect her to talk to you. She will be sleeping for many hours. All is well. Go home now and come back tomorrow to visit."

Papa thanked them sincerely. As the doctors started to leave the room, another man pushed Mama's gurney into the waiting area where we all stood. Papa and I moved immediately toward her, and the bed stopped in front of us. Mama opened her eyes, smiled at me, and said to Papa, "Take good care of the children. I will be home soon."

Behind me I heard one of the doctors exclaim, "This cannot be possible. She just spoke!"

The other doctor replied, "She told me her uncle Chaim would be with us to watch over her."

I turned to the doctors and said, "My mama is never wrong!"

"Your mama's surgery went well, but it will be a very long recovery." With that, they left the room.

Papa and I went quickly outside to the frightened boys and told them Mama was going to be well again and back home soon. We all hugged each other with joyful tears and felt closer to each other in that moment. We left the hospital to return to our home in Tel Aviv.

At the entrance to our building, a nice man had a table set up where he sold things like razor blades, shoelaces, gum, and other small items people could purchase without having to go to a big shop down the street.

He was the first person to ask how Mama was doing. Papa assured him Mama would be back home again in a few weeks. Reaching into his pocket, the man pulled out a telegram that had arrived for us. Papa was much too nervous, and not being able to read Hebrew very well, he handed the telegram to me.

I read it to myself several times before I could read it aloud to my family. I was in shocked disbelief! The telegram had come from Holland. It informed us that the great *Tzadik* (righteous man) Chaim Schotland had passed away. The date and time of his passing was precisely in the middle of Mama's surgery!

I looked at Papa after reading the telegram aloud a few times and I reminded him what Mama had said. "Mama told me how Uncle Chaim came to her in a dream and said that if someone must die, he will go in her place so she could continue to be a mother to her children! Papa! He kept his word!"

Papa stood in shock. "Yes, I remember you telling me about that dream. Do you really believe in such things, Anna'le?"

"Well, Papa, the important thing is Mama believed the dream. It helped her stay positive, and it got her through the worst of the operation."

I felt great sorrow for Uncle Chaim's passing. I loved my mama's uncle very much; he was always very good to me in the camp.

The next morning when the kids were off to school, Papa and I took the long bus ride back to Beilenson Hospital to see Mama, who was now in intensive care.

Over her bed was a structure like half of a wooden tunnel. It was there to immobilize her and to keep anyone from touching her. Staff could remove it for her care, but she would have to remain in it for at least three weeks.

The kicks of Nazi boots had injured her back and ribs previously. Now the fall down the stairs and the broken vertebrae had greatly magnified her injuries.

Surgery had fused her fractured vertebrae, but her very pale face still registered considerable pain. I felt her pain, and pity arose in me. I knew I could forgive all of her transgressions against me. All I wanted at that moment was to have her back home with us. I wanted to see her smile again. I wanted to witness at least a few good days, weeks, or, if we were very lucky, even years in which my mama would finally know some joy and happiness.

I also knew this would not happen until Mama could get us all safely to New York City, to her America. That day I made up my mind to do everything possible to help her achieve her goal.

When we went back to visit Mama two days later, Papa and I met first with the doctor. I immediately asked, "Did you have a big problem around eight thirty in the morning during Mama's surgery?" Before he could reply, I handed him the telegram and said, "Mama's Uncle Chaim in Holland promised to die for her."

Doctor Ashkenazi looked shocked as he nodded his head yes. "We did almost lose her at that time. We worked very hard to bring her back!" The doctor looked at the telegram again and then at us. "Do you believe in this?" he asked.

"I know I believe G-d can do anything that pleases Him, and it pleased Him to let Mama live! As to the dreams and Uncle Chaim passing away the moment that Mama almost died, I will never attempt to explain G-d's miracles."

Shaking his head in amazement, the doctor gave us a good report about Mama. "Some day she will walk again with a cane, but walk, she will!"

"Doctor, I am a dancer, and I know I can help Mama strengthen her muscles and teach her to walk again one day without a cane."

"Well, it will be lots of hard work and take a very long time, but I won't discourage you from trying once she has healed from the surgery," he conceded.

We went to Mama's room then, and though she was still in pain, she was able to talk with us. To our amazement, she told us another dream she had while she was in surgery.

"Uncle Chaim came to say good-bye and told me to enjoy a good life with my children. He then kissed me on my forehead and told me he was going to take my place and would not be back again to see me. When I awoke, I was no longer in surgery. And I saw your two frightened faces outside the operating room."

Papa and I looked at each other. I knew what he was thinking, and I shook my head no! This was not the right time to tell Mama that her beloved uncle, a survivor of the Holocaust, was no longer with us—that he had indeed saved her life that very day!

We talked then about the children and made plans for her return home. I felt Mama needed a reason to get better, and she would be happy and get well faster if she could look forward to something of great importance. Nothing was more important to her than going to America. So at that moment, I made a very important decision. I told Mama I would no longer stand in her way but would instead help with anything she needed to get us all to America.

Mama finally came home from the hospital. I worked with her every day, helping her with stretching exercises and gradually building up her strength. She managed to walk slowly with the help of a cane, but soon she put that aside, and life eventually went back to normal. Mama never complained, and she got well much faster than anyone expected. Her determination to get back to life was amazing.

Chaim and I gave Mama every penny of our part-time work so we could save as much money as possible. We wanted to help any way we could to establish our new home in the United States.

In preparation for leaving, Mama hired a tailor shop to make several suits for the boys and Papa and three new dresses for me. She also ordered a fur coat for herself—a full-length, black, broadtail lamb coat. We needed shoes and some personal items, and we got them new this time—not from the flea market as before.

For Israelis immigrating or even leaving on vacations, the government allowed them to take only ten America dollars per person out of the country. Therefore, many people looked for ways to get around this regulation. My parents had been sending money back with visitors from America, and even with friends of friends. One of Papa's uncles in America stashed it away for us, a nest egg awaiting our arrival in that country.

Now we were only weeks away from sailing, and we still needed to sell our beautiful furniture and other items that were impossible to take. Two suitcases per person is all we were allowed. One of my big suitcases was full of my books, which I refused to leave behind.

Tension and excitement were building in our home. Mama was so happy her dream of taking her family to her "golden land of America" was nearing fulfilment.

# Chapter 41

# Graft and Corruption

*Haifa—1952*

Once settled in Haifa, Mama and Papa dreamed of opening a small bakery. They believed that with just twelve sacks of flour a month and lots of hard work, they could build up the business to employ others just as they had done in Warsaw. All they needed was a business license.

Mama, ever hopeful, set her mind to getting the necessary paperwork done—a daunting process. She could converse in five languages, but Hebrew was not one of them so she found herself redirected to many different departments and offices. Often, staff seemed to ignore her when they couldn't understand her, or she waited endlessly for someone to translate the application forms.

She returned many times to the same licensing office, despairing of ever having all the documents required for this small business. One particular supervisor who often served her always seemed to need more documents filled out and gave her more attention than one would expect from a manager in a government office. Mama became very uncomfortable when he asked personal questions.

My mama was a beautiful woman in spite of the scar across her face. With her bright olive complexion, sparkling black eyes, and thick, wavy jet-black hair cut in a short and bouncy style, she was a wonderful sight. She added black eyebrow pencil and bright red lipstick for special occasions. Getting her business started was definitely a special occasion.

One day Mama told Mr. Golkin she had had enough of running around every day without receiving her business license. He hinted there were other ways to get things done much faster! When she did not respond in the manner he hoped, he informed her it might take forever to get her papers.

She was shocked and left his office. Necessity brought her back again, but Mr. Golkin was usually unavailable.

One day Mama returned to check on the progress of her application. She took a seat in the waiting room where she would be able to see into Mr. Golkin's office if his door opened. After a while, he opened his door and, not noticing Mama, asked his secretary if the envelope with the Ze'ev Markus license had arrived from upstairs.

As she handed it to him, she replied, "Yes, it is here, and the license had been issued."

Mama, overjoyed, stood up. Still he did not see her, and before she could say a word, Mr. Golkin announced, "I have Mr. Kline in my office; *he* will get this one." He returned to his office, closing the door behind him.

Mama was stunned. Her license, the one she had been running after for more than two years was being stolen right from under her nose!

With tears stinging her eyes, she ran to his door and threw it open. As she marched in, Mr. Golkin said to Mr. Kline, "I see you have 5,000 *lirot*."

There he stood behind his desk counting a big envelope full of money. Bribe money for a license that cost fifty Israeli *lirot* (plural of *lira*).

The two men looked at her in disbelief. "What are you doing in my office?" yelled Golkin. "I told you I can't do anything for you!"

Mama shouted back, "You are a thief and a liar; you are stealing the bread from my children's mouths! You dare to take my husband's license and sell it to Mr. Kline for 5,000 *lirot*? I am going straight to the police. Your secretary knows all about this. I will make sure you are out of a job for this, and I will get our license from you!"

Mr. Kline grabbed the envelope with his money out of the furious Mr. Golkin's hands and ran past Mama as if fearing for his life.

Golkin screamed at Mama to get out of his office, but she walked to the door, closed it, and went back to his desk. She demanded he hand over the envelope his secretary had just given him—the envelope with her license. He opened his desk drawer, took out a small revolver, and pointed it at my mama.

Although Mama had had guns pointed at her before, it was never by a Jewish gangster in her homeland Israel. "I will give you your cursed license, but if you ever say a word of what happened in this office this morning, I will find you and kill you and your family."

Mama took the envelope from his desk and looked inside to make sure it was Papa's name on the license and that it indicated he was entitled to twelve sacks of flour per month. She turned and marched from the room.

Mama told my father all about her frightening morning. Papa wanted her to go to the police, but Mama was not so quick to trust police when she could not explain herself in Hebrew and did not have any proof of what had happened.

"Let's start our new life, Ze'ev, and let someone else put that thief in prison."

The new Markus one-room bakery was on its way.

Press reports later revealed a fraud scheme in which business licenses were being denied to legitimate bakery and restaurant applicants. Unscrupulous officials made huge profits by diverting these licenses, with the goods then purchased legally and sold on the black market.

*Tel Aviv—1959*

In February 1959, Mama had an appointment at the taxation office in Tel Aviv to obtain statements confirming we had paid all our Israeli taxes in full. We required these to get final clearance documents from the American consulate allowing us to leave Israel and immigrate to America.

She was stunned when the official told her it would take him months to locate the documents unless she was willing to exchange "favor for favor." Mama was not naïve. She understood clearly that if she rejected his proposition, she and her family would literally miss the boat! He told her to think it over and come back to let him know.

How dare he? This was Israel, and he was a Jew, not a goy! She was so very disappointed. All she wanted was what was rightfully hers; all he must do was hand her the documents.

That evening, Mama came home devastated, more miserable than I had seen her for some time. When Papa came home, she told him what had happened that morning in the government office. Papa was furious and threatened to go with her to that office the next morning, confront the vulgar little man and box his ears! This time Mama insisted they go to the police. After a long conversation, Papa relented and agreed to go with her to the police station.

Years later, Mama told me of the visit with the police and the very strange plan they suggested. Mama would go back to see the supervisor of the tax department and agree to his advances. She was to tell him the best place for them to meet would be her home, because the kids would be in school and her husband would be at work until later that evening.

One morning about a week later, Mama dressed up very nicely. I noticed she had taken all the clothing out of the large wardrobe in her bedroom. She used her eyebrow pencil and eyeliner and then applied the special red lipstick she only used when going out with Papa to a movie or to visit friends. I told her she looked very pretty.

Mama said, "Anna'le, you must care for the kids after school and do not come straight home. You must stay away until after four o'clock." She gave me four little apples without any blemishes. She also gave me some money for a movie and ice cream. That would be a great treat for us after school. What a great surprise for my brothers!

After we left for school, two police detectives arrived. They stepped into the large wardrobe, leaving the doors ajar so they could see and hear everything. And they waited.

Promptly at ten o'clock as agreed, that little mouse of a man arrived with flowers, a bottle of vodka, and a box of chocolates. "I am so very happy you saw this my way. I promise to be very good to you. We can meet like this as often as you can make time for me until you leave for America," he said.

"When will I get my papers? You promised them to me today. I must have them now, or I will not go through with this plan!"

"Don't get upset. I will keep my word. I have the envelope in my pocket, and I will give it to you as soon as we make love and have a few drinks."

With that, he started to undress himself and told Mother to do the same. Mama was wearing several layers of clothing, including a sweater, a blouse, a skirt, and a long slip. She slowly started to unbutton her sweater, waiting anxiously for the two detectives jump out. Mama was a very modest woman; only in the hot Israeli summer would she bare her arms with a short-sleeved blouse.

Mama realized the detectives were waiting for him to get as close to naked as possible and dare to reach out and touch her. She knew she would have to bring this about as quickly as possible before she lost her nerve.

The detectives later said Mama gave an Oscar-winning performance as she approached the man, now clad only in his underpants. Mama was still fully dressed, so he offered to help her. She agreed, and he removed her blouse and skirt. Mama stood before him in her full-length slip and her underclothing, as he started to caress her shoulders and back.

At that moment, the doors of the wardrobe burst open. The two men jumped out, yelling loudly and ordering the startled man to get to the floor, where they promptly handcuffed him and photographed him in his state of undress.

Mama immediately grabbed his jacket and found the envelope containing her precious documents. When she was sure all was in order, she nodded to the detectives that she now had all that was hers.

"Mrs. Markus, you did well to remove this criminal from his job. He will never again take advantage of people like you. We will meet you at the police station to take your statement."

With that, they gathered up his clothes and marched him out of our home.

Mama was relieved that soon she would be leaving behind the graft and corruption she had experienced so personally in her husband's beloved Israel.

# Chapter 42

# A Family Treasure

*April 1960*

Mama had been especially busy the past few weeks. She sold all of the furniture, which purchasers would pick up later. She had sold the apartment and purchased our tickets. New owners would take possession after we left.

Preparations for our trip to America were finally complete. All we had to do was last-minute packing. Excitement echoed through our almost-vacant home.

In late morning a few days before our departure for the ship, many friends and neighbors came by to wish us well. Some were very happy for us, while others promised to join us soon when they had all their documents in order. Others told me we were traitors to the dream of our forefathers. I nodded my head and agreed with them all, wishing for them to just go away and leave me to wallow alone in my sorrow.

In my heart, I did not wish to go away. I did not want to leave Israel, the land of my Zionist dreams. On the other hand, I eagerly anticipated living in a new land and learning a new language. Mama's excitement had been contagious, and now we all dreamed of America and all the possibilities for a peaceful future.

The knock on the door brought two people I had not seen for some time—Papa's cousin Rosa and her husband, Moshe Hofaizen. Rosa, a sweet, gentle woman, and her very kind, quiet husband had come to say good-bye and bring us a parting gift.

Papa received the large bundle from Rosa and placed it on the dining room table. What could it be, all rolled up in many layers of paper? I stood watching curiously with my brothers as Papa, with Mama's help, slowly removed the wrapping.

There, to my surprise and Mama's delight, was a small Torah scroll purchased specially for us to take to America, a memento from Jerusalem. Papa stood in silence for a moment and then solemnly declared, "We will have to guard her and keep her safe."

The words from Aunt Rosa will stay in my heart for the rest of my life. "Remember who you are and where you came from. Do not allow the American glitter to assimilate you! This new family treasure must stay in your family to bring joy to each member for generations to come."

While Papa thanked them, Mama and I hurried to the kitchen to prepare tea and cake for our loving guests. I listened as Rosa told Papa her vision for the future of the Torah. It was to stay in our home with my parents until the first bar mitzvah of the family. Then the bar mitzvah boy would receive the Torah and become her guardian. As each future son in the family reached the age of his bar mitzvah, he would take guardianship of our new family treasure.

Some time later in New York City, not long after Mama passed away, my brother Yitzhak finally had his belated bar mitzvah. He was next in line to receive the Torah scroll. He was the youngest of my brothers.

Because Yitzhak lived at home with all of us, I decided to keep the Torah safe with me, waiting for the next bar mitzvah boy. It would be many years before Yitzhak married Tzipora. All the while, the family treasure remained in my care. Then their son Doron reached bar mitzvah age.

Doron, my dear nephew and godson, was to be the next recipient of our family Torah.

On the way to the Catskill Mountains for the weekend celebration of his bar mitzvah, I told Doron of our family treasure and of his responsibility as her new guardian. I reminded him that he must pass her on eventually to the next generation. Doron, a fine young man, promised he would take his new responsibility very seriously and carry out the wishes of his grandparents, Devorah and Ze'ev. That weekend, I gave the Torah to his care.

Doron was the first of the grandchildren of my parents to receive the special family treasure. I hope he will not forget his promise to me to guard her well. Aunt Rosa and Uncle Moshe *zt"l* (of blessed memory) would be very proud indeed to see their gift passed down with love through the generations.

No one may give away this Torah or donate it to anyone. She must always go on to the next bar mitzvah boy in our family.

The next recipient and guardian of the Torah will be Ezra Cohen, the grandson of my brother Chaim and son of Sherry and Neil Cohen.

From generation to generation. May you go from strength to strength. (The blessing given to a bar/bat mitzvah child at the conclusion of his or her special ceremony.)

# Chapter 43

# A Surprise for Chaim

*April 1960*

The muffled ring of the alarm clock under my pillow startled me, and in an instant I remembered—I had big plans for today. I jumped out of bed and was dressed in record time.

Chaim was fast asleep in the bed across the room from me. I moved quietly to his bed and shook him awake, warning him to be silent. "Chaim, Chaim. Get dressed quickly! Don't make a sound. We have to leave the house without waking anyone."

"What is wrong? Why? Where are we going?" he whispered. "It is still dark outside!"

"I know. Don't talk; just trust me and get dressed. I have made plans for the day. I have saved money for a long time, and we have food. Now move!"

It didn't take us long to tiptoe out of our apartment and down the four flights of stairs unseen by anyone. We had to walk a great distance, as the local buses were not running this early. I planned for us to be on the first long-distance bus of the day. I would not tell Chaim where we were going. I wanted it to be a surprise. I was happy with my plan.

"Anna, are we going to the bus station?"

"Yes, my brother, we are going to the bus station. We must not leave Israel without you first making this one very special visit! And I will take you there."

When we arrived at the central bus station, I led him to the stop we needed. He read the sign. "We are going to Jerusalem?" he asked with surprise and joy.

"Yes, we are! I will show you the holiest and most beautiful city in the world. Many years ago, Mama told me it is the duty of every Jew to visit and love her in person, even if it is only once in a lifetime. Today, my dear Chaim, you will have the opportunity to love her and admire her, and then, for the rest of your life, in your heart you will remember this day and the holy city Jerusalem!"

I had been saving for this trip for some months, holding back a bit of my earnings from Mama's eager hands. Now that the day was here, and with the food I had packed, I was happy. Within three hours, we were at the downtown Jerusalem bus station.

From the bus terminal, we walked and sometimes took local buses to visit all the historic places and museums.

We started with Hadassah Hospital on Mount Scopus. We sat for a while on some rocks, mesmerized by the beauty of the view. There was talk at that time of creating a synagogue in the great room of Hadassah Hospital at Ein Karem. (The stained glass windows of Marc Chagall would one day light the room when he generously donated them to the hospital. They were installed in February 1962.)

We walked, climbing many hills and mountains all over Jerusalem. We visited the military cemetery and toured the German Colony with its many beautiful homes.

The city was full of budding and blossoming trees and bushes. The colors of the springtime flowers added to our festive mood. The intoxicating perfume of almond trees, covered in pink and white flowers, filled the air.

We visited the famous King David Hotel, and from the wonderful vantage point of the big terrace, we admired the panoramic view of the new and old parts of the city. We stopped for juice and cake on the grand balcony. We saw many impressive homes and businesses built of Jerusalem stone, gleaming bright in the spring sunshine. Three thousand years and more of Jewish history had only brightened her beauty. Knowing this might be the last time to view our historic, eternal capital city brought tears to our eyes, and we hugged as we silently left the hotel.

Walking through the narrow streets was a special experience. Modern office buildings stood next to ancient houses, seemingly out of place. The city's diverse architecture was overwhelming, and we wanted to see more.

From many places in the city, we could see the golden Dome of the Rock. I told Chaim that on that mountain once stood our holy temple, built by King Solomon. It was the greatest and most beautiful structure ever built. Before the Romans destroyed it, our beautiful temple housing the Holy of Holies was located in the immediate vicinity of that Moslem shrine. Because the exact location of Solomon's Temple is not firmly established, our rabbis forbid Jews from walking in that area lest they inadvertently tread on that holy place. The top of the Western Wall, a portion of the gigantic retaining wall of the temple courtyard built by King Herod, is near the mosque.

Chaim was always a very good student and knew our Bible well; it was a pleasure to talk with him on that subject.

Everywhere we went in the city, we thought of another paragraph from the scriptures. We walked in the footsteps of the prophets. We spoke of Jeremiah, Ezra, and Daniel and of how Daniel's dream of the return from the Babylonian exile had come true.

"The prophets can now rest in peace," Chaim declared. "Israel is alive and well!"

We stopped on Jaffa Street to visit Mama's cousin Pola Fogel Kornblum, whose family owned a big grocery store. I wanted to see her for one last time before we left Israel. Though we told her we had our own food with us, she insisted on feeding us yogurt, fresh buns, vegetables, and fruit. When I told her our plans for the rest of our day in Jerusalem, she made big sandwiches and put fruit into paper bags for our supper on the way back home.

"Does your Mama know where you two are?" she inquired.

"No, Auntie Pola, I will tell her this evening. I did not wish to take the chance she would say no, and then Chaim would never have been able to see Jerusalem. She probably thinks we just went for a long walk and will return eventually."

Later, on the bus ride home, Chaim was very quiet. I didn't interrupt his thoughts. After a good while, he spoke my name and looked at me with tear-filled eyes. "Anna'le, this is the greatest gift anyone has ever given me, and I am sure no one will ever be able to surpass this gift of yours. In the future, whenever you may need or want anything at all from me, just ask. I will be happy to grant your every wish!"

Our time in Jerusalem was wonderful—a very emotional day—and I am certain neither of us will ever forget it.

We arrived home late, and of course, Mama asked where we had been. My answer: "I took Chaim to Jerusalem. He could not leave Israel without a visit to our holy city!"

Mama smiled and agreed. "Anna'le, you have done the right thing."

It was a day well spent.

Next year in Jerusalem! Amen.

# Chapter 44

# Our Last Day in Israel

*April 1960*

A light citrus perfume arrived on the breeze outside our fourth-floor walk-up apartment in Tel Aviv. Every spring morning since arriving here, I had stood on our terrace in the warm sunshine, delighted by this wonder. This would be the last time.

Early in the morning on April 29, 1960, two large taxis stopped in front of our building at 100 Hertzel Street. They would transport us with our few suitcases to the port city of Haifa to begin our journey to America. When we walked through those big exit doors, we knew it would be a final good-bye to our beautiful home—the home where we had lived for the past six years—and good-bye to our life in the only Jewish country in the world.

Eleven years and two months earlier, we had landed in Haifa. My papa, the sworn Zionist, had finally, joyfully arrived in the land of his hopes and dreams—Israel, his golden Holy Land. This morning, however, there was only one joyful person in our family. Mama, our mama, could not, would not stop talking. Her excitement overwhelmed us all. She talked about our great new life and the truly great and happy future we would all have in America.

"You will see! Papa will love our new future, and we will all be happy." Mama kept talking as she checked every room repeatedly to be sure we had not forgotten anything.

For the first time in my life, I saw Papa emotionless. He was disillusioned with his broken dreams of life as a Zionist in Israel. He had nothing to show for eleven years of hardship and hard work. He was bitter about the graft and corruption he had witnessed and felt he had no other choice than to leave this country to make a life for our family elsewhere. He told me he would never forgive or forget, and he vowed never to return to Israel. He never did. According to Mama, America was the only place to go.

With the taxis now loaded, we began our final journey to Haifa. Each of us quietly thought of all we were leaving behind—friends, a few family members, others we loved and would probably never see again.

Entering the city of Haifa, I was in awe at how much it had changed since I was last there. Tall, stately trees were everywhere, and the city had grown with many large buildings all around and on top of the Carmel Mountains. It was so beautiful.

However, my heart was troubled. I wanted to stay. *I should not be listening to Mama. I should run away.* Many thoughts tumbled through my bewildered brain. The port was now in sight, and my last chance to escape was all but gone. On this bright spring morning, we had come full circle, back to where we started. We were leaving the land of Zion. Papa's grandchildren would be born in America.

I recalled one evening soon after we moved to Tel Aviv. Yakov and I went for a walk to acquaint ourselves with our Hertzel Street neighborhood. There on a street corner stood a group of young men in their twenties, talking loudly about sports. Typical Israelis. They were all handsome to this fourteen-year-old. One of them was particularly handsome—tall and broad-shouldered, with wavy black hair and gorgeous black eyes. My heart stopped; I was captivated. I fell in love and promised myself that one day I would marry him. As that thought ran through my mind, he looked in my direction and said, "Here's the new little Markus girl with one of her brothers. They just arrived from Haifa."

I was so embarrassed. There I stood in my short shorts, little blouse, and sandals. *Me? A child?*

"Yakov, do I look like a little girl?" I whispered. He replied that I looked like a girl of fourteen.

When we returned home, I ran into the washroom to give myself a closer examination. In my mind, I was almost a woman! But as I looked in the mirror, I did not see any signs of womanhood—no hips, no breasts, not even a hint of curves. I had the face of a young girl with a full lower lip and unruly blond hair flying everywhere.

*How very sad,* I thought. *In this condition, I can never compete for his attention.* My dreams were dashed at that moment. *I will go back to the Yarkon River and the stables. I love the horses, and they love me. They will fill my lonely heart for now. I will go riding whenever I have some money.*

I learned his name was Shlomie, but I didn't see him again for many months. He seemed to have disappeared from Tel Aviv. I pined for him and inquired of his friends where he might be. They only said he was out of town. While longing for Shlomie's return, I threw myself into many activities—attending school, taking dancing classes, reading adventure stories, and making new friends.

Time passed, and I turned fifteen. One day while walking home from school, I was startled to see Shlomie walking toward me. My knees almost gave out, and I could scarcely breathe from the shock and joy of seeing him again. He reached me just as I began to faint and caught me before I crumpled to the ground. When I opened my eyes, I was in his arms, mere inches from his face—such a beautiful smile and gorgeous lips that I wanted to kiss. I didn't! I didn't know how! His eyes seemed to gaze right into my soul, and I knew then I would always love him and be his.

We started dating when I was seventeen. A year or so later, we discussed having our families meet each other and speak of marriage plans.

Shlomie, without my knowledge, asked Papa for my hand in marriage. Because Shlomie was a Sephardic Jew, Papa, who was of European Ashkenazi descent, would not give his permission. I was heartbroken when I learned of Papa's refusal. Respecting Papa's decision,

Shlomie stopped seeing me and began to date other girls. Bitter and angry with my parents, I also began to date others.

Eventually, we began seeing each other in secret. When it became clear my family was going to America, I begged to stay in Israel and live with his mom and family until we could marry. No amount of pleading would change my parents' minds; Papa threatened to call the police. They told us to forget each other—our love was not meant to be. Our entire family was going to America. Mama would never leave anyone behind. Papa warned Shlomie not to return to our home or lives. He never did.

Or did he?

I learned later that he waited for five years for me to come back to Israel and to him. He even came three times to look for me in New York City. A friend in Israel alerted my parents that he was coming, so each time they shipped me off to stay with Aunt Mindy in Toronto. With a broken heart, I resumed my life in America without the love of my life.

After a wait of some hours in the refreshing ocean breeze, several hundred people, all excited, talking, and laughing, boarded the beautiful ship *Zion*, sister ship of the *Jerusalem*. April 29, 1960 was a day of mixed emotions. For some of us, it was a final good-bye, the last time we would see *Eretz* Israel, the land of our ancestors.

The ship was more luxurious than anything I had seen before, and my spirits lifted. We searched for our staterooms on a lower deck. Papa and the boys had a nice, big room with four bunk beds for themselves, so different from the wooden plank bunk beds with thin mattresses in the little ship *Caserta* that had brought us to the shores of Israel. Mama and I were in a room with two other ladies, though I don't remember much about them.

We put our luggage down, and I reluctantly made my way to the rail as we sailed away from the lovely port city of Haifa.

It was a bright day, one that under normal circumstances would make me very happy with its beauty. Not that day. As I stood watching the shore and my Carmel Mountains slowly recede from view, I felt so very alone and sorry for myself.

There I was, leaving the man I loved and a country and life that I wanted. How would I survive in a new land with a new language and new people? Mama could no longer live in our Israel. It was too hot and humid in the summer, and with too few jobs, she could no longer see a future for us there. Soon all her children would reach the age to join the military, and Mama would never allow that! For her health, survival, and peace of mind, we all had to leave our home and life in Israel. I looked about to make sure no one could see my tears.

I was not the only one on this part of the deck. There, leaning against the railing, was my papa, his eyes brimming with tears. Deep in thought, he did not see me. I could always read his dear face very clearly, and I now stood watching him through several transitions.

*Sorrow.* He was leaving the only land he had ever loved and wished to live in forever. *Is he remembering his dreams of a great future, a life in Israel? Does he recall our escape from Poland, Russia, and other countries into Germany, then on to France, and finally Israel?*

*Anger.* The tears stopped, his face changed, and he looked very angry. *What is he thinking? What is he remembering? What does he see as the shores of Israel slowly move away and Mount Carmel grows smaller?* In the distance, I could still see some of the taller buildings, none of which were there when we first arrived. In the past eleven years, our beautiful Haifa had changed so much. She had grown into my heart's beautiful city. My eyes returned to Papa.

*Despair.* Papa's beloved Israel, the land of the Zionists, was getting away from him. A look of despair came over his face, and my heart was devastated. I could see him thinking: *Where did I go wrong? What could*

*I or should I have done differently? What else could I have given you, my Israel? I gave you everything but my life and almost did that as well while serving in the army in the Sinai Campaign. I proudly served in the army and fought for my country.*

*Resolution.* I am not leaving you, Israel. You have forced me to escape to preserve my life and sanity. The graft and corruption in our land have kept my children hungry for years.

Poor Papa. My heart went out to him. I feared he might never recover from this near fatal blow. *I hope America will be kind to him and life for all of us will improve.*

The shore became a tiny white ribbon of sand on the horizon. Turning away from the rail, I did my best to cheer myself up. I told myself that soon I would be seeing the Statue of Liberty. I would learn English and meet new people. I would take dance, opera, and acting classes. I would do my best to make a new life for myself. Maybe someday I would even fall in love again.

As we traveled through the Mediterranean, I was thrilled to see the Rock of Gibraltar, pictures of which I had seen in my books. I even posed for a photograph with a couple of new friends on board as we passed that historic location. Then we moved on, into the Atlantic.

For the next two weeks, there were lineups for the washrooms, day and night. Papa brought us tea and toast, because we were usually too sick to go to the dining room. With the rocking motion of the ship, many became seasick, and the staff could not keep up with the cleaning. The stench was suffocating all over the ship.

It took us two weeks to reach Brooklyn, New York, America.

No one was there to meet us.

As I write this chapter in 2010, this year marks our fiftieth anniversary as a family in North America. I am grateful to G-d that my mama and papa brought our family to the golden land of America where most of our dreams did eventually come true.

My parents' big dream of a good education for their family has happened. All seven of their grandchildren are university graduates. Deborah (Debbie) is a vice president of international programming with one of the three major television networks. Sherry is a judge. Shana is a fashion consultant and owner of a chain of stores. Doron has a PhD in education and is vice principal of a high school. Shane manages a few vintage clothing stores and is a fashion consultant for Broadway theaters. David and Benjamin are attorneys, and Benjamin is active in theater productions. All live in New York State.

# Chapter 45

# The Uncles in America

Papa's parents are Yitzhak and Esther Markus. Esther's brother, Gershon Rogove, was an artist and a painter. In the early 1900s, he had worked and apprenticed in Palestine in the prestigious Bezalel School, learning art and design as well as gold- and silversmith skills. Life was very hard during those years. Arriving in the Holy Land from Poland as a young man, just a teenager, he worked fourteen- to sixteen-hour days with very little food. He was often cold and lonely, far away from family and friends. He received little recognition for his efforts and accomplishments. At the first opportunity after graduating from Bezalel, he left by ship for New York.

Uncle Gershon was very happy to immigrate to the United States. In the late 1940s, he made a living as a jewelry designer in the diamond center of New York City. He also worked diligently on his paintings, of which he was very proud. He married and had a little girl who was born with some disability.

Another uncle was my grandfather Yitzhak Markus' brother, Solomon Markus. We called him Uncle Markus. He had become a rabbi; he had a wife and two children. That is all Papa told me about him while we were in the camps.

Then there was Shimon Goldwasser, who married my father's aunt, Esther Markus. Over time, he had collected twelve hundred dollars that my parents had sent with visitors to Israel for safekeeping until we would arrive in America. We called him Uncle Goldwasser.

When we arrived in America that May, Mama's dream had finally come true. Papa would now have the joy of being near his relatives—his two sisters, his uncles, some cousins, and their families. Papa was a lucky man to have so many family members living in America.

Friday morning, May 13, 1960, we arrived in Brooklyn, New York. All of our belongings, two suitcases per person, sat on the dock to await the arrival of some of Papa's family with whom we were to stay for a few days.

We needed to get our money back from Uncle Goldwasser. The first thing Papa wanted to do was to call his dear Uncle Markus, whom he had not seen since he was a young boy.

As we waited for someone to come meet us, morning turned into lunchtime, and we four kids were hungry. Papa had just six dollars cash in his pocket. A hot dog cart was the only place for us to get some food. Papa paid the man two dollars for four hot dogs. Now he had just four dollars left.

As late afternoon approached, Papa realized that neither of his two sisters, one living in the Bronx and the other on a chicken farm near Margate, New Jersey, would be coming to take us in for a few days as promised. Papa had a telephone number for Uncle Markus in Brooklyn, so Papa and I set off to look for a phone to call him for help.

We found a police officer. Papa handed him a dollar bill and gestured for him to dial the number for us, as we had not seen letters on a phone before and did not know how to use a pay phone. He seemed to be asking for something else, something we didn't understand. Taking coins from his pocket, he indicated the one he needed from Papa. My father had none, so the officer used his own coin, a kind offering.

Placing the call, the police officer waited until a man's voice answered and then handed the phone to me. I held onto the phone, and the two of us could hear every word from that point on:

Papa: "Uncle Solomon, is that you? I am so very happy to hear your voice!"

Uncle Solomon: "Do you have anyone to go and stay with?"

Papa: "No, Uncle. No one came to pick us up from the ship; not my two sisters or my cousins."

Uncle: "What do you plan on doing now that you only have five hours before Shabbat?"

Before Papa had a chance to say anything, we could hear in the background the voice of his wife—a shrilly, loud voice I came to call the "fishwife-of-Brooklyn" voice.

Aunt: "Ask him what he brought with him."

Uncle Markus repeated the question to us. Papa looked at me and whispered, "What should I say?"

I whispered back into his ear, "Tell him you brought with you a wife and four children." Papa repeated my words, and Uncle repeated Papa's words to his wife.

Aunt: "Tell him to go back where he came from. They will never make it in *America!*"

Uncle: "If you do not have a big fist full of money in your pocket and more in the bank, you should not have come to this country! I am busy now getting ready for Shabbat. Call me again after you have jobs and are settled."

Stunned by this rejection, Papa responded that in time, he and his family would have the life in America of which most people only dream.

Papa's words came true. Papa and Mama's children have a dream life in America. *We made it!* The first time I met this ugly little man in person was at my mama's funeral about two-and-a-half years after this conversation.

Papa's last resort was to try to contact his cousin Tzipke, daughter of Uncle Goldwasser who had our money. Because her father was in Florida for Passover, Tzipke came to the port. She hired two taxis and accompanied us to the Bossert Hotel where (with her husband's permission) she guaranteed payment of our bill. In addition, she gave us twenty dollars cash to buy some food and candles for Shabbat. Tzipke then invited me to go with her to her home for the weekend.

When Uncle Goldwasser returned a couple weeks later, he sent Tzipke to us with our money. In the two weeks we spent at the hotel, Papa found a job and an apartment to rent. I went with Papa to find some furniture and household goods.

We moved into our first Brooklyn apartment. Mama registered the three boys to attend school, and I found a job in a factory earning forty-two dollars per week making Christmas corsages. I hoped to learn a bit of English there and save enough money to pursue a career in the arts. Unfortunately, most of the workers there spoke Spanish.

So our life in America began.

In spite of the poor welcome we received from Uncle Solomon Markus, I had a burning desire to locate my great uncles. I was now a young woman, and he and Uncle Gershon Rogove were the only family members of my grandparents' generation still alive after the Holocaust. I knew I must meet them as soon as possible, for they were now elderly.

For two years, I phoned Uncle Gershon without much success. He made it clear he wanted no contact with any of us, especially with my father. I could not understand why all I got was a sneer and accusations about Papa when I asked him about our extended family.

"He is the son of that terrible Yitzhak, my sister's husband. A wonderful, gentle woman was my sister Esther, and how he made her suffer! No, I do not wish to meet any of you!"

I reminded him that my brothers and I were the grandchildren of his own sister, but he would not hear it. I learned later that he did see my father several times in those two years, but he continued to refuse to meet me.

Finally, after numerous phone calls and repeated rejection, Papa's uncle Gershon, upon learning of my mother's death, finally took pity on me and agreed to see me. He asked me to meet him for lunch in an automat cafeteria in Manhattan. For all I knew, this might be the only time we would meet.

While we were in the camps in Germany, the Red Cross had located him and Uncle Markus for us, and I wanted to thank him for confirming our relationship. I wanted to love him as I would have loved his sister, my grandmother Esther.

I dressed with great care in my best garments. After two frustrating hours of getting lost on the subway, I finally arrived, still on time to meet Great-Uncle Gershon.

I walked into the cafeteria with joyful expectation but also with a strange sadness. I would finally be meeting my grandmother Esther's brother. So many wasted years!

As I walked into the unusually big hall, I wondered why it was so noisy. People stood in long lines in front of a big wall full of hundreds of pigeonholes with small windows. Beside each was a place where you could insert coins. The window would then pop open, and you could reach inside to take out a small plate with the food you had selected. What a wonderful sight—a wall full of food! *I must have one like that in my home when I am rich,* I thought.

I was distracted for a few moments. I just *had* to look into one of the pigeonholes to see how the food got in there. I passed all the lines saying, "I only look, no eat, please, thank you." People nodded and smiled. I think my accent and "great" English told them I was a foreigner.

Looking into the windows, I saw some had soup, some had sandwiches, and others had salads. I did not recognize many other wonderful things.

A man near me inserted his coins, and when the little window/door popped open, he took out a plate. Cake! It looked wonderful! I reached for the little door and held it open, staring into the tiny compartment. Just then, a big black face looked in from the other side, saw me, and smiled as she refilled the space with a big slice of pie. I had kept the little door open, and she told me to take the pie. I stood in wide-eyed silence. Once again, she smiled at me and said, "Take it! It is good. You will like it!"

She waited for me to take it, but I had no coins with which to pay, and I told her, "Sorry, no money." She assured me that when the little window/door was open, it meant someone had already paid, and I could have the pie now. She would replace it with another one she held in her hand.

I took the pie. I was feeling a little guilty, but food is food, and I was always hungry! It was a happy day and my first American apple pie—two years after arriving in New York City.

With my slice of pie in hand, I looked all around the big room. I soon saw my father's uncle. I had no difficulty recognizing him—he was just a much older version of my papa.

There he sat in the middle of that large dining room full of people all talking and eating. It sounded more like a marketplace or a bazaar in Russia than a big-city restaurant. I looked at my great-uncle as I walked toward him. His hair was grey. Although his face looked very tired, his eyes were bright and alert, looking in all directions like a bird of prey. All at once, his eyes focused on me with a questioning look. I nodded my head up and down in recognition. I would have known him anywhere!

As I approached, I rehearsed my plan. *First, I will give him a big hug and a kiss on each cheek. I will ask about his health and his family. Then I will ask to meet his wife and daughter and invite them all to our home for dinner, so he can meet the rest of my family. I will cook the best meal I know how.*

As I approached, he eyed me very carefully. I stood before him, smiled, and said, "Shalom, Uncle Gershon."

He didn't move; he didn't say a word. Though I found his reaction rather strange, I said, "If I am to give you a hug and some kisses, you will have to stand up!"

Surprise registered on his face. He seemed taken aback by my boldness, but a familiar twinkle was in his eyes—the same twinkle I had seen many times in my father's eyes.

Smiling in amazement, he exclaimed, "You look so much like my sister!"

Taking his time, Uncle stood up and extended his hand. Ignoring it, I stepped closer and put both arms around him for the big hug that I needed. I kissed him on each cheek. The love I felt at that moment was greater than anything I had felt for many years.

Uncle Gershon, a tall, slender man, slowly squirmed out of my hug and sat down, motioning for me to sit. His gaze never left my face. He cleared his throat and in a quiet yet strong voice he asked, "When do you plan to pay me back the ten dollars you have taken from me?"

I looked at him in shocked surprise. "Uncle," I exclaimed, "this is the first time we have met! When was it you gave me money?"

"Then you will not pay it back?"

"Uncle, if you tell me how I came to receive money from you, I will be only too happy to give it back."

"In that case, I will tell you. At the end of the war, I think it was 1947–48, your father's uncle Solomon and I received a call and then a visit from an official with the CARE organization. They told us our nephew, his wife, and four children had survived the war and were looking for family and any help we may be able to offer. That man said it would cost each of us ten dollars so the CARE people could send a package to Germany with food and necessities for your family."

Angry tears gathered in his eyes.

"I had a very sick little girl and did not make enough money for food or medicine for my own family. Still, they insisted if we did not each give ten dollars, they would cross your names off their list and let you starve. They said everything they could to extort the money from us! Uncle Solomon and I did not have money to spare, as we were also very poor! Somehow, with great effort, we gave them the money they demanded. I even had to ask the bank to help me with that. I do hope all of you had lots of good food while we went hungry!"

As I listened to his bitter memories, my mind traveled back to the DP camp and that day when all the CARE trucks came to our camp to give us food. My uncles in America had contributed money at great cost to their own families so we could survive. They could not possibly know the tragedy and disappointment we had endured with the arrival of those "gifts" from CARE.

# Chapter 46

## On the Steps
## of the Legislature

*Edmonton, Alberta Canada—November 16, 2000*

The call from the doctor came on a cold and dreary November morning in 1962. I went to Columbia Presbyterian Hospital in uptown Manhattan in New York City to visit my mother for what was to be the last time. My poor mama had been in the hospital dying of colon cancer for the past three months. Though I didn't know then that I would never see her alive again, my mama knew she would not see me. She asked for my solemn promise that I would take care of my father and my brothers.

On her deathbed, she also made me promise to do many other things not in my power to accomplish, but I promised to do them all. I didn't realize then what a tall order it would be. She painfully declared, "As my generation and then yours dies out, we and the Holocaust will all be forgotten."

I promised her that telling our story would be part of my life's work for as long as I lived. I begged Mama to believe me. I told myself that if it took the rest of my life, I would not stop telling everyone what happened to us, to my family, and to my people. The world *must* know and remember.

One bright, cold November morning, we gathered at the Jewish Center in Calgary with our rabbi for a bus trip to the Alberta Legislature in Edmonton, the capital city of my province of Alberta, Canada.

Earlier that year, I had undergone a serious surgery. I had wondered if this emotional trip would be just too difficult for me. *Can I handle it?* All the horrors and the pain of the past would come rushing to the foreground yet again. *Should I go, or not?* It was a short-lived battle I fought with myself. I knew I *must* go, not only for me but also for all those in my family who had not survived the Holocaust.

The small convoy of two buses was carrying what is quickly becoming a rare and precious cargo—thirty Holocaust survivors with some members of their families and friends, fifty people from my home city of Calgary. Though I had brought along some entertaining musical tapes for all to enjoy, the trip itself was mostly quiet and subdued.

As we made our way north, thoughts of my dead twin brothers flooded my mind yet again. I tried to imagine what those two young boys would have become had they not been murdered by the Nazis. As I pondered, I glanced across the aisle of the bus and noticed a woman who I knew to be a survivor of Auschwitz. She was discretely wiping tears from her eyes. *What lost loved ones does she recall?* I knew I was not alone in my pain.

Edmonton in the winter is just as lovely as it is in the summer. I do like the city, and I am happy to return for a visit whenever I can. That day, however, was not to be just a visit. It will stay in my memory for as long as I live. The accomplishment of our mission would affect Jewish Albertans for all time.

The government edifice looming on the hill was a majestic sight. As we got off the buses not far from the legislature, our people started to walk in small groups toward the building. Family and friends who lived in Edmonton met some of our travelers for a quick visit before going on to the House together. There was nobody to meet me, as I have no family in Canada, so I felt especially alone that day.

I shivered in the cold. As I looked around and did not see anyone else near the bus, I began to walk alone toward the building. As I drew closer, I became even colder than before. Something very strange was happening to me. I was unable to hear any sounds or see anyone. As I neared the stairs of that great building, I looked up, and the entrance appeared almost unreachable. Everything around me seemed to disappear, as if a thick fog had rolled in all around the hill.

Suddenly, I could no longer feel the cold. The only sound was that of my recently repaired heart, beating faster. It pounded with excitement and joy. As I put my foot on the first stair, I heard a child's voice speak to me: *You made it! I knew you would.*

I knew I might have difficulty walking up the many stairs in the cold air, but then the child's voice came to me again, in Yiddish: *You know these stairs are only a small obstacle in your journey. You have been at war for years for your survival. You have always worked with the hope that the day would come when the world would accept its responsibility for what has happened. Now is the time to be happy.*

The little voice spoke again. *You have lived to see this day! In just a few hours, it will become law in your province!*

As I looked around me, eyes brimming with tears, I realized that the voice of the little girl belonged to me at age seven, when I had looked at Europe for the last time. I had stood with my papa on the deck of the *Caserta* on our way to our Jewish homeland, Israel. Our Land, *Eretz Israel*, was less than one year old.

Thanks to the diligent work of then-Premier Ralph Klein and Mr. Ron Stevens, member of the Legislative Assembly of Alberta, the Assembly passed into law Bill 26 on November 16, 2000, bringing about a yearly Holocaust Memorial Day—*Yom Ha'Shoah*. This solemn anniversary is now remembered in Alberta every year in April or May, according to the Jewish lunar calendar—a fulfilment of Mama's and my dream.

Dear Mama, you can now rest in peace. You and all our murdered Jewish families will not be forgotten.

# Chapter 47

# Not a Dream after All

"*It was only a bad dream!*"

That sentence was a curse to me through much of my childhood. My mother, wanting to protect me from witnessing her attack on the road to the church, said those words. Then the "nice" priest said the same when Galena died. Papa said that my long stay in the church and every other manner of hell I lived through was all "just a bad dream." "In time, you will forget all about this and have a good life. You will see, I promise you!" Papa said. "It was all a bad dream!"

Crossing the river into Russia was a bad dream? Time spent in prison as a little girl in Russia with my mother and baby brother was a bad dream? Escaping from Russia on a military train full of soldiers? The long stay in the church, the rapes of boys and girls by Nazi officers and priests—these were also bad dreams? The displaced persons' camps in Germany? Hunger, starvation, lice, filth, diseases in the camps—bad dreams as well? My poor mama's bleeding face, having been beaten with a whip and fists and worse? These were *all* just bad dreams? No, I think not.

My life began unlike any other child I have known. The trauma of my mother's life coursed through my veins while I was still in her womb. I was born under the streets of the Warsaw ghetto. I did not have a childhood. For the first four years of my life during the war and for the next four-and-a-half years after the war ended, I had too many years of bad dreams.

Though we cannot turn back the hands of time, I am still looking for all that could have been and should have been my life. I still hope and dream of peace before I die.

My Torah tells me of our Joseph, the great dreamer. All of his dreams came true. Most of the children I knew did not have an opportunity to dream; others died before they could fulfill any dreams they might have had. I hope other child survivors have fared better than I.

For my twin brothers whose names and faces I never knew (they are known to G-d); for my grandparents, uncles, aunts, cousins, and numerous other family members who did not survive to tell their stories; for all the children in the church; and for me—none of this was a dream! This nightmare really happened to us. It is still reality for many of our people all over the world.

Papa survived the Holocaust. Mama survived physically but wished she had not. Emotionally, she did not survive. Her mind was not able to believe or accept all that had happened to her, including the premature death of her own father and brother.

In spite of all that happened between Mama and me, I really did love her. I loved her love for our family and her desire to laugh and be happy. After everything that hurt and tormented her, she still maintained an air of innocence. I loved to see her in a pretty, new dress, wearing bright red lipstick, eyes outlined with the black eyebrow pencil. Her eyes sparkled with joy when I smiled and told her she was beautiful. I wish we could have been friends.

I stopped talking to my brothers about this subject many years ago. Even in our childhood, it seemed they had no interest in knowing anything of our family's personal history. From my perspective, it seems they have chosen to deal with our family's past by ignoring it.

For years, I measured my self-worth, self-respect, and the possibilities for my future life by the abuse and brutality I experienced as a child and youth. The rapes and beatings, and especially the pain inflicted on me by my mother's fists—these are some of my most vivid memories.

How could anyone else love and respect me if my own mama did not? Instead, she had hurt me. I had no one to protect me from her illogical and hysterical anger. She was often very unkind to my father as well, though he loved her very much. He helped me when he could, but her rage intimidated him.

How would I ever rise above all of this? Could I? After the abuse of those early years, I was suspicious of any expression of love from anyone. Fearing another disappointment or painful trap, I was always on guard.

One afternoon many years ago, I tuned in to one of my favorite TV programs, *The Oprah Winfrey Show*. She was speaking on a subject that had been taboo for me for too many years. Oprah revealed that as a young girl she had been raped. She spoke of the emotional problems that followed and encouraged survivors to be brave and to tell a trusted friend or counsellor. "It is not our shame. The blame belongs with the abuser." She said it had taken her many years to understand it was not her fault.

It was as though Oprah spoke directly to me. I responded to her image on the screen and told her the same thing had happened to me. Because Mama had warned me I must never reveal the shame of rape, I had hidden the experience for many years. Oprah's words that day confirmed for me that I was just as innocent as she was. It was not *my* fault either. I was only a little girl.

As the show concluded, I thanked Oprah for her honesty, which helped open my eyes to my true innocence. I no longer needed to be ashamed about what had happened to me. That day, she gave me courage to write about my own abusive and painful experiences.

For many years, I would not even consider forgiving all those who had hurt me. They do not deserve my forgiveness or kindness. However, since G-d extends his mercy and grace to me, maybe someday I will choose to forgive. The issue still rages within me; it is a constant struggle. Perhaps one day G-d will win, and I will forgive them all.

For more than fifty years I was warned—first by my mother and then by my father—never to tell or write anything about our family's history for as long as they were both alive. My three brothers are unaware of most of the events I have written in this book. "It is too horrible for your brothers to know this truth," Mama said. "Wait till they are much older, and we are no longer alive!"

"Mama, they won't believe me, because you have made me wait much too long already! Now you must talk to them or write it all down, and tell it all!" She would not agree to that.

After Mama passed away, I did all I could to keep our little family together. However, the environment in our home made me quite unhappy in the role of substitute mom, and I soon came to realize it was time to move out—not as an act of selfishness, but rather one of self-preservation. I needed to take control of my own life and assume responsibility for only myself. I did not wish to adopt my mother's role as a martyr.

The year following Mama's death in 1962, I began to speak publicly about our life, as she insisted only in her final days. Though Papa lived many years after Mama's passing, he could no longer stop me from talking. I would no longer allow him to hide my suffering behind his silence.

For forty years, I have been giving lectures in Calgary and the surrounding communities and cities. I have participated in minisymposiums in Catholic and other denominational schools and churches, for Hadassah Wizo, B'nai B'rith, and other Jewish organizations and synagogues—wherever people would listen. This year, 2013, while in India, I found a Chabad House in Manali in the foothills of the Himalayan Mountains. There I addressed, for the first time in Hebrew, an audience of 250—rabbis, visitors from Israel, and young Israelis who had recently completed their army service. It was a great honor to share our Shabbat meal in that faraway place. When I traveled as a dancer from one country to another, I organized opportunities with local clergy to speak to groups of people, telling them of the Holocaust and of what happened to my family, my people, and me personally.

The writing of this book, while incredibly painful and draining, has given me back a measure of control. I have spent many agonizing hours writing my memories and accumulating thousands of notes and hundreds of typewritten pages. The early years, while helping to shape who I am today, are becoming less of a hindrance to my life. My mama's legacy of remorse, regret, tears, anger, and pain is becoming increasingly a thing of the past.

Most of my life I have worked on projects to help make children's and adults' lives happier, hoping to make a difference. This is no doubt in response to the powerlessness I felt as a child.

I am learning that living the life of a victim is not beneficial to me. I no longer blame myself for things that were or are beyond my control or feel shame for the wrongs others have inflicted on me.

I am well aware that all survivors have stories to tell, and tell them they must. Some have said that my stories as I tell them are much too graphic. To them I say, "I survived that hell. I experienced that pain in my body and soul. I relive it even now in the telling. Please listen and just try to understand."

Mama feared that with her death, the Markus family story would soon be forgotten. On her deathbed, she beseeched me to break a conspiracy of silence to erase our past and to tell the story of all that happened to us and to our people. To honor Mama's dying wishes and to shine a light on a very dark period in our world's history, I tell my own story. I feel compelled to speak for those who can no longer speak for themselves.

I speak for my twin brothers. I speak for Uncle Aaron whose life was cut short by hatred. I speak for Mama and Papa who were too busy merely surviving to consider how they might pass on the message of "never again."

I speak in the face of Holocaust deniers who would silence the truth. Even now, more than sixty years after the events recorded here, the skies are once again darkening with rabid anti-Semitic hatred and violence all over the world. All I know is I must speak.

Now, through these pages, I have kept my promise.

Shalom
Sahbra Anna Markus

# Author Notes

My family and I immigrated to the United States from Israel in 1960. Hoping to learn to speak English, I took the first job I could find—doing piecework in a factory making Christmas corsages. With most of my coworkers speaking only Spanish, I soon moved on to my first love, dancing, where fluency in English was not required. I not only loved to dance—I *needed* to dance. The accolades I received began to fill up some deep hunger in my soul to be loved, accepted, and appreciated.

My first professional dancing contract was with a modern jazz, Afro-Cuban dance troop from New York. We worked at the Paddock Nightclub and Lounge in Atlantic City.

I began my belly dancing career at La Bistro in Atlantic City, followed by an engagement with the 500 Club, also in Atlantic City. I subsequently performed at the Taft Hotel in New York City. Warmly received, I continued performing all over New York City, and for many years, I spent weekends dancing in many major and smaller hotels in the Catskill Mountains.

I preformed solo only, dancing and doing a comedy routine in large convention centers, hotels, nightclubs, and casinos, often accompanied by large orchestras. I shared the same bill with many world-famous singers and comedians. I thrived on the recognition afforded me by huge audiences and famous people. It gave me joy to witness the pleasure my performances brought to often packed houses. Yet I wanted more. More than money to pay my bills, I craved the attention I drew with my colorful and creative onstage acts.

I performed at the Waldorf Astoria with Henny Youngman and for special events hosted by Wall Street stock market organizations.

Needing a rest from belly dancing, I joined the Zigani (Gypsy) Ballet, performing with world-renowned Hungarian artists Nora Kovach and Isvan Rabovsky at the Latin Quarter on Broadway in New York City, the Cattlemen Club in Huston, Texas, and at the wonderful Rooster Tail Club in Detroit, Michigan. Barbara Walters visited us at the Latin Quarter and told me she loved my show. I returned to the Rooster Tail Club months later to perform belly dancing on the same bill with the very funny comedian Tom Patterson.

I eventually traveled to many countries around the world, performing a wide variety of dance genres and as a belly dancer and actor. I danced in most of the states in the United States, as well as in South America, South Africa, French and British Guyana, three engagements in Surinam (formerly Dutch Guyana), Puerto Rico, all of the Caribbean, the Bahamas and Antilles Islands, Nassau, and the French islands of Martinique and Guadeloupe. I also danced in Israel.

My favorite nightclubs were the 500 Club, the Round Table in New York City, and the Latin Quarter on Broadway—prestigious clubs where New York's beautiful people met to enjoy quality shows.

In August of 1963, I joined a busload of entertainers in Atlantic City to join the March on Washington. Hearing Dr. Martin Luther King Jr.'s *I Have a Dream* speech was one of the most moving events of my life.

In the summer of 1969, I attended the iconic Woodstock Music Festival with a group of friends. The three-day concert lasted for four days and was one of the biggest events in music history.

I lived in New York City for twelve years, during which time I married Edward Salem, who owned a talent agency. He arranged a three-month contract for me in South Africa.

After New York City, Edward and I moved to Los Angeles, where I did the *Scoey Mitchell TV Show* and performed as a belly dancer in nightclubs. We resided in LA for two years. With a lucrative contract to perform at a nightclub in Calgary, we moved to Canada in 1974 where I became a Canadian citizen. We divorced in 1982.

Continuing my career in the arts as a dancer in Alberta, I performed in most major hotels in Calgary as headline entertainer for many major oil companies and organizations, including Shriner's Conventions. I did shows at the Banff Springs Hotel and the Jasper Park Lodge and in the capital city of Edmonton.

I taught fitness and belly dancing in my home as before, until I opened a dance and fitness school where I was the choreographer and principal teacher. I produced, directed, choreographed, and hosted my own TV shows, *Sahbra's Dance into Fitness* and *Sahbra's Belly Dance School Presents,* which was dedicated to Jeannie and Tommy Millar, my "Canadian mom and dad." My dancers and I performed on *The Marie Hortenz Show* several times, and I participated (dancing and cohosting) in Jerry Lewis' March of Dimes telethon along with Leonard Nimoy of *Star Trek* fame.

During this time, I performed in the movie *Days of Heaven,* starring Richard Gere, filmed in Calgary and Lethbridge, Alberta.

Calgary's St. Francis High School and St. Mary's University drama departments presented *Fiddler on the Roof,* for which I was the advisor for Jewish rituals, culture, costumes, and dance.

In the past few years, I have had several of my stories published in the Jewish Free Press in Alberta and have been interviewed on local television and radio stations.

I have been a volunteer with the Calgary Zoo for the past thirty-six years. During the 1988 Winter Olympics in Calgary, I served as a volunteer translator with the Foreign Press. I have served numerous times with *Sar-El* (In Service for Israel), a program in which 160,000 civilian volunteers from around the world perform a variety of important duties on army bases in Israel.

As an active participant at Beth Tzedec Synagogue in Calgary since 1974, I have been involved with fund-raising, have served on the board of the Sisterhood, and am now on the Board of Directors with the Synagogue. For many years, I served on the Board of Directors of the Jewish National Fund, and since 1976, I have been a life member of the Hadassah Wizo organization, helping sponsor the youth village of Hadassim in Israel. I am a member of the Mercaz Zionist organization. In 2001, I created the Yiddish club at Beth Tzedec in conjunction with the Sisterhood and have directed and taught Yiddish faithfully on a volunteer basis ever since, much to the joy of the participants. Bimonthly, I present remastered movies in Yiddish with English subtitles provided by the Canada-based National Center for Jewish Film.

For twenty-nine years, I have participated in annual Holocaust symposiums at Mount Royal College/University in Calgary, Alberta.

In the past forty-five years, I have been the keynote speaker lecturing about the Holocaust in churches and synagogues throughout the world. I have been an invited guest speaker in schools, colleges, and universities, addressing many thousands of high school and college students and others, always warning of the dangers of hatred and prejudice.

Now with the imminent publication of these memoirs, I am receiving more invitations to share my story and will be doing lecture tours. Ninety-one percent of Poland's Jews perished in Hitler's war. I am one of the nine percent who lived to tell about those years.

# Photographs
# and
# Documents

| | | |
|---|---|---|
| | | CLAIMS CONFERENCE - FORMER SLAVE |
| Reference No: | DML91089912C0001 | AND FORCED LABORS AS PER |
| | | THE FOUNDATION "REMEMBRANCE, |
| Issue Date: | JULY 29, 2004 | RESPONSIBILITY, AND THE FUTURE" |

Send To:

SAHBRA ANNA MARKUS

CALGARY AB

Beneficiary:

SAHBRA ANNA MARKUS

Bene Acct Info:

| | | | Batch: | 49765 |
|---|---|---|---|---|
| | | | Seq: | 00079 |
| Amount: | CAD ***************8,149.48 | | ICN No. | 0000000 |
| Cheque No: | 026502163 | | | |

Details of Payment:

Dear Sir or Madam:
Enclosed please find the one-time payment for which you were approved under the Claims Conference Program for Former Slave and Forced Laborers in in accordance with the Foundation "Remembrance, Responsibility, and the Future." Depending on the total number of eligible former slave and force laborers under this program, you may receive a second payment. At such time, we will notify you.
Please note that the waiver you signed on your application form becomes effective with this payment. However, the waiver does not apply to claims or payments under German law on the consequences of war or indemnification measures. Applicants should note that claims under other components of Foundation law, including claims under the insurance, medical experiments (other personal injuries) or property sections of the German Foundation are still being reviewed.

Sincerely,

Bettina Seifert, Program Director

This document is vindication! It acknowledges the validity of my claims of abuse in the church. They categorized it as "Slave Labor". The Claims Conference was established in 1951 as a means of seeking a measure of justice for Jewish victims of Nazi persecution. They administer various programs, and payments are made from the recovery of unclaimed and looted Jewish property, and from funds received as restitution from the German government.

**Canada** Yad Vashem

**The Government of Canada**
is honoured to present this certificate of recognition to

# Sahbra Markus

**a Holocaust Survivor**

## on April 23, 2013

to pay tribute to your profound courage, strength, and dignity.

During Canada's chair year of the International Holocaust Remembrance Alliance, the Government of Canada will
work with community partners to preserve survivor testimony as an invaluable resource for Holocaust education.

Few can fully understand the unimaginable suffering, cruelty, and loss that you witnessed and endured.
Your remarkable story serves as a compelling reminder to all humankind of our obligation to learn from the past.

By sharing your story, you strengthen the Canadian Society for Yad Vashem's mission
of ensuring that the universal lessons of the Shoah are never forgotten.

Your passing of the torch of remembrance encourages future generations to be
vigilant against all forms of hatred and intolerance and to embrace inclusiveness and pluralism.

**Jason Kenney**
MINISTER OF CITIZENSHIP,
IMMIGRATION AND MULTICULTURALISM

**Mark Adler**
MEMBER OF PARLIAMENT

**Fran Sonshine**
NATIONAL CHAIR OF THE
CANADIAN SOCIETY FOR YAD VASHEM

Four of five Efroimowitz sisters and niece. Clockwise from front left: Esther, Mindel, Devorah, Rachel, and Mindel's daughter Shifra. Bluma not present.

Devorah Efraimowitz and sister Esther, circa 1936

מדינת ישראל

בבית הדין הרבני האזורי
תל אביב-יפו
לפני כבוד הדיינים:
הרב א. גולדשמידט - אב"ד
הרב י. קוליץ
הרב ש. מזרחי

חיק מס.4004/תשי"ח

בענין: איסור נשואין

המבקשים: זאב וולף מרקוס
ת.ז, 332427,
דבורה לבית אפרימוביץ
ת.ז, 332428,
גרים: רח' הרצל 100
ת.א.

פ ס ק   ד י ן

על סמך החומר שבתיק מאשר בית הדין:

כי הנשואין בין המבקש זאב בן יצחק מרקוס ובין
המבקשת דבורה מרקוס בת חיים אפרימוביץ נערכו כדת בעיר
בז'ז'ין (פולניא) בשנת הרצ"ח (19.12.1937).

מנשואין אלו נולדו למבקשים ארבעה ילדים:

1) אננה נולדה בעיר ורשא בשנת תש"א(14.7.41),
2) חיים נולד בעיר מרי (תוקמניה-רוסיה התיכונית)
בשנת תש"ד (24.7.44),
3) יעקב נולד בעיר מרי הנ"ל בשנת תש"ו(19.12₪45),
4) יצחק נולד בעיר סטראובונג(גרמניא) בשנת
תש"ז (12.3.47).

ניתן ביום י"ד אייר תשי"ח
(4.5.58)

Court document from Tel Aviv, affirming the marriage of Ze'ev Markus and
Devorah Efroimowitz in 1937. (Original lost in Holocaust.) Court asserts that
there are 4 children born of this marriage - Anna, Chaim, Yakov and Yitzak.

Center front, Rabbi Chaim Schotland (Sahbra's Grandmother
Rivkah's brother); seated left, his wife Sonya; with family members.
Back row, second left, Joseph; behind Chaim, daughter Galina

Anna (Sahbra) in Poland

Mama Devorah with Anna in Russia

**My brother Chaim writing a letter to me while I was in the church in Poland**

**Mama, Anna and Chaim in DP camp, circa 1946**

Papa, Mama, Chaim & Anna in DP camp, circa 1947

Mama with Anna, Chaim and baby Yakov in DP camp, circa 1947

Anna, Mama, Chaim, baby Yitzhak and Yakov in DP camp, circa 1948

From left, Mama and Papa at a labor meeting in Haifa, circa 1952

Devorah and Ze'ev Markus at a party in Tel Aviv, 1955

**Yakov (Jack) Markus, school photo, Haifa**

**Yitzhak (Joe) Markus, school photo, Haifa**

# Going to America – Passport Pictures

Ze'ev Markus

Devorah Markus

**Anna Markus**

**Chaim Markus**

Anna at Kibbutz Ein Harod, 1949. Summer visit
with Uncle Aaron Schotland and family

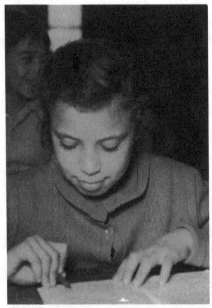

Anna, school photo, Haifa, circa 1952

Anna with brothers Chaim (left), Yitzhak, cousin Avi
Hofaizen at his bar mitzvah in Ramle, and Yakov

Anna with fellow travelers passing the Rock of Gibraltar, April 1960

Mama's headstone at Beth David Cemetery, Long Island, NY

Sahbra (Anna) with Papa at PGA Golf Club, Florida, 1967

Papa, Joe (Yitzhak) Markus and Sahbra at Joe and Michelle's wedding,
January 19, 1969, New York City

Papa and groom Joe on wedding day

Papa and Tzippi (new daughter-in-law, Michelle)

**Sahbra and Joe at Joe's wedding**

**Wedding of Michelle & Joe Markus**

Clockwise from back: Sahbra, Papa, bride & groom, Chaim, and other family members. Seated, from right, Rabbi Solomon Markus (Papa's uncle), Sol and Fela (Papa's sister) Gelnick, and other family members.

Sahbra while performing at nightclub, 1968

Sahbra on beach in Puerto Rico, taking a break from
performing at the Sheraton Hotel, 1968

**Sahbra while dancing in Port of Spain, Trinidad, 1967**

**Sahbra, the dancer**

**Sahbra Markus - modeling headshot for agent**

Family group at bar mitzvah of Doron Markus (son of Joe and Tzippi) at Homowack Hotel in the Catskill Mountains, upstate New York. Seated at table: center, Joe (Yitzhak) and Tzippi (Michelle), her parents Mrs. and Mr. Laufer. Continuing left, Papa Ze'ev, Sahbra, Jacob (Yakov) and Mona Markus.

From left, Uncle Yosef (Papa's brother), his daughter Dora with her husband, Yosef's wife Hannah and son Yitzhak, in Uruguay

Group of bride's family at Shana Marcus' wedding to Baruch (Bobby) Moscovici. Sahbra stands beside her niece, the bride. Groom is seated on floor at right, with bride's father Chaim Marcus in center; Behind Chaim is Papa Ze'ev and left of him is Papa's sister, Fela Gelnick.

Family group

(Zelochevski, Turi, Markus, Markus, Gelnick, Marcus) at cousin's wedding, New York. Sahbra is seated in front of the bride.

Sahbra Markus - Graduate MAGNA CUM LAUDE from
St. Francis High School, Calgary, Alberta, 1996

## St. Francis High School

This Certifies that

SAHBRA MARKUS

has qualified as a member of the graduating class
of 1996 and is therefore entitled to this
MAGNA CUM LAUDE

Diploma

Dated this 30th day of June, 1996.

Principal

Sahbra with Leopold (Poldek Pfefferberg) and Mila Page. He is Schindler's
List survivor No. 173 and Ludmilla is No. 195. Prof. Page was instrumental
in bringing the story of Schindler to the attention of Steven Spielberg.
After a chance meeting with Page, Australian author Thomas Keneally
wrote Schindler's Ark, which was later adapted for the screen as Schindler's
List. Page, who died in 2001, was a technical advisor to the movie.

Sahbra with Alberta Premier Ralph Klein at
the Legislature in Edmonton, 2000

Sahbra with Professor Elie Wiesel

**Sahbra with Lieutenant General of Alberta, Norman Kwong and his wife at a Holocaust Memorial event**

Sahbra, serving with Sar El, receiving Blue Epaulettes

Sahbra serving with Sar El in 2002 with IDF tank
at Israeli Independence Day celebration

**Sahbra at Knesset Menorah in Jerusalem, 2003**

**Sahbra with Brig. Gen. Aharon Davidi, founder of the Sar El program of voluntary military service in Israel, 2008**

**Sahbra (center) with Sar El volunteers on a base in Israel**

Sahbra (serving with Sar El) with Dr. David L Dunn (left) of Three
Hills Bible College, Alberta with students at Eilat, Israel

Sahbra at wedding of Yossi, son of Chabad Rabbi Matusof, Calgary, Alberta

BJ (Benjamin) Markus and Jessica Bittner's wedding. BJ is Sahbra's nephew.

Sahbra's nephew Doron Markus with family. Baby Micah was the first baby born in New York City during Hurricane Sandy, 2012.

**Sahbra at Moulin Rouge, Paris, France, 2011**

Sahbra at Golden Temple, Amritsar, India, 2013

Sahbra with fellow travelers, the Bhatti family,
at the Golden Temple, Amritsar, India, 2013

Sahbra at Taj Mahal, Agra, India, 2013

Sahbra at dinner with Bhatti family in Heritage Park, Jaipur, India, 2013

**Sahbra wearing her Mama's antique crystal rose pendant.**
*Photo courtesy Penny's Hotshot Photography*

**Shirley Knapp, with Sahbra celebrating completion of manuscript.**
*Photo courtesy Penny's Hotshot Photography*

# Genealogy Charts

# Family Tree Information Compiled by Sahbra Markus

Names in **BOLD** are mentioned in book. *Italics* denote alternate names or commentary. Names <u>Underlined</u>: Perished in Holocaust. Spelling of some names may be inaccurate, and unknown names are denoted by **? mark**.

| Generation 1 | Generation 2 | Generation 3 |
|---|---|---|
| **SAHBRA'S LINEAGE on PATERNAL GRANDFATHER'S SIDE** | | |
| *VOLFE Ze'ev BROMBERG (m. unknown) | Yaacov JACOB MARKUS | Alte MARKUS |
| Changed name to WOLFE MARKUS | (m. Reva ?) | (m. 2 wives, names unknown) |
| *Resisted service in Polish army; visited cousins in Warsaw, saw marquee with name Markus and adopted it to hide Jewish identity. (Not certain if this is father or grandfather of Yaacov JACOB MARKUS.) | | Esther MARKUS (m. **Shimon** Hersh **GOLDWASSER**) |
| | | Eliazar MARKUS |
| | | Chava MARKUS (m. Moshe Joseph {C}RAVITZ) |
| | | ***YITZAK MARKUS** (m. <u>**ESTHER ROGOVE**</u>) |
| | | *Sahbra's paternal grandparents |
| | | (see Esther Rogove's lineage below) |
| | other children unknown | |
| | | SHLOMO Solomon MARKUS *'Uncle Markus'* |
| | | (m. Bashah Fege) |
| **SAHBRA'S LINEAGE on PATERNAL GRANDMOTHER'S SIDE** | | |
| | SHLOMO Yitzak ROGOVE | **GERSHON ROGOVE** (m. ?) *Uncle Gershon*, NYC |
| | (m. Rachel Leah) | <u>**ESTHER ROGOVE**</u> (m. <u>**YITZAK MARKUS**</u>) *above |
| | *Ostro, Poland* | Hershel ROGOVE (m. ?) |
| | | Shimon ROGOVE (m. *Chaya* ) |
| | | <u>*Chaya ROGOVE*</u> (twin) (m. Nahum Y ZEIGELBOIM) |
| | | <u>Chinkah ROGOVE</u> (twin) not married, no children |
| | | <u>Shifrah ROGOVE</u> (m. Benjamin ?) |
| | | Miriam (m. Emil TOURNER) |
| | | another dau. Name unknown |

| Generation 4 | Generation 5 | Generation 6 | Generation 7 |
|---|---|---|---|
| **SAHBRA'S LINEAGE on PATERNAL GRANDFATHER'S SIDE (cont.)** | | | |
| MARKUS: Joseph, David, Fege, | | | |
| Chaia Rachel (m.?) | son and daughter | | |
| GOLDWASSER: Israel Joseph, Pashke, | | | |
| Zipporah *Tsipke* (.m.?), Golda | | | |
| no children | | | |
| no children | | | |
| Abraham Samuel MARKUS (m. Tatsha ?) | MARKUS: Stachek, Lutek, Sveyek | | |
| Chava Sarah MARKUS* | Chaim, | | |
| (m. Yaakov GOLDCART) | Hannah | | |
| *(father sold her as bondservant; redeemed by brother Abraham) | | | |
| Yoseph MARKUS (m. Hannah ?) | Dora, *(m. man with children)* | | |
| *moved to Uruguay* | Yitzak - *married with children* | | |
| **MIRIAM MARKUS** | Ami - *(m. ?)* | son and daughter | |
| **(m. Ze'ev TOURI)** - *They walked to Israel* | Carmella (m. Mike ?) | 2 daughters | both with children |
| Jacob MARKUS, *no info* | | | |
| ***ZE'EV** *Volfe* William **MARKUS** b. 1913 | **Twin sons**, names unknown | | |
| (m. 1937 **DEVORAH EFRAIMOVICH**) | | | |
| * *Sahbra's parents* | **ANNA** *(Sahbra)* **MARKUS** b. 1941 | *(no offspring)* | |
| | (m./div. Edward SALEM) | | |
| | ****CHAIM MARCUS** | Deborah *Debbie* MARCUS | Phoebe OSTLANDER |
| | (m. Renee nee ? ) | (m. Kenneth OSTLANDER) | |
| | ***Changed spelling of last name* | | |
| | | Sherry MARCUS | Gabrielle COHEN |
| | | (m. Neil COHEN) | Ezra COHEN |
| | | Shana MARCUS | Ethan MOSKOVITCI |
| | | (m. Baruch MOSKOVITCI) | Charlotte MOSKOVITCI |
| | **YAKOV** *Jacob Jack* **MARKUS** | David MARKUS | |
| | (m. Mona Helen MILLER) | Benjamin *BJ* MARKUS (m. Jessica ?) | |
| | **YITZHAK** *Joe* **MARKUS** | Doron MARKUS | Noah MARKUS |
| | (m. Tsipora *Michelle* LAUFER) | (m. Julia ALEMENY) | Micah MARKUS - born NYC during Hurricane Sandy |
| | | Shane MARKUS (div. KELMAN) | Zachary MARKUS-KELMAN |
| Zipporah *FELA* **MARKUS** | Yitzhak *Ira* GELNICK (m. Sima ?) | 5 children, *Israel* | |
| (m. Stacheck *Sol* **GELNICK**) | Helen GELNICK (m. Jacob YOEL) | YOEL: Sherri and Dina - *NJ* | |
| Ezra MARKUS, *died young in US* | | | |
| Lily *Charlotte* MARKUS (m. Maurice J. RUBIN) | | | |
| | | | |
| **SAHBRA'S LINEAGE on PATERNAL GRANDMOTHER'S SIDE (cont.)** | | | |
| I daughter, name unknown | | | |
| | | | |
| ROGOVE, 1 son name unknown | | | |
| Rivka ROGOVE | | | |
| Rivka ZEIGELBOIM, and another | | | |
| daughter name unknown) | | | |
| **Rosa ROGOVE** (m. **Moshe HOFAIZEN**) | Abraham *Avi* *HOFAIZEN (m. ?) | son and daughter | |
| one son, one daughter | *changed to Israeli *HARPAZ* | | |

# Family Tree Information Compiled by Sahbra Markus (cont.)

Names in **BOLD** are mentioned in book. *Italics* denote alternate names or commentary. Names <u>Underlined</u>: Perished in Holocaust. Spelling of some names may be inaccurate, and unknown names are denoted by **? mark**.

| Generation 1 | Generation 2 | Generation 3 |
|---|---|---|
| **SAHBRA'S LINEAGE on MATERNAL GRANDFATHER'S SIDE** | | |
| | Aaron SCHOTLAND (m. Shifra) | Heinik SCHOTLAND (m. wife unknown) |
| | *He was a 'schochet'- slaughterer* | Esther Leah SCHOTLAND (m. Shaul FOGEL) |
| | | |
| | | |
| | | |
| | | |
| | | |
| | | <u>Mindel SCHOTLAND</u> (m. Moshe Pincas ZELEG) |
| | | |
| | | |
| | | <u>Miriam SCHOTLAND</u> (m. Moshe Pincas ZELEG) |
| | | Rivka SCHOTLAND * see below for lineage |
| | | *(m Chaim Meir EFROIMOWITZ)* |
| | | **Chaim SCHOTLAND** (m. Sonja) |
| | | *('He took her place')* |
| | | |
| | | |
| | | Aaron SCHOTLAND (m. Miriam) |
| | | *Kibbutz Ein Harod* |
| **SAHBRA'S LINEAGE ON MATERNAL GRANDMOTHER'S SIDE** | | |
| Abraham Labe EFROIMOWITZ | Efraim EFROIMOWITZ | **Chaim Meir EFROIMOWITZ (m. Rivka SCHOTLAND)\*** |
| (m. Miriam ?) | (m. Miriam ?) | *\*Sahbra's maternal grandparents* |
| | other offspring unknown | |
| | | |
| | | |
| | | |
| | | <u>Devorah EFROIMOWITZ</u> (m. Yonah TANNENBAM) |
| | | <u>Sarah EFROIMOWITZ</u> (m. Bunim ZELEG) |
| | | <u>Fremet EFROIMOWITZ</u> (m. Alta TEEGE) |
| | | <u>Esther EFROIMOWITZ</u> (m. ? INSHAL) |
| | | <u>Aaron EFROIMOWITZ</u> (m. Zipporah /w id/ remar.?) |
| | | |
| | | |
| | | |

| Generation 4 | Generation 5 | Gen. 6 | Gen. 7 |
|---|---|---|---|
| **SAHBRA'S LINEAGE on MATERNAL GRANDFATHER'S SIDE (cont.)** | | | |
| 6 children (as noted by Esther's oldest son Aaron) | | | |
| Aaron FOGEL (m. Esther) *Tel Adashim* | 2 sons, and dau. Michal | | |
| Israel FOGEL | | | |
| Rosa FOGEL | | | |
| **Pola FOGEL** (m. ? KORNBLUM) - *lunch in Jerusalem* | a son, an Ambassador | | |
| Rachel FOGEL | | | |
| David FOGEL *lives in USA* | | | |
| | | | |
| Bunim ZELEG | | | |
| Yitzak ZELEG - (*His mother died after his birth and father* | | | |
| *married her sister Miriam.*) | | | |
| ZELEG: Yosef, Leah, Rachel, Shimon | | | |
| | | | |
| | | | |
| **Galina** *Gala* **SCHOTLAND** (m. **Baruch KOGAN**\*) * WWII pilot | | | |
| Avraham SCHOTLAND | | | |
| **Yoseph SCHOTLAND** (m. ?) - *lives in Holland* | SCHOTLAND, Baruch & Alexander | | |
| Yakov SCHOTLAND (m. ?) - *lives in Israel* | | | |
| Moshe SCHOTLAND (m.?) - *moved to Germany* | children unknown | | |
| 2 sons, and dau. Batya | | | |
| | | | |
| | | | |
| **SAHBRA'S LINEAGE ON MATERNAL GRANDMOTHER'S SIDE (cont.)** | | | |
| Rachel EFROIMOWITZ (m. Aaron BROWN) | BROWN: Shifra, Esther and Miriam | | |
| **Devorah EFROIMOWITZ** b. 1913 (m.1937 **Ze'ev MARKUS**)\* | | | |
| \*(*Sahbra's parents - see their children and ensuing generations in Paternal Grandfather's Side above* | | | |
| Mindel EFROIMOWITZ (m. Moshe HORN) | Shifra HORN | | |
| Esther EFROIMOWITZ | | | |
| **Bluma EFROIMOWITZ** - *killed at Auschwitz, age 22* | | | |
| **Aaron EFROIMOWITZ** (*First Martyr of Brzezine, age 19*) | | | |
| TANNENBAUM: Mayer, Esther, Hersh, Malka, Menachem, dau.? | | | |
| ZELEG: Mendel, Meir, Mindel (**Aunt Mindy**) KLEIN, Abraham, Gina, Efraim | | | |
| TEEGE: Miriam GOLDSTEIN, Devorah , Belka, Chaia, 2 dau unknown | | | |
| INSHAL: 2 sons, names unknown | | | |
| EFROIMOWITZ: , David, another son ? | | | |
| Deborah EFROIMOWITZ | SRABROLOV: Zipporah, Shoshanah | | |
| (m. ? SRABROLOV) | ? SILVER, *half-bro. changed last name,* | | |
| | *Canada* | | |